ADVANCE PRAISE FOR LOUIS DIAZ AND *DANCING WITH THE DEVIL*

"Few of us get to share the real world of a top-notch undercover agent. *Dancing with the Devil* not only provides an inside look at the cases, most of which made front-page headlines, but a haunting portrayal of the psyche of the guy who made them. Louie Diaz has bared all to tell a thoroughly gripping story."

—Nicholas Pileggi, *New York Times* bestselling author of *Wiseguy*

"Louie Diaz put his life on the line, going undercover to develop evidence that was crucial in the conviction of the thretofore 'untouchable' narcotics kingpin Nicky Barnes. *Dancing with the Devil* recounts this story and many others in a graphic, colorful, and explosive first-person account of an extraordinary law enforcement career."

—Robert B. Fiske Jr., former United States Attorney for the Southern District of New York

"Louie Diaz took down the biggest heroin dealer in the country and did it under extraordinary dangerous conditions, but with extraordinary success. He demonstrated character, commitment, and courage at a time when heroin was killing thousands of American citizens. Louie Diaz turned the tide . . . he is a hero."

—Peter Bensinger, former DEA administrator

This title is also available as an ebook

Dancing with the Devil

Confessions of an Undercover Agent

Louis Diaz

and Neal Hirschfeld

G

GALLERY BOOKS
New York London Toronto Sydney

This work is a memoir. It reflects the author's present recollections of his experiences over a period of years. Some dialogue and events have been re-created from memory and, in some cases, have been compressed to convey the substance of what was said and what occurred. Certain names and identifying characteristics have been changed.

Gallery Books
A Division of Simon & Schuster, Inc.
1230 Avenue of the Americas
New York, NY 10020

First Gallery Books trade paperback edition December 2010

Designed by Davina Mock-Maniscalco

Manufactured in the United States of America

10 9 8 7 6 5 4 3 2 1

Library of Congress Cataloging-in-Publication Data is available

ISBN 978-1-4391-4882-2
ISBN 978-1-4391-6326-9 (ebook)

For Iris, my parents, Henrietta and Alfonso,
mi abuelita Adela, and Benito and Mercedes.

For my wife, Maria Jose,
all my love and sincerest thanks
for giving me a second chance at life.

For my son and daughter, Louis John and Maria;
my grandchildren, James, Grant, and Julia;
my brothers, Rigel and Alfonso Jr.;
and the rest of my family and friends here and in Spain.
My eternal thanks to all of you for your love, support,
and belief in me.

PROLOGUE

THE MOMENT I SPOTTED the cars, I knew it was trouble.

Four of them bearing down on us, all coming from different directions. Dark-colored sedans, two or three guys riding in each. Two pulled in front of me and two zoomed up from behind, boxing me up like a take-home pizza.

No warning, just a cold stop.

I had known they'd be on the lookout for strangers, particularly strangers who looked like we did. Julio, my informant, was a tall, mulatto Dominican with a semicrippled left arm, a gift from the Dominican secret police. He was wearing denim pants, a dark work shirt, construction boots, and a black beret. I was dressed in a black polo shirt and denim vest embossed with the likeness of a black panther. The panther, set against a round, red background, had yellow death rays shooting out of its eyes. I also wore a black beret and big, heavy motorcycle boots. Together, we looked like major trouble.

We had been cruising Bed-Stuy in Brooklyn, looking for Julio's connection, a heavy-duty gun and drug runner. Julio had planned to introduce me to him as a Mafia-connected Cuban who brokered big-money deals.

As soon as the four cars cut us off, I told Julio to put his hands on the dashboard. I placed my own on the steering wheel, taking care to keep them in full view.

Nothing would piss them off more than not being able to see our hands. I knew the drill.

"Stay cool," I said to Julio. "These guys are gonna toss us."

Out of the unmarked cars poured eight or nine plain-clothes cops, all with guns drawn, all crouching in combat stances. Taking cover behind their car doors, they began yelling their jingle: "Police! Don't move, motherfuckers!"

After a minute, one cop moved to the passenger side and yanked Julio out. Another, the biggest of the bunch, moved to the driver's side and aimed his pistol at my left temple. Six feet-plus, 230 pounds, short-cropped hair, Irish from head to toe, he resembled the old-time heavyweight Jim Braddock. He looked a decade older than I did.

With my hands glued to the steering wheel, I quietly turned to him and said, "Hey, not for nuthin', but I'm on the job."

Eyeing me with about as much credulity as if I had declared myself to be Mother Teresa, he shouted to his backups, "Hey, asshole over here says he's on the job!'"

Then he spat at me, "Get the fuck outta the car!"

I opened the door slowly and, with my hands up in the air, I stepped out. The moment I did, the cop grabbed me by my vest, whirled me around, and slammed me up against the side of the car. He banged my head on the hood and kicked my feet apart.

"Listen, officer," I said, "I'm packing."

The cop shouted to the others, "Hey, now this shithead says he's carrying!"

Then he threw a couple of stiff shots to my head, rattling my brains around my skull. After that came half a dozen punches to my kidneys. I winced from the pain.

While I struggled to keep my wits about me, he patted me down and came up with my gun, which inspired him to throw a few more roundhouse blows to my kidneys. For several days after, I would piss blood.

"Go easy, willya?" I said with a gasp. "I'm a Fed. My credentials are in the trunk, under my spare."

The cop shouted to his backups, "Now he claims he's a Fed!" Then he yanked me off the hood and shoved me toward the rear of the car, his gun to my head. I stumbled to the trunk.

Screwing the barrel into the base of my skull, he said, "Open it, motherfucker."

I used my key to open it. Shoving me into the arms of his backups, the cop began poking around under my spare.

"Do me a favor," I said. "Keep my creds outta sight. I'm still working this area undercover."

"Shut the fuck up," he replied. A moment later, he came up with my shield and my identity card.

"Huh!" he grumbled. "Howd'ya like that? This guy is *for real.*"

"Please, can you just leave my credentials there?" I said.

His response was to give me an ass-reaming, "You fuckin' Feds are all the same. High and mighty, think your shit don't stink. Too good to even give us a goddamn courtesy call, telling us that you'd be working our turf."

"Yeah, you're right," I said apologetically. "But you know how shit gets sometimes. We had to move quick on this one."

What I neglected to tell him was that I had expressly been ordered by my superiors at the Bureau of Alcohol, Tobacco, and Firearms *not* to alert the local cops, since many of them were suspected of being on the take.

The cop put his gun away and told the others to stand down. He gave me back my own gun, and I got into my car with Julio, who, fortunately, had not been roughed up too badly. The cops let us drive away. We continued to cruise the neighborhood for half an hour but could not find his connection. So I dropped Julio off at a local watering hole and went on my way. We'd look for his man on another day. If he got wind of what the cops had done to us, it would probably boost my credibility.

But I was still hurting and angry about the abuse I had taken. Not that I faulted the police for stopping us. They did right. But when I told that one cop I was a Fed, he'd crossed the line.

My kidneys ached like hell. And I was getting more pissed off by the minute. I had gotten into plenty of dustups before with cops, including one humdinger during my youth that nearly landed me in the slammer. I disliked many of them. The way they could abuse their authority. The way they victimized civilians who couldn't fight back. Their big-mouth, big-shot bullying attitudes.

It wasn't anything new. Hell, I had grown up with the king of the bullies.

Alfonso Diaz Canellada.

My old man.

Whether it was his bull-like pride, his hot Spanish blood, his rigorous machismo, or the five awful years he had spent in Franco's prison camps during the Spanish Civil War, Papa had been a brute.

CRUISING AROUND BROOKLYN after the "tune-up" I had received from the cops, I thought about all this. And I seethed about the way that one big-mouthed, muscle-headed donkey had crossed the line and put a beating on me.

I knew that these cops worked out of the Brooklyn North Division. Because of the time they had stopped us, I figured they were working an 8:00 a.m. to 4:00 p.m. duty tour. I looked at my watch. It was now 3:15 p.m. Some of them might be getting off duty.

Heading over to the headquarters of Brooklyn North, I spotted a few of their cars. I pulled into a spot across the street and waited. At 3:45 p.m. I saw the big Irish palooka come out and head toward his car. I stepped from my own car.

He was fiddling with his door lock when I came up behind him, so at first he didn't see me.

"Hey, officer," I said. He turned to face me.

When he recognized me, he gave me this big shit-eating grin. "What brings you around here?" he sniffed. For an instant, a vision of my old man flashed before my eyes.

"This," I replied.

And throwing the full weight of my body into it, I hit him with a thunderous left hook to the liver, a shot that could have dropped a horse.

He fell to one knee, the air whooshing out of his lungs.

Holding his ribs and gasping, he managed to croak back at me, "I guess we're even now."

"Yeah," I said. "I guess we are."

I stuck out my hand. He took it, like a man. I turned, walked slowly back to my car.

At least he had a sense of fair play.

But as far as what had happened earlier that day—the car stop, the verbal abuse, and the beat-down—well, that was a whole other story. So, in the end . . .

Fuck 'im.

CHAPTER ONE

YOU HAVE TO WORK your way in slowly. Otherwise your targets can get suspicious. So the first few times you come onto the set, you can't appear too eager.

I was casing a bar in the Williamsburg section of Brooklyn. The word on the street was that the bar was a regular bazaar for stolen guns and dope, swag off the piers, you name it. And I was looking for a piece of the action.

The bar itself was not much different from any other in this neck of the woods. Dark wood. Fake Tiffany lamps. Old-fashioned jukebox to one side. A couple of pool tables in the back. Sullen, rheumy-eyed customers enveloped in a permanent cloud of cigarette smoke, bending their elbows up front. The clientele consisted of longshoremen, truck drivers, construction workers, and wiseguys. Along with the usual deadbeats, drunks, and drifters.

To the side of the bar, a fat guy in a stained apron and a white cardboard cap was slapping slices of fatty meat on pieces of rye for sandwiches. Next to his slicer, a glazed ham sat in a quarter-inch pool of greasy gravy.

If you want to hunt elephants, you gotta go where the elephants go. And if you want to bag an elephant, you gotta have the right equipment. Dressed as I was in my old army fatigue jacket, hooded sweatshirt, dungarees, work boots, and a black longshoreman's cap, I fit right in with the rest of the mooks.

I took a seat at the bar, ordered a beer. I made sure to sit facing the bar and drink my beer from a glass. Customers who stood with their backs to the bar scanning the room and who shunned the glasses to drink directly from bottles, as if to fend off the germs of criminals, could be made for undercover cops.

I finished my drink. I spoke to no one. And then I left.

The next time I came in, same thing. A few drinks, then I was out of there.

The third time, I said hello to a couple of familiar faces, but nothing more. Then I finished my drink and headed home.

After that, I made a point of staying away a little longer than usual.

When I finally did come back, one of the regulars, a tough-looking hood named Frankie, sidled over. With his cauliflower ear, mushroom nose, and clotted speech, it was obvious he'd done some boxing. And probably a few other things as well.

He was curious about my absence. "Ain't been around in a while, have ya? Whattya been up to?"

"Little of this, little of that," I said. It was street jargon, a code for telling him something about myself. If he picked up on it, he'd know I was dirty. And I'd know that he was as well. At a time when Richard Nixon was trying to convince the nation that he was "not a crook," Frankie and I were trying to convince each other of the exact opposite.

Frankie shot me a knowing smile. I smiled back. The hook was in.

"New in the neighborhood?"

I eyed him warily. "Not exactly."

He waited. So I filled in the blank. "Just lookin' for a new place to hang my hat. Last place I was hangin' out . . . well, let's say I had a bit of a problem."

Frankie nodded. "Hey, tell me about it," he said. "So, where ya from anyway?" he asks.

"Red Hook," I answered.

"Oh, yeah?" said Frankie. "You know Joey the Chink? You're from Red Hook, you *gotta* know Joey. Everyone in Red Hook knows Joey. Big fat greaseball Chinaman with that jagged scar over his nose. From that time up in the joint, when he got cut up by the niggers."

It was the old wiseguy trap, and I smelled it instantly. If I told him I knew Joey the Chink, and there was no Joey the Chink or he got whacked three years earlier, I was fucked. Frankie would smell a cop in the blink of an eye.

So I gave him my stock answer for these kinds of impromptu field tests. "You know what? I know this guy out there, but to tell you the truth, I'm not sure the guy I have in mind is him."

I left Frankie guessing.

"Yeah, sure," he said, continuing to size me up. "Could be Joey, could be somebody else."

But I had given him an honest answer, and he knew it. He started to relax. In his mind, I had passed the litmus test. For now.

I looked at my watch, as if I had someplace important I needed to be. "Hey, I'll see ya later, okay?"

"Yeah, sure thing," said Frankie. I could feel his eyes following me like lasers as I walked out the door. The courtship had begun.

The next time I popped by, I brought some cartons of cut-rate cigarettes to peddle, making it appear that I had either heisted them or my connection had. Either way, I looked like a player.

"How about a little pool?" Frankie said.

We racked them up, played a couple of rounds, and shot the shit. And Frankie tried to pump me a little bit more.

"So, apart from this and that, what kinda other stuff you into anyway?" he asked.

"A little construction work, some gigs down by the piers. And these cigarettes when I can get 'em."

"Anything else?"

Hunched over the pool table with my cue as I sized up my shot, I lowered my voice. "You don't wanna know."

The art of seduction. Always leave 'em hanging on what *could* be. Always leave 'em hungry for more.

Later, when the two of us were back at the bar, Frankie pressed for details. I'd only been taking sips off the top of my glass, never finishing my entire drink, but at this point I started to make it seem like the alcohol was loosening my tongue.

"Yeah, well, long story short, me and my crew knocked off a load of booze from a truck down on the piers that was already promised to the 'boys.' So, uh . . . I hadda get lost for a while, y'understand? So, anyway, now I'm back and just tryin' to get my shit together."

"Got ya," said Frankie.

But a little while later he said, "Well, since you're into this and that, maybe you know somebody whose looking to buy pen guns."

"The fuck is *that*?" I said.

Frankie crooked his finger and motioned me to follow him into the bathroom, which I did. Inside, he bolted the lock behind us. Then he pulled out what looked to be a writing pen, made of stainless steel. Pulling back the head, he stuck a .25-caliber bullet inside. Then he pushed the head back into position and wrapped the pen in a rag to muffle the noise.

"Press the head straight down and . . ."

Bam! He fired a round into the toilet bowl.

"Fuck me!" I exclaimed.

"Forty bucks a pop," Frankie said. "You interested?"

Still playing it cautious, I put my hands up, defensively. "Whoa, not me! I'm outta that line of work. Just tryin' to keep a low profile, y'understand what I'm sayin'?"

But the truth was, he had given me an instant hard-on. I continued to string him along, however, telling him I'd ask around, I might know of someone who was.

"You know where to find me," said Frankie.

This time I let Frankie leave the bar first. Then I followed right behind.

He looked over his shoulder at me. "Where you goin'?" he asked.

"Catch a smoke," I said. "Burns cooler outside."

"Sure thing," he said, then started walking toward his car.

As I stood watching, slowly drawing in the smoke from my cigarette, I shot a glance at his license plate and made a mental note of the number. Later I would run the plate through DMV to get his *real* name and address. Then I'd head over to Police Headquarters to run the name through their computers to see if he had a rap sheet. If he did, it would facilitate the opening of a criminal case file on him.

Back at the bar a few nights later, I bumped into Frankie again.

"Hey, Lou," he said to me. "You think about that thing we discussed?"

I made a show of snapping my fingers, as if suddenly jarring my memory back to our earlier conversation.

"Jesus Christ, Frankie, I never gave it much thought. But

you know what? Now that I think about it, I actually got a guy in mind. I'll get back to you, okay?"

"Sure, Lou, sure," said Frankie. By now he was so hot for it, he had a case of blue balls.

So the next day, when I came back in again, I told Frankie, "You know what? I got someone may wanna do some business with us, maybe in a week or so." But I left it at that, nothing more.

Then I took Frankie over to another bar I was casing, in Queens, and showed him off to the clientele over there like he was my new best buddy. With his punched-up face, thickened and calloused knuckles, and tough-guy style of speaking, he impressed the hell out of everyone in the joint. And, pleased with all the attention he was drawing, I impressed the hell out of Frankie for looking like I was well connected in more than just one part of town.

The following week, I told Frankie my buyer was ready to do the deal for his pen guns. Matter of fact, I could even bring Frankie around to meet him.

"Fuck that," said Frankie. He pulled a pen gun out of his coat pocket and handed it to me. "Take it. Just show it to him."

I took the gun and thanked Frankie for his trust. "I'll get back to you in a few days," I said.

When I returned to the bar that weekend, Frankie was there, waiting for me. "My guy went crazy for the pen gun," I said. I passed him his forty dollars.

"I can get more," Frankie said.

"That's good, Frankie, 'cause my guy wants another ten."

Frankie was ecstatic. "Fuckin' A! When, Lou? When?"

"Whenever you're ready, I'll bring him over," I told him, knowing I could easily get one of my fellow agents to pose as "my guy."

"Listen, Lou," Frankie said. "I'd rather deal just with you."

I put my hands up like big red stop signs. The wiley ex-con looking to avoid any new jams.

"Ah, you know," I said with a sigh, "after what I been through, I can't really take that kinda chance. I'd rather just set up the meet, introduce you to the guy, y'know what I mean?"

Frankie looked crestfallen.

"All right, lemme run it by my guy," I told Frankie. "I'll get back to you."

We slapped high fives and said good-bye.

The next night, when I returned to the bar, I suddenly changed my tune.

"You know what?" I told Frankie. "I hadda chance to sleep on it, and, fuck it, I'll do it. I'll make the buy for him *myself.*"

Frankie could have creamed in his jeans. We set up a meet outside his place of work, a factory in Long Island City, and it was there, in the parking lot, that we made the exchange—his ten pen guns in return for my four hundred bucks. It all went down without a hitch.

A few nights later, when I met up again with Frankie at the bar, I told him my buyer had "offed" the ten pen guns like hotcakes, and he was itching to buy at least forty more. Frankie was hot to trot, but he said he'd have to run it by his connection. This got me even more jazzed, since now I might be able to "buy up" and flush out his connection, too.

I gave Frankie my phone number. Expecting that we would embark on a long-term and mutually profitable relationship, he happily took it. He had no idea that every time he called that number, he would be recorded and anything he said about his criminal activities would constitute prima facie evidence that could be used against him.

The next day I got a call on my undercover phone from

Frankie. He had squared away the deal with his connection and would have the forty pen guns for me the following day. We arranged to meet outside the Long Island City factory at noon to make the exchange.

I withdrew $1,600 in official advanced funds to make the buy.

My backup team moved into position outside the factory an hour early to case the area for any potential threats to my safety. The "rip" signal would be the customary one. If anybody but me went to the trunk of my car, it was a rip-off, time for the cavalry to charge. If I opened the trunk, it meant the deal had gone down and it was time to make the bust.

At 12:05 p.m. I pulled up to the factory. Frankie was standing outside, anxiously shifting his weight from one foot to the other.

Milking my act a little more, I asked him if he could cut me a better price on the guns.

"No way," said Frankie, "the price is the price. But I'll throw in a few extra pen guns as a show of good faith."

"Okay," I said.

He walked into the factory, returning a moment later with a brown paper bag containing the forty pen guns, plus an additional two. I led him around to the trunk of my car, where I had stashed his sixteen hundred bucks under my spare tire.

Before I opened the trunk, I peeked into the bag and counted the guns again. Then I opened the trunk and reached inside for the cash, signaling my backup team that the deal was down.

I waited for the net to drop.

Nothing happened. No charge of the light brigade. No backup agents. Nothing. I was standing out there by myself with my thumb up my ass. My balls shrunk to the size of peanuts. Yet again, I realized that the only person I could ever totally rely on in these situations was *myself.*

So, acting on instinct, I dropped the cash back inside the trunk. Then I spun around, pulled my revolver from my army fatigue jacket, aimed it at Frankie's chest, and shouted, "Police! You're under arrest! Don't move!"

For a moment, Frankie stood stunned. But then he came right at me, challenging what I had just told him. "Fuck *you*, you're the man! You ain't no cop, motherfucker!"

He was convinced I was trying to rip him off.

Frankie started to reach behind his back for something, so I tackled him and we both went down hard. At this moment, I heard sirens approaching. Thank God. My backup units. Finally.

Frankie and I were still rolling around on the ground when the other agents pulled up. Just as Frankie was about to take another swing at me, Kenny Coniglio, my ATF supervisor, screwed his gun barrel into Frankie's ear.

"Give it up," Kenny announced. "Federal agents. You're under arrest."

Frankie's body went slack, the fight drained out of him. The other agents cuffed him.

But he still kept glaring back at me with disbelief.

"You ain't the man, no way," he said. "You're a snitch, right? Level with me, Lou. C'mon, level with me!"

No matter how many times I told him otherwise, Frankie simply couldn't believe I was a cop.

CHAPTER TWO

PLAYING TOUGH CUSTOMERS WASN'T much of a stretch for me. I already walked the walk and talked the talk. Given my upbringing, it came second nature.

My biggest teacher in all this was my old man, a guy who wouldn't take crap from anyone. Alfonso Diaz Canellada was a fierce Asturiano from the north of Spain, known as "El Rubio" because of his blond hair. But if Papa gave me a set of brass balls, the Borough of Brooklyn gold-plated 'em.

I grew up in a section of Brooklyn called Red Hook, which was one of the settings for the film *On the Waterfront*. In Red Hook, you were either the meat eater or the meat. Everybody was itching to prove how tough he was. Usually by beating the crap out of the next guy. Most of us were first- or second-generation Americans—Sicilian, Neapolitan, and Irish, with a sprinkling of Spanish, Lebanese, and Jewish thrown in for seasoning. Our fathers were working stiffs—seamen, longshoremen, truck drivers, construction workers, physical laborers, the kind of hard-wired, blue-collar guys who would belly up to the bar for a beer and a shot. Like our old men, we, too, were looking for respect, a reputation, a place in the sun. Meanwhile, there was always some other guy looking to snatch away your rep so he could jack up his own. Because the more of a rep he got, the higher up it put him on the totem pole of the not-to-be-fucked-with.

Life started out peacefully enough. We lived in a tiny

walk-up apartment above Leo Sacco's Italian deli, for which Papa paid $30 a month in rent. This, after all, was the early 1950s, when a loaf of bread cost 16 cents, a pound of hamburger meat 50 cents, and a new car $1,500. The apartment, barely five hundred square feet, had one bedroom, a ten-by-ten-foot living room, a space for the bunk bed in which my brothers and I slept, a dingy little bathroom, and a two-by-nothing cramped kitchen with an icebox and a black cast-iron stove that burned both gas and wood. The drab walls, shmeared with a yellow enamel paint, were bare save for a single painting of Hernando Cortés, the Spanish conquistador who defeated the Aztecs, sitting atop a magnificent stallion.

For the first few years of my life, while Mama was working for the government, sewing parachutes for the U.S. Army, and Papa was off at sea with the merchant marine, my Basque grandmother, my Abuelita Adela, was my guardian angel. She brought me with her to buy sour pickles on Delancey Street, letting me stick my hand in the barrel to fish out the tart, crunchy pickles, a nickel apiece in those days. She bargained vigorously with the old Jewish merchants on the Lower East Side, all of whom seemed to adore her. She bought me toy soldiers. She filled piggy banks with spare change just so she could buy me gifts. She gave me my first puppy. When that dog became sick and we had to give him up, she even brought me a new one—Butch, a reddish half shepherd, half huskie who would become the family pet for the next fifteen years.

Abuelita Adela made everything seem sweet and beautiful and rainbow-like. All I knew was love and affection. Peace and innocence reigned. All men were good. God's plan for us was working.

But, of course, all of that was about to change.

* * *

EARLY ONE MORNING when I was five, I was playing with my toy soldiers in our living room. I had gotten up extra early so my younger brother Rigel wouldn't interfere with my war games. I set up my soldiers on opposite sides of the living room into two opposing armies, then tried to be fair to both on the battlefield. After one side took a shot with a pea or the head of match stuffed into my plastic toy cannon, the other side would get its turn. Whichever side had more men standing at the end would win the battle.

On this morning, I must have been playing too loudly. Papa, who had been resting, arose in a fury, charged into the living room, and began kicking my toy soldiers aside. Then, yanking his belt through his pants loops—I can still remember the sickening, snapping sound the leather made—he began whipping me. I wailed in horror as he brought the belt down on my tender flesh.

"No, Papa, no!" I cried.

But either he couldn't or he wouldn't hear me. Again and again he lashed me. Rigel screamed in terror. Charging into the living room, Mama begged Papa to let up.

"Stop! *Stop!*" she shouted. But to no avail.

Fueled by a rage that could not be controlled, Papa smacked away without letup, drawing an extra jolt of adrenaline that pushed him to superhuman fury. When his anger finally subsided, his whole body went slack and he looked dazed and depleted, as if his entire being had been drained of its life force.

This first beating was an eye-opener. At the tender age of five, I learned that if I displeased my father, there would be consequences. Ugly, brutal consequences. Up until this point and thanks to Abuelita Adela, life had been sweet and carefree. But after the beating, I was robbed of my innocence.

Six months later, I provoked Papa into another vicious

beating. Once again I was playing with my toy soldiers, but one of the match heads I had stuffed into my plastic cannon accidentally ignited and set fire to the living room curtain.

Terrified, I screamed for help. When Papa rushed in, he grabbed the glass terrarium in which I kept my baby turtles and flung it—water, rocks, turtles, and all—onto the fire. He tore down the curtain and stomped out the flames. Then he turned his fists on me. The beating was awful, but mostly I cried for my turtles, all of whom were burned into charred stubs of cartilage.

"Why? Why did you do that?" I yelled at him. "What did *they* do?"

He raised his hand to hit me again, then suddenly stopped himself, grunted, and went back into the bedroom. I never got an answer from him.

STRONG, RUGGEDLY HANDSOME, bearing a distinct resemblance to Burt Lancaster, Papa was a troubled and angry man. He spoke broken English, and although he was a voracious reader, he had never finished grammar school. He'd left all his family behind in Spain, many of them then still jailed in Franco's prison camps. He could not use words to express how he felt, so he showed his feelings in a different way.

With his fists.

When our upstairs neighbor was being pummeled by one of her Mafia boyfriends, Papa, clad only in his boxer shorts, charged out of our apartment, grabbed the thug, and flung him down the stairs. Shaking off the fall, the wiseguy went for his pistol, but Papa was too quick for him. Disarming him, Papa threw the hood into the street and threatened to blow his brains out with his own gun if he ever returned.

When another boyfriend got liquored up and barricaded himself inside the same lady's apartment—we could hear her pleading for her life—Papa actually shinnied up the outside of our building and jumped through her third-floor window. The abusive Romeo was soon hanging from the window by his ankles, begging for his life, as Papa threatened to drop him to the sidewalk. Once he skedaddled, he was never seen again.

And when a fellow dock worker uttered a perceived insult, Papa, in an act of violence that sickens me to this day, literally knocked the man's teeth out. His rage was volcanic, terrifying, something beyond human.

Worst of all, it was often turned on me.

Papa would beat me for annoying him. He would beat me for being disrespectful. He would beat me for not raising a hand to him in self-defense.

"I'm your father!" he would exclaim as he was raining his blows down on me. "What I do is okay because *I'm your father.*"

Often the whole neighborhood could hear or see him beating me, since he would routinely go after me on the street, in front of other people. None of them ever called the police or contacted social services. Dropping a dime on a neighbor was not done in those days. A man beating his own son was considered to be a private family affair, not police business. Besides, many of the cops were considered to be bigger brutes than the people they locked up.

But I would plead with Papa not to beat me in public. "Papa, *my friends,*" I would beg. "Not in front of my friends."

"Never mind your friends!" he would say, throwing another hard fist my way. "I'm your father. Let them mind their own business."

Mama, whose Spanish name was Enriquetta but was known as Henrietta, was no pushover either. Of Basque descent, she had been raised to be tough, yet was beloved for her wicked sense of humor and revered in the neighborhood as the Spanish Carol Burnett. But she also had stinging hands and a dead-eye aim, i.e., a slipper with eyes. Wherever you might be cowering, it would find you.

But Mama would never resort to the level of violence inflicted by Papa. And when he beat me, she tried as valiantly as she could to make him stop without putting herself in harm's way, for she, too, feared Papa.

"*¡Bruto! ¡Bruto! ¡Animál! Te voy a dejar! ¡Voy á irme con los niños!*" she would scream at him. Bully! Bully! Animal! I'm going to leave you! I'm going to take the children and go away!

Chastened by her outburst, Papa would grunt or shake his head. Although he would never admit it, I knew he was filled with disgust for his own lack of self-control. Once the beating had ended, he would take out his frustration by pounding a fist into a wall.

The walls in our apartment acquired countless imprints of his knuckles.

WHEN I WAS seven, I was entrusted to keep an eye on my younger brother Alfonsito. With chubby red cheeks and blond, curly hair just like my dad's, "Fonsi" was an adorable baby. But Alfonsito had contracted meningitis as an infant and was prone to epileptic seizures. Mama taught me, and later my brother Rigel, to recognize the smacking, swallowing sounds he would make when he was struggling to breathe so we could use a taped-up spoon to keep him from swallowing his own tongue.

As we got older, I became Alfonsito's protector. Everyone in the neighborhood knew that if they ever fucked with Alfonsito, they would have to deal with his big brother, Louie D.

Being able to fend for yourself and protect your loved ones was essential for survival in Red Hook. Nearly every day, from our window over Leo Sacco's Deli, Rigel and I could see the local citizenry beating the shit out of each other. One got both his kneecaps busted by mobsters wielding baseball bats. Most likely he owed money to Leo's brother Frank, a mustachioed, slicked-back Don Ameche look-alike who ran numbers for the mob while Leo busied himself at the counter making his overstuffed prosciutto, pepper, and provolone heros.

When I was about ten, Leo handed me a brown paper bag containing policy slips and cash. "Hey, kid," he said, "take this over to my brother Frank. Here's a buck for your piggy bank." And that was how I was recruited to become a policy runner for the mob, which I did for a while.

When I turned eleven, the Dodgers played their last game in Brooklyn before moving west to Los Angeles . . . and I scored my first TKO. I was walking with my Abuelita Adela to buy fresh crumb buns from the local bakery. Whenever we passed by the corner near the bakery, this one Italian kid, a few years older than I was, would always start giving me shit. He was a wiseguy in training, a real *jabone,* a moron with all the trimmings—black leather jacket, motorcycle boots, garrison belt, cigarette dangling from his mouth, greasy hair in his eyes, and shit in his future.

"Hey, here comes the mama's boy," the *jabone* would taunt. Deaf as she was, Abuelita never heard him. But I sure did. I wanted to rip his fucking lungs out.

Now, Abuelita was a tender, beautiful, elegant lady—all European charm and Old World class. And for the first few years of my life, she had sheltered me from the harsh realities of an ugly world. But she still had a good bit of the Basque in her. And she wouldn't allow her loved ones to take shit from anybody.

On one of my first days at school, she had pulled me aside and recited her three Golden Rules: *Never snitch on anyone. Never come home crying that you caught a beating. And if you get into a fight with a kid who's bigger than you are, pick up a stick and break it over his head.*

So when I finally fessed up and told her that the punk on the corner had been taunting me, she said: "Why didn't you tell me, Luisito? Go! Go! Go do something about it!"

Fortified by her blessing, I walked over to the bully. He looked down at me with contempt, as if to say, "Just what are you gonna do, Pee Wee?" So I busted him a shot to the face, bloodying his nose and sending him running home to *his* mama.

That night, when Abuelita told Papa what I had done—and that she had sanctioned it—Papa beamed with pride. In his eyes, I was a chip off the old block, now worthy of being the son of El Rubio.

Meanwhile, the neighborhood continued to offer an ongoing lesson in survival of the fittest. When I was twelve, I actually saw a wiseguy get whacked outside a social club. His porkpie hat flew off his head and seemed to stay suspended in midair, even after the bullets had knocked him to the ground.

It was the first time I ever saw anyone get killed, but it came as no big shock, given where we lived and the street violence I'd already seen and was sometimes subjected to. In fact, I remember thinking, "Hey, this is just like in the movies. Only this time, I got a front-row seat."

IN 1957, PAPA had left the merchant marine to take a job as a night supervisor at the Spanish-language newspaper *El Diario-La Prensa*, and we were able to move around the corner to our own brownstone. Papa bought the building with fourteen thousand bucks he borrowed from my Uncle Casimiro, a mob-connected loan shark. In our new home, we were able to upgrade to a two-floor apartment because Mama and Papa rented out furnished rooms on the upper floors to fellow Spaniards who literally had just gotten off the boat. The boarders would stay for a couple of months before suddenly vanishing, trying to stay one step ahead of the U.S. immigration authorities who, at one point, actually raided our house.

One of the few non-Spaniard tenants, Mr. Olson, was a master carpenter from Scandinavia. A quiet, unassuming man, Mr. Olson used to help Papa with woodworking tasks around the house. But he was a heavy gambler, always in debt to the bookies and the numbers runners.

One day in 1958, just as my brother Rigel and I were about to go off to school, we heard a loud *pow!* coming from the direction of Mr. Olson's room. Rushing up the stairs with me at her heels, Mama was sure that Rigel and I had set off a cherry bomb. Using her master key to unlock Mr. Olson's door, Mama peeked her head inside. I stuck my head in, too, just below hers. There on the floor, surrounded by a widening pool of dark, red blood, lay a lifeless Mr. Olson. Unable to pay his debts, the poor man had taken a long-barreled .38-caliber revolver and blown his brains out. For me, it was like a scene straight out of *Alfred Hitchcock Presents,* which at the time was one of the more popular crime shows on television.

"Get out!" Mama snapped, pulling the door shut in my face. *"Get out!"*

She quickly relocked the door with her key. Then, as if nothing had ever happened, she hustled Rigel and me off to school. She then called the police, who arrived to cordon off the room. It was still cordoned off when I came home for lunch. It wasn't until late in the day that the coroner removed the body. I still don't know who cleaned up all the blood.

At the dinner table that night, Mama and Papa talked in hushed tones about Mr. Olson's demise. Rather than express shock or horror, they spoke with the detached resignation of two people already hardened to life's miseries.

Papa simply sniffed, "One more reason to stay away from gamblers," thus ending the discussion.

AT ST. PAUL'S grammar school, I received a sobering education. Forget the math, the history, the English, and catechism. It was the survival training that really counted. And it came from the nuns, most of whom had mustaches and were meaner than spit. On Broadway, gentle, lighthearted nuns such as Sister Maria were being idolized in the *The Sound of Music*. But out in Brooklyn, the nuns were a whole other breed.

Sister Rose, who measured about four-feet-nine, was a feisty, hot-tempered little pit bull with a large brown mole on her cheek, out of which sprouted ugly black hairs. Whenever she confronted me, I tried not to look at the mole, but invariably I would end up speaking directly to it, as if it were a second head. If I goofed around in class—hitting her in the back with my pea shooter or twanging a girl's hairpin under my desk—she would grab me by both sideburns and shake my head from side to side like a cocktail mixer. It was a counterterrorist tactic that many of the nuns utilized, and it made you feel like they were about to rip your face off.

The repeated physical abuse infuriated me. So when Sister Anselm ordered me to stand by my desk and began slapping me on both sides of my face, winding up like a baseball pitcher to put a little extra mustard on each delivery, I snapped, firing two hard fists straight into her belly. And over she went, flat on her ass, undoubtedly helped on her way by my pal Mikey Howard, who stuck his foot out behind her to make sure she went down for the count.

Naturally, I was hauled into the principal's office, smacked around some more, and given a week's suspension, which was a bitch and a half what with all the makeup work that awaited me. Ordinarily, Papa would have beat the hell out of me for this kind of insolence. But after a bunch of my classmates came to our house and vouched for me, even he felt sympathetic.

The nuns knew that their physical abuse was wrong. They might even have felt ashamed about inflicting it. But if so, they never admitted it. They certainly never asked for forgiveness. Instead their attitude was, "It's done. It's over. Now stop your moping and get back to work."

As for us kids, we never said anything either. If you caught a beating, you learned to take it. That was the deal. But I for one vowed never to cry. *Ever.* No matter how hard or how often any of the nuns hit me, I wouldn't let them break my spirit.

Of all the nuns, the very worst was Sister Margaret. An industrial-size version of the Wicked Witch of the West, she was a mean, mannish-looking behemoth with watermelon breasts, fire in her eyes, and the smell of must and mothballs wafting up from her black habit. Maybe it was the tight chinstrap she wore to keep her Sisters of Charity cap in place or it was high blood pressure . . . she was always red in the face.

I don't know why Sister Margaret hated the boys as much as she did, but she was absolutely vicious toward us. Every day she would torture one of the boys while he struggled to work out a math problem on the blackboard, smacking her wooden pointer sharply in her palm, just waiting for him to make a mistake, which, under that kind of pressure, he invariably would. And then, with a twisted little smile, Sister would whack the shit out of the kid's back, reducing him to tears.

When I was about thirteen, me and my pals Eddie and Mikey hoodwinked Sister Margaret into thinking that the whole class was following her up the metal staircase from the playground and back into the building. Instead, as she advanced up the stairs, too proud to look back, all of us began making loud stepping sounds at the bottom of the landing, but never going beyond the first step. When she finally realized the joke and who was behind it, she was livid.

Sister smacked the three of us around pretty good, but, unlike Eddie and Mikey, I refused to cry. I wouldn't give her the satisfaction.

Eyeballs nearly popping out of her face, she seethed, "If I can't get you to cry, I'll just get your father to do it."

Sure enough, Papa appeared at the classroom door the next day. Sister Margaret said he had been asked to come to school and "teach Louie a lesson."

I was sitting in the back row, in front of the classroom cupboard. For what seemed like an eternity, Papa stood at the head of the class, frozen in place like an animal caught in headlights. For the first time maybe ever, I sensed that this was too much, even for him. To beat his own son in front of the entire class? Even he couldn't be that monstrous. But Sister Margaret kept egging him on. He had no choice.

Walking to the back of the room, he stood over my desk, staring down at me with a terrible sadness in his eyes. I could tell that he didn't want to do it. I didn't deserve this shit. Crazy as it sounds, I actually felt sorry for him. Which was probably why I did what I did.

Picking up my books, I slammed them down defiantly on my desk.

"Come on!" I said. "Do it!"

It was like waving a red cape under the bull's nose.

Grabbing my tie with his left hand, he jacked me up out of my seat. Then, still holding me with his left, he fired a savage right into my face, propelling me backward and through a cupboard. I stumbled to my feet, blood pouring from my lip and my nose.

The class exploded with hysteria. The girls, and even some of the boys, started to cry. Sister Margaret went blank—even she was mortified by what she had unleashed.

As I shook off the punch and straightened my tie, I could see that Papa was embarrassed and ashamed. He took me by the collar, led me out of the classroom, and walked me home, saying nothing along the way. For a long time after, not a word passed between us—both of us knew what we wanted to say, but neither of us ever said it.

OUTSIDE OF SCHOOL, I flirted with danger. I'd play "chicken" over on the abandoned barges by the docks with my friends, leaping from one floating barge to the next while tiptoeing around the discarded used condoms—"Coney Island flounders," as we used to call them. On Halloween I'd fill old socks with colored chalk sticks, bang them on the sidewalk to pulverize the chalk, then use the powder-filled socks to vandalize some poor sap's front door. I'd set off fireworks every July Fourth—cherry bombs and ash cans bundled together like grenades and sky rockets—and when I got older and made trips into Little Italy, I became the fireworks supplier for our neighborhood. I'd have fights with eggs and water balloons, and when I really wanted to be a little prick, I'd find an old roll of negative film, wrap it around some wood matchsticks, bind it up with rubber bands, and jam it under the front door of an apartment building before lighting it with another match. The thick, billowing cloud of black, sulfurous-smelling smoke would throw the tenants into a panic and bring the Fire Department.

I fooled around with girls, but I'd never go beyond first or second base or venture into "the forbidden zone," since my strict Catholic upbringing made that completely taboo. If one of our guys ever got serious with a girl, we'd write him off as a wuss—playing ball, hanging out in the streets, and being tough were my priorities, not mooning and swooning over a woman.

In the end, though, my childhood was colored by one overriding impulse: the desire to fight. In my battles, I would be guided by a set of iron-clad rules Papa taught me: *Never think about what the other guy can do to you, think only about what you are going to do to him. Never fight in the wrong or for wrong. Right makes might. If you're fighting a bigger guy, make sure to hit him first.*

Unlike Papa, I'd never hit or kick a guy once he was down. And I hated bullies, especially two who ganged up on some other guy. When I was about thirteen, I got into a real street brawl with an older kid who started ragging on a girl I knew. We fought toe-to-toe, down on the ground, rolling from the sidewalk to the gutter, then back up on the sidewalk again, while all around us grown men stood around stupidly rubbernecking. The other kid was bigger and stronger than I was, and I actually was praying that somebody would stop the fight and I could save face. Instead, all these knuckleheads just stood around and enjoyed the free show. When I managed to get a headlock on my opponent, he bit into my arm like a pit bull.

Enraged, I picked him up off the ground and flung him headfirst through the plate-glass window of a dry-cleaning store owned by some locals.

The two of us stumbled off before the police showed up, neither of us giving a thought to making restitution to the owners. The other kid was cut up and bloodied. I came away with bruises and a bite mark on my arm. Instead of going straight home, where the sight of me might incite Papa to go after my opponent, I went to my Abuelita Adela's house, which was close to our own. Whenever I had been roughed up in a fight, I would always go to her first for medical attention. Later I might let Papa know that I had been in a fight, but I could fudge the details.

In about 1958 I took a leave of absence from my regular friends by the piers to join a local street gang, the Gowanus Dukes. One member of the Dukes, Little Nunzio, had challenged me by saying, "You know, you're a pretty tough guy around here, Louie, but I don't know if you could make it with the gang." So naturally, I had risen to his dare. The initiation required me to walk into a pitch-black hallway where five guys jumped me. I went ape-shit, punching back, kicking, flailing away like some lunatic. When the beating ended, I walked back outside again, bloodied and bruised, but officially a member of the Gowanus Dukes. Within a couple of months I became the gang's wartime consigliere.

We were real-life versions of the gangs in *West Side Story*. Chains, sticks, and knives were our weapons of choice. The Ambassadors, the Kane Street Midgets, the Playboys, the Mau Mau Chaplains, and the Bishops were our mortal enemies. My job was to formulate war strategy, scope out the terrain, assign decoys, and launch us into battle. Later, after one of my pals taught me how to make a .22-caliber zip gun from wood, a piece of car antenna, a door latch, and rubber bands, we did a test-fire in his apartment, putting a hole in his bedroom floor.

Another gang, the Rebels, tried to recruit me away from the Dukes when I was fourteen. By way of initiation this time, three guys came up to me outside my house, put a gun to my head, and said, "If you know what's good for you, you'll join." I called their bluff and didn't join, but down the line I settled the score with the recruitment committee, beating the shit out of all of them.

During the six months I spent with the Dukes, I was slashed, knifed, and ice-picked in assorted fights.

When Puerto Ricans started to move into our immediate neighborhood, we often competed with them for playing time on the local ball field. Naturally, the way to decide who would get first dibs was to duke it out. Whoever was left standing got to play ball. The rules of the street.

As a teenager, I was on the short side and weighed only 145 pounds. But I was broad-shouldered and muscular and developed a reputation as a kid who could use his fists. So much so that, whenever word got around that I was going to go at it with some other kid, the neighborhood wiseguys would troop down to the ball field with their folding chairs and their bottles of Rheingold and set themselves up in comfort while placing bets on me to bring home the bacon.

One summer day when I was fifteen, my brother Rigel and I were having a late lunch with Papa. My other brother, Alfonsito, had eaten earlier and already gone over to the ball field. Suddenly my friend Jimmy McMahon appeared outside our door, out of breath.

"Louie!" he gasped. "Look what the spics did to Fonsi!"

Behind him stood Alfonsito, his T-shirt torn, his lip busted up and bloody, a hangdog look on his face. I told Alfonsito to remain in the vestibule, out of sight of Papa. Then I stepped back into our kitchen and motioned Rigel to come away from the table.

After Rigel came out and got a look at Alfonsito's condition, I said, "Fuck it, let's go kick some ass."

I stuck my head back into the kitchen without letting on what had happened and said, "Goin' over to play some ball, Papa. See ya later."

Papa merely grunted.

Back down the street we headed—me, Alfonsito, Rigel, and Jimmy McMahon. As we turned the corner, marching side by side, we must have resembled the steely-eyed gunfighters from the O.K. Corral.

Near the ball field I could see a sizable crowd gathering. The moment that Jimmy had announced he was gonna "go get Louie," everyone had known the shit was on. Neighborhood regulars, old people, young people, even toddlers had shown up. And, of course, the usual wiseguy contingent with their folding chairs and bottles of beer. "Fuggedaboudit, here come the Diaz brothers," they said, snickering. Their words filled me with both pride and fury.

As we neared the ball field Jimmy said, "There they are."

Alfonsito pointed out the kids who had jumped him. One of them, his jaw jutting out as if daring us to try something, stepped toward us. My brother Rigel, who ordinarily hated to fight, didn't even hesitate. Without a word, he lunged forward and tore into the challenger with both fists—*boom, bam, bing!*—a regular raging bull.

I hung back at first, but when three older kids tried to step in, I grabbed a stickball bat and cracked it over each of their heads. Pretty soon it was a free-for-all, twenty to thirty guys whomping the shit out of each other. President Kennedy might have been trying to gets his new Peace Corps up and running, but we were out there kicking ass. Outnumbered by Diaz supporters, the others turned tail and beat feet.

When it was finally over, we were all pretty scuffed up. But we had settled a score and could return home with our heads held high. I lovingly yoked my brother Rigel, keeping my arm around his neck the whole way back. Never had I felt as much love and pride for the kid as I did at that moment. One for all and all for one. We were the brothers Diaz, the Three Musketeers of Red Hook.

When we came back home and Papa finally realized that we had been in a rumble, his only comment was, "So how'd you do?"

"Kicked their asses," I replied.

Satisfied that we had upheld the family's honor, he snorted his approval, then went back to reading his paper.

BY THE TIME I turned fifteen, my success with my fists began to catch the eye of the wiseguys—many of whom reported to "Crazy Joe" Gallo, the mob chieftain who ruled the roost in Red Hook and lived half a dozen blocks from my own house. A few doors down from Joe's place was Mondo's Social Club, a mob watering hole run by Mondo the Midget—a local celebrity, mascot to the Mafia, and Joe's favorite little man. Joe Gallo spent much of his time at Mondo's and kept his pet lion Cleo caged in Mondo's basement. Cleo was reputed to be a highly effective member of Joe's delinquent-debt collection crew. According to local folklore, Joe used to walk through the neighborhood with Cleo on a leather leash and once brought him into a nightclub. Terrified, one patron demanded to know how such behavior could be permitted. The headwaiter supposedly replied, "Because that guy is Crazy Joe Gallo. I'd rather deal with the lion than mess with Crazy Joe."

A couple of times when I walked by Mondo's, I could hear Cleo roaring. It sounded like it must be his feeding time.

You could usually find Joe's corner guys loitering near Mondo's, at the intersection of President and Columbia streets. The heavy hitters wore multicolored sweaters, nice slacks, and three-quarter-length coats, some with fur-trimmed collars. When they dressed up, it was full-length dress overcoats, dress shirts, and fedoras. When it was warm, they would pare down to nylon or polyester shirts and leisure suits. Meanwhile, the wannabes wore dark shades, chino pants, and T-shirts, one sleeve rolled up tightly to hold a pack of Lucky Strikes.

One of Joe's corner guys, Perky, was a muscle-bound Sicilian fireplug, maybe five-foot-five and possessing a kick-ass set of biceps. Having seen me do battle over at the ball field, Perky had taken a shine to Louie D.

"Hey, kid," he'd say. "How ya doin'? Come on over here, ya think you're so tough."

Then he'd grab me by the back of the neck or throw a few feints in my direction and some soft punches to my chin and my chest. "Real tough monkey, eh?"

I'd go into my Rocky Marciano shuffle, bobbing and weaving, volleying shadow punches until he'd throw a headlock around me and say, "Ayyyyyy, you're all right, kid."

The palsy-walsyness that Perky and the other Gallo soldiers bestowed on me burnished my street rep. And God, I loved it.

Because of the attention I was garnering from the wiseguys, I began to mimic them. In speech and in body language,

I became a wiseguy in training, even using Italian expressions in my everyday conversations.

Since Gallo was known to be generous to the neighborhood kids, I asked Perky if I could hit him up for a donation to help us buy T-shirts for our stickball team.

"Go see Tony over on the corner," Perky told me.

It was standard operating procedure when you dealt with the mob. The corner was where you got the latest news and left messages. Whenever you wanted to do business with the mob, you had to talk to some guy about some other guy and then go see some third guy over on some corner.

Tony-on-the-Corner arranged a sit-down for me, and when I finally did meet Joe Gallo, I was struck by his appearance. Stringbean slender, he had piercing blue eyes and, just like Sister Rose at St. Paul's, a large, ugly mole on his left cheek. Unlike his dark-haired cohorts, he was a blond, just like my old man. The resemblance gave me the willies.

I sat there and made my case. And true to his rep, Joe peeled off a bunch of crisp twenties for our stickball team.

Afterward Perky told me, "Joe knows all about you, kid. The way you handle yourself on the street. You get a few more years on you, come back and see him. He'll give you advice on what to do with the rest of your life."

How about *that* for career counseling! I filed the invitation away in my head. There was no mystery about what it meant.

I WASN'T READY to totally cross the line, since I knew Papa would kill me if I ever did. Papa disapproved of Joe Gallo's criminal ways, and was once rumored to have faced him down over by the docks. No doubt Crazy Joe realized that Papa was even more insane than he was.

Papa was still my conscience and my king. And as I got older, he imparted more of his Old World wisdom to me, including:

Never ask a favor, only give a favor. That way, they owe you.
Avoid lending money to a friend because you are bound to lose your money and your friend.
Never enter a man's house if his wife is there by herself.
Always wear a shirt in the presence of a lady.
Never, ever bring discredit to your name.
Always treat others as you wish to be treated.

Over the course of my life, I would try to follow his code. And I would emulate Papa in other ways. The way he would pinch a cigarette between his index finger and thumb, then tuck it under the remaining three fingers to cuff the smoke. The way he would roll his shoulders when he walked. The way he would stare down other men when he wanted to intimidate them. The way he would never, ever back down from a fight. He was my shining knight, my El Cid and my Don Quixote, my hero.

I worshipped him. It was all a son could do for his father.

STILL, WHILE I worshipped him, I feared him. I loved the principles and ideals he stood for, but I loathed the way he could behave, especially toward me.

When I was about fifteen came the very worst beating of all.

It was a Saturday morning and Papa sat in the kitchen, having coffee with Mama. Papa, who could be as tough on my mother with his words as he was on me with his fists, was rebuking Mama about some opinion she had dared to express.

"Achhh, what do you know, woman?" he scoffed. "Shut your mouth! You don't know what you are talking about." It was awful to hear him speak to her this way.

As I entered the kitchen, Papa suddenly leaped out of his chair and began yelling at *me*: "You walked over it! You walked over it! You want your mother to pick it up?"

His eyes were bulging and his nostrils flaring. "Respect begins at home," he snarled at me.

What the hell? I thought he had gone stark, raving mad.

He pointed over my shoulder. I turned, glanced back down the hallway, and saw that Papa's seaman's watch cap was on the floor. It must have fallen off the hat rack. I hadn't seen it when I came into the kitchen.

Pursing my lips, I made a *tssst!* sound. It's a sound that many Spaniards make when they feel something is insignificant or of no account. It was a sound that Papa himself often made in conversation . . . but for me to address him like that was akin to saying, "Yeah, fuck you, too."

Papa sprang at me like a big cat, throwing a vicious blow to my jaw and knocking me to the kitchen floor. Pouncing on top of me, he began to pummel me with closed-fist punches. I covered up as best I could, but he easily penetrated my defenses.

Just as I managed to get to my feet, he hit me again, throwing me clear into the living room. Down I went, reeling, hurt. This time I couldn't get up. My legs felt like jelly. Papa continued to throw punches to my head. I could actually feel my brain rock back and forth in my skull, hear the sickening *thump* each time his fist connected with my flesh.

By now my mother and my abuelita were yelling at him to stop. "*¡Assesino! ¡Cabrón!* Murderer! Good-for-nothing!"

Together, they began tearing at Papa's shirt, trying to pull him off me. But he was too crazed to hear or even feel them. Suddenly my abuelita lost her balance and fell.

The sight of my abuelita lying on the floor enraged Papa even more, and he continued unabated, beating me about the head, the chest, and the stomach. The blows left me feeling faint. I didn't lose consciousness, but I knew it was better to keep my eyes closed and stay down till it ended.

Later, I felt hands caressing me. Gently. Opening my eyes, I saw my mother and my abuelita kneeling over me, both of them sobbing. And I knew that finally, blessedly, it was over.

Mama and Abuelita Adela helped me to my feet and led me to the kitchen table. They soaked towels in vinegar and put stinging cold, wet compresses on my face. They gave me sips of hot black coffee to revive me.

Not once during the beating had I allowed myself to cry. But now, as I started to revive, my defenses crumbled. I began to weep. Great, heaping, gasping sobs. Not because of the blows my father had inflicted, but because of the humiliation and the shame. And the terrible pain he had caused my mother and my abuelita.

It was the first—and last—time I would ever let that man break my spirit.

From that day on, I decided I would never, ever allow him to hit me again. I also promised myself about what kind of man I would become in this world. Gentle and compassionate on the inside, fierce on the outside. Capable of withstanding any blows, any insults, any humiliations. And when confronted by bullies and brutes, annihilating in my counterattack. I wouldn't look for trouble. But if it came my way, I wouldn't run from it. In any fight, I would be an animal, tougher and meaner than the next guy. Nobody, but *nobody*, would put me down. If they did, they would have to kill me. Because I would fight to the death.

Rising slowly from the kitchen table, with both my mother and my abuelita watching, I limped over to the icebox and opened its door. Inside were a frost-covered box of peas, some chorizo sausages, and half a chicken.

Wiping a tear from my eye, I dabbed the tear on the interior wall of the icebox. I studied the tear for a moment, etching its outline in my memory. Then I closed the icebox door.

Soon that tear would freeze. And it would become an enduring symbol. I never looked at it again, but I always knew it was there.

For me, it would be a permanent reminder.

All hell would have to freeze over before I would ever hurt anyone I loved the way Papa had hurt me.

SCARRED BY PAPA'S brutality, consumed with an inner rage that never, ever seemed to cool, cursed with an overexaggerated sense of self-righteousness, a hair-trigger temper, and a knee-jerk reaction to perceived slights, I was, for better or worse, very much a chip off the old block.

And sometimes it got me in real hot water.

When I was about sixteen, a bunch of my regular friends were shooting the shit on our favorite corner when two plainclothes detectives came by in an unmarked car, rolling up right in front of us. The detectives were known to take graft from the mob, shake down shopkeepers, and beat up local kids. They got out of their car and started to push my pal Jimmy Reilly around. Jimmy was tall, blond, and Irish; the cops were short, stocky, and Italian.

"Hey, lay off the guy, would ya?" I said to the cop. "He ain't doing nuthin'."

The detective shot me a menacing look. "Who asked *you*?" he fired back. "You the *lawyer* for this group?"

"No, man," I said, "I ain't no lawyer. But you're supposed to be the cops."

"You know, wiseguy, you got a big mouth. You're some kinda wiseguy, right?"

"No, I ain't no wiseguy," I said. "But you guys ain't right."

"So whattya gonna do about it, huh, punk?" the detective challenged, prodding me sharply in the chest. "Huh, punk? Huh?" He prodded me again.

And then he knocked my wool longshoreman's cap off, which was one of the biggest insults anyone could throw down in Red Hook. Everybody on the docks knew that the one thing you never, ever did was forcibly remove a cap from some other guy's head. It was a slight on someone's manhood.

Instinctively, I caught the cop with a left hook. It sent him staggering back against his unmarked car.

His partner was on me like a fly on horseshit. The two of them banged me around pretty good, then cuffed me and tossed me into the backseat of their car. Although the rest of neighborhood tried to protest on my behalf, some people even running alongside the car and screaming at the cops to release me, I was hauled off to the nearby Eighty-second Precinct station house.

The station house was one of those fortresslike concrete structures, painted green on the outside, with heavy green entrance doors, and adorned with old-fashioned gas lamps near the entrance. It was surrounded by a heavy picket fence. Half a dozen green and black squad cars sat parked out front.

As the two detectives hustled me inside, a dozen people and friends outside continued to shout, "Let him go! Let him go!"

Inside, the lobby of the station house was empty except for the white-haired sergeant who sat behind the raised wooden desk. When he looked down at us, one of the detectives shoved me forward, my hands still cuffed behind.

"We're gonna book this punk for assaulting a police officer," he told the sergeant.

Once I had been booked and fingerprinted, I would be placed in the precinct's holding cell, then driven to the courthouse and marched before a criminal court judge to be arraigned on the assault charge.

I kept totally silent.

As the precinct desk sergeant started to write up the arrest, the two asshole detectives walked into the back room to get themselves coffee.

The moment they were out of earshot, Sergeant John McCarthy looked down from his high desk and said, "What the hell have you gone and done this time, Louie?"

The sergeant remembered me from the Police Athletic League. He knew I wasn't a bad apple, just a raw one, full of piss and vinegar. I told him how the two detectives had roughed me and my friend up without justification.

He nodded disdainfully in their direction, as if he had just gotten a whiff of stinky cheese. "Those two bulls have a hard time calling themselves cops."

Tossing the arrest forms in the trash, Sergeant McCarthy told me he would handle things with those two . . . but in return, I would have to enroll in a local boxing program at the Trinity Club run by an ex-cop, Sergeant Pat Kennedy.

When I showed up the next day at the boxing club, Sergeant Kennedy, a six-foot-two, 230-pound bruiser with a broken nose and scarred eyelids, handed me gloves and headgear and put me in the ring with a skinny Puerto Rican kid named

Kiki Costoso. I figured I could put this stringbean on his ass in two seconds flat, and when the bell rang for the first round, I bull-rushed him. But every time I'd go to throw a punch, Kiki wouldn't be there. Meanwhile, he kept popping me in my nose—*bam! bam! bam!*—and jabbing my eyes—*biff! biff! biff!*

"The fuck was *that*?" I said to myself.

It was like fighting three guys at once. By the end of the first round, my face was swollen and bloody. The second round was worse. At the start of the third round, I charged Kiki like a linebacker, grabbed him around the neck with my left glove, and started pummeling him with my right. Eel-like, Kiki slipped out of my grasp, spun me around on the ropes, and threw what must have been a hundred punches, all of which found their mark. When the round mercifully ended, I tore off my headgear in disgust. Kiki had taken me to school.

As Sergeant Kennedy began to unlace my gloves, Kiki came over and flashed a big grin.

"You got a lotta heart, kid."

It was only later that I found out Kiki Costoso had won three straight Golden Gloves titles and was well on his way to a fourth. Eventually he would go on to become a professional fighter and top-ranked welterweight.

I had thought I could fight. But now I realized that I was only a street brawler, not a real boxer. If I wanted to know what Kiki knew, I would have to learn. And over the next few months, with Sergeant Kennedy's help, I did.

Along the way, my romance with boxing blossomed. I fell head over heels in love with the sport and anything that came with it. The feel of my mitts as they hit the heavy bag. The popping sounds of leather on leather. The sense of power as the bag swung from side to side. The thrill of a good sparring session, taking a guy to the inside, working over his body. The meeting and colliding of the flesh. The sweat, the grunts, the sweet combinations.

I went on to win the Police Athletic League welterweight championship, which gave me a nice leg up on the neighborhood's not-to-be-fucked-with totem pole.

MEANWHILE, MY EDUCATION on the mean streets of Red Hook got even meaner.

Along with two of my friends, I got into a dustup with some trash-talking young punks over by the Red Hook public swimming pool. When one of them dissed me as "a guinea who could speak Spanish," I dumped him on his ass. Then the three of us ran like hell. It wasn't over yet.

A few days later, as I sat with my crew on our favorite stoop, a black sedan with several passengers drove by. Someone pulled a gun. Shots rang out. Donnie, the youngest kid in our crew, fell to the ground. I dove on top to protect him. The sedan sped off, leaving rubber.

When Donnie picked his head up, I could see that my shirt was covered with his blood. We rushed him over to the hospital, where the doctors found that the bullet had only passed through his cheek, and they stitched him up. Just under my high school medallion, I had a slight gash on my chest, which they painted with antiseptic and covered with a bandage. Detectives came to the emergency room to question us, but none of us had gotten a good look at the car or the shooters, so they sent us all home.

That night, however, as I lay in my bed, the gash in my chest began to throb. Pulling up my T-shirt, I felt around and found a hard lump. When I touched it, it moved. I could actually feel something rolling around in there.

"Holy shit!" I said to my brother Rigel, who was lying in the other bed. "That's a bullet! I've been shot!"

Rigel ran over to feel the lump. Then he began to cry. "Jesus, Louie, Jesus! Don't die!"

We ran and told Mama, who became hysterical. She immediately telephoned Papa, who was working that night at *El Diario-LaPrensa*. When Papa came home, he rushed me back to the hospital, where he went berserk and threatened to kill everyone in sight. Not content to wait his turn in the emergency room, he nearly started a riot by grabbing one of the doctors by the throat and demanding to know how the hell they could have released me with a bullet still in my chest. Fortunately, one of the security guards, who knew Papa from the neighborhood and spoke Spanish, calmed him down and made sure I was attended to promptly.

As I lay on a gurney, a Spanish-speaking doctor used a scalpel to dig into my chest and remove a .22-caliber bullet. It had nestled just above my sternum. Fortunately, it was just below the skin.

At the last second, the doctor figured, it must have been slightly deflected by my high school medallion. Just enough to detour it away from my heart.

A quarter inch to the left, I would have been a goner.

CHAPTER

THREE

FOR A WHILE, I figured I could punch my way to prominence.

At age seventeen, I advanced to the Golden Gloves competition in the welterweight division, won three fights in a row, and was on the fast track to the citywide championship.

But right around that time, my beloved Abuelita Adela took sick and, fearing that I might get seriously hurt in the ring, begged me to quit.

Abuelita had never asked me for anything before. Yet she had done so much for me over the course of my life, sheltering me, mentoring me, caring for me, I felt I had no choice. On the other hand, it would have been unthinkable to admit that I was hanging up my gloves because of my Abuelita Adela; the other guys in the hood would never have stopped giving me shit. Meanwhile, despite my string of consecutive victories, I worried that I might one day lose a bout. And I suspect that Papa, who was always concerned about his standing in the eyes of others, was secretly hoping I would retire undefeated as well.

So to save face, I made my decision and pounded my right hand into a brick wall enough times to make it swell up to three times its size, requiring that it be set in a plaster cast. To cover myself, I told everybody that I had been in a tough street brawl. And my boxing career came to a sudden, albeit semirespectable, halt.

* * *

I FINISHED MOST Holy Trinity High School in the spring of '63, but thanks to an ongoing feud with one of the Marianist brothers on the faculty—a shuffling little doofus named Brother Diodotti, who liked to suck on chalk and put everyone to sleep in his Latin class—my final year was less than stellar. During a schoolwide Mass, when I turned to whisper to a friend, Brother Diodotti handed me a slip with three demerits. When the Mass ended, I threw it right back in his face. As punishment, I was banned from both graduation and the prom, and I had to go with both Mama and Papa to the principal's office to collect my diploma in private.

Remarkably, Papa, who had never finished grammar school but always preached the importance of formal education, did not haul off on me for this indignity. Actually, he was rather relieved that I hadn't been kicked out of school altogether.

So when the principal proposed to quietly give me my diploma in his office, Papa quickly said, "We'll take it," snatched the document from his hand, and hustled me out the door.

I went off to St. Francis College in Brooklyn that fall, joining the baseball and rifle teams and the navy ROTC program. I had been a good ballplayer all through high school and, thanks to numerous visits to the shooting galleries at the Coney Island amusement park and my experiments at home shooting at tree branches with a Daisy pump-action BB gun, I had developed a fascination with firearms. At St. Francis I took courses in history, math, English, and science, but all my extracurricular activities left me overextended, and I quickly started to screw up my grades. Given that Papa was footing the bill for my college studies, this was something that *did* set him off.

"All my-hard earned money for you to go to college, and you waste it!" he would rant. "You good-for-nothing! You bum!"

Meanwhile, I was still living at home, chafing under Papa's suffocating rules. Having turned eighteen, I wanted to come and go as I pleased. Papa had very different ideas, and we butted heads about this, too.

Adding to the friction, I didn't know what I wanted to do with my life. One minute, I would talk of becoming a doctor, a lawyer, a diplomat, or a cop. The next, I would see myself traveling to exotic destinations in Central America with my childhood buddy Nicky Estavillo, maybe even joining up with some guerrilla revolutionary group, given that this was the early 1960s and nearly everybody was revolting against something. Here and there I picked up part-time work—as a longshoreman, a construction worker, and, thanks to Papa, a mailer—tying, stacking, and loading newspaper bundles at the *New York Times* and the *New York Herald Tribune*. But I had no real plan for the future, and this seemed to enrage Papa most of all.

Meanwhile, the Vietnam War was heating up. A lot of my old pals started enlisting. When Nicky Estavillo changed course and signed with the Marines, I gave up my dream of becoming a Mexican revolutionary and decided to follow suit. Of all the uniformed services, the Marines were the toughest shit-kickers of the bunch, and that suited me just fine. By joining the Marines, I felt I could both emulate and please Papa, who was a veteran of combat in both the Spanish Civil War and World War II. I longed to see combat in Vietnam, wanting the respect that came from being on the front lines, as well as the medals and the bragging rights when I eventually returned to Red Hook. I wanted to be like Papa. More than anything else, I hungered for his approval. And, in my mind, facing the bullets and bombs in Southeast Asia would compel him to finally give it to me.

But when the Marines learned that I was still in the Naval

Reserve as part of my ROTC requirement, they told me to take a hike, and my mood went straight into the shitter.

I had come to loathe the navy. One weekend each month, as part of my ROTC commitment, I had to ship out on a destroyer escort in the Atlantic Ocean for submarine search-and-destroy exercises. Every time I did, I would get seasick. Instead of acting like a real sailor, I was puking my guts over the side railing.

An old naval petty officer tipped me off that I could ask the draft board to "push" my draft status, accelerating a call-up by the army—once I was drafted, the navy couldn't lay a finger on me. I followed his advice, and not long after, I got a cheery letter from President Lyndon Baines Johnson ordering me to report to Whitehall Street in Manhattan for induction. They even included a subway token for the trip downtown.

I dropped out of St. Francis, got all my affairs in order, and prepared to go off to serve my country.

Papa was disappointed that I wouldn't be finishing college, but given his own short-lived experience with schooling, he was still relieved that I had gotten my high school diploma, since he had never expected me to get even that far. I had seen him cry only once in my lifetime—when he learned that his mother had died back home in Spain—but that day in early 1964 when I left for the army, he actually got teary-eyed. I hugged Mama and my Abuelita Adela good-bye, along with my beloved shepherd-husky Butch, then caught the subway into Manhattan to board the bus that would take me that very night to Fort Jackson, South Carolina.

Although much of the ride was shrouded in darkness, the trip south was an adventure. The farthest I had ever been from Brooklyn was the Catskills.

During the ride south, I made friends with Tony Ramirez, a six-foot, 220-pound bruiser whose parents came from the same northern part of Spain as mine.

We arrived at Fort Jackson before dawn. And right away, the shit started.

"Okay, you disgusting maggots!" screamed a voice at the front of the bus. "Get your asses off this bus *now!* Move! Move! *Move!*"

The speaker, a pint-sized sergeant with a southern accent, had a pinched face, a Smokey the Bear hat, and creased, starched fatigues.

We piled out of the bus, bleary-eyed and exhausted. The sergeant ordered us to stand in three lines. Walking up and down the lines, he commanded everyone to sound off and tell him where we were from.

"Louie Diaz, Brooklyn, New York, sir!" I shouted.

The sergeant stopped dead in his tracks. Squinting as if he had just smelled a skunk, he pushed his nose so close to my own that I could smell the wieners and baked beans he had eaten for dinner. "Brooklyn, eh? So we got us a tough guy here."

"Jesus Christ," I told myself. I couldn't believe this. It was just like in the movies.

"No, sir," I answered. "Only when I have to be."

With that, the sergeant screamed into my face, spraying flecks of hot-dog-scented spittle across my chin: *"Who told you to speak?! You speak when I tell you to speak, maggot!"*

He kept up the screaming for a few more minutes, then ordered me to stand off to one side at attention. Me being me, I began to fantasize about rearranging his nose. But I managed to hold myself in check.

In front of everyone else, the sergeant announced that I

would be polishing every fire extinguisher and piece of brass on the base. One of his goons escorted me to an empty billet, handed me a can of polish and some rags, steered me toward the first fire extinguisher, and told me to snap to it. Then he left.

I began polishing. By now, it was 4:00 a.m.

After about an hour of this horseshit, I put aside the rags and polish and darted into another barracks. There, I rolled up my coat for a pillow and plopped my ass down on the floor next to Tony Ramirez, who I was relieved to find. By now it was obvious that nobody cared whether I rejoined the original group of recruits. The whole polishing exercise had been sham, a way to bust chops. There were no consequences to me walking away from it since everybody had already forgotten I was even there.

It seemed like only a few minutes later that I was awakened by a fresh chorus of shouting and screaming. Another sergeant had entered the barracks and was bellowing, "All right, ladies, drop your cocks and grab your socks! Fall out!"

When Ramirez rolled over on his cot and saw me on the floor next to him, he exclaimed, "Shit, Louie! I thought they had shipped you to Siberia!"

From Fort Jackson, I was sent to Fort Gordon, Georgia, while Ramirez was shipped elsewhere. At Fort Gordon, armed guards patrolled the front gate and, with its high-intensity domed lights, its chain-link fence, and its rolled coils of heavy barbed wire, the place looked more like a Nazi concentration camp. Plus it was manned by even more barkers, screamers, and spitters who started in with the same old refrain the instant we stepped off the bus.

"Move, maggots, move, move, move!"

It was here at Fort Gordon that I did my *real* basic training. For me, the physical part was a breeze. Before being inducted, I had been playing a lot of baseball. And after my self-inflicted hand injury had healed, I had begun training again as a boxer. Thanks to all my roadwork, I could run for miles without getting winded. I could do sixty push-ups in less than a minute. I was in the best shape of my life.

The one thing I wasn't in shape for was all the chickenshit. I had passed the real test of manhood long ago, surviving the mean streets of Red Hook and the beatings from Papa. I did *not* need the army to make me into a man.

During one exercise, we had to belly-crawl under simulated barbed wire while a machine gun fired blanks over our heads. A fat guy in front of me freaked out. I tried to encourage him on, but he would periodically choke on the dirt and stop dead.

One of the drill instructors, a real southern peckerwood, walked over and planted his boot on the back of the chubby soldier's neck, pushing his face deeper into the soil. I could hear the poor guy spitting up and gasping for air. The DI finally let him wriggle forward, but then he stepped on his neck again and made him eat even more dirt.

I could feel my anger rising. Picking my head up, I yelled: "Hey, why don't you let up on him?!"

Turning in my direction, the drill instructor broke into a demonic grin. "You want some of the same, maggot?" he said, stepping into my path.

"No, sir," I replied. "How about just letting me get by?"

His grin widened. "Make your move, boy."

When I tried to crawl around him, he stepped over me so that he now straddled my head. Then he tried to bring his boot down on my neck, too.

Big mistake.

With my head still between his legs, I went for a wrestling move I had learned as a kid. Reaching slowly behind his heels, I yanked his feet forward toward my shoulders, sending him ass-over-end. Then I jumped up and went into a boxing stance. When the DI scrambled to his feet, I could see he wanted to throttle me.

Seeing the commotion, the company sergeant came running over. "Is there a problem here, gentlemen?"

Simultaneously, the drill instructor and I barked back, "No, sir!"

"Then carry on," the sergeant ordered. And he walked away.

The moment he did, the drill instructor hissed, "It ain't over, punk."

"Call it," I shot back.

"Behind the barracks. After chow."

"Don't be late," I answered.

That night, after dinner, I headed over behind the barracks. It was cold, dark, and nobody else was in sight. Out of the corner of my eye, I saw the DI approaching. He had donned tight-fitting, black leather gloves, the kind you might wear if you were going to pull a caper and didn't want to leave fingerprints. And he was standing tall, with that same shit-eating grin on his face, just knowing he was gonna give me a tattooing. He began to wave me on, taunting me with his gloved fists.

The DI was bigger, but that didn't faze me. Most of the guys I had fought were always bigger than I was. Because of their height and their big mouths, they always thought they had the edge. They hardly ever got challenged, so they usually didn't have to fight. They got by on their size and their bluffs.

I was the bluff buster.

As the DI began to circle me, I knew exactly what I was going to do. With one nasty left hook to the body and another to the side of his head, down he went, falling on his face, out cold. I waited a minute until he came to. Then I put my foot on the back of his neck and pushed his face into the ground. He began gasping for air, spitting out dirt. When I eased up, I could see his eyes pleading for mercy.

"Are we good?" I asked him.

He nodded.

I extended a hand to help him to his feet. "By the way," I admitted, "I'm a trained boxer."

He grunted sheepishly. I walked back to my barracks while he dusted himself off. Not knowing any of the other recruits well enough to trust them, I kept mum about my knockout victory. And desperate to save face, the DI kept quiet about it, too. We never had any more problems with each other.

Unfortunately, there were plenty of other dickheads in this man's army only too ready to step into his shoes.

Periodically, I was detailed to KP duty, picking up trays off the tables, cleaning and mopping the mess hall, washing the pots and pans, etc. Passing in front of the chow line one day, I was spotted by a second lieutenant who was sitting at one of the tables.

"Hey, you there, soldier!"

I stopped and pointed to myself. "Me?"

"Yeah, that's right, *you.*"

I walked over to the lieutenant. "Yes, sir, what can I do for you?"

"You will bring me a tray of food." His accent was as southern as fried chicken and pecan pie.

"I will?" I said.

"Yes, soldier, *you will.*"

"Yes, sir, right away, sir," I said through clenched teeth.

So back to the chow line I went and fixed him a tray. But then my pride kicked in and my resentment rose like a tidal wave. Here was one more swaggering numbnuts with bars on his shoulder and turds in his cranium who liked to boss people around.

When I came back to the lieutenant with his tray of food, I smiled. "Here you are, sir."

"Well, set it down, boy," he commanded.

"Yes, sir." And I dropped the tray, food and all, right in his lap.

"Sonofabitch!" the lieutenant exclaimed as he jumped from his seat, beef stew, string beans, and mashed potatoes cascading slowly down his pants legs. "Donkey-ass 'cruit!" Then he shouted across the room: "Mess sergeant! On the double!"

The mess hall sergeant trotted over. "Yes, sir?"

"I want this 'cruit put on company punishment forthwith!" the lieutenant commanded.

The mess sergeant took me outside and led me to a twelve-by-twelve-foot hole in the ground reinforced with concrete. It was the pit where all the grease from the kitchen collected. It reeked like vomit.

Pointing to a steel drum receptacle, he handed me a shovel and nodded at the hole.

"Clean it," he ordered.

And for the next several hours, I had to shovel all the shit out of the grease pit and into the steel drum, hoping not to ruin my lone pair of army boots since that would only lead to more punishment when inspection rolled around.

* * *

IF ONLY THAT was the end of it. No such luck.

When my platoon lined up to file into the mess hall, a lot of us would horse around with each other as we waited to enter. One DI corporal, who was tall and lean, with a bony face and a short-cropped military haircut, would always single me out for discipline.

"Diaz!" he would scream. "Drop down and gimme twenty!"

Just to shove it up his ass, I would fall to the ground and do thirty instead.

But the DI continued to ride me. He particularly liked to fuck around with my name. "Diaz," he'd sneer. "How do ya like that? And here I thought you was Eye-talian, but it turns out you ain't nuthin' but a Mexican."

Well, that really pressed my buttons. So soon after, while standing on line, I murmured to another soldier that the DI was a dumb, shit-for-brains hick . . . and I said it just loud enough that he overheard. He immediately marched over and ordered me to meet him in the company staff office as soon as chow was over.

After lunch, when I showed up at the staff office, the DI corporal was there waiting for me. He opened the door to a small room, which held a desk and a couple of chairs. My radar and self-defense systems went into full alert.

"Tell me, Private Diaz," he began, a sick smile slowly creeping across his storm trooper face, "you like to play games?"

Uh-oh.

"Depends," I answered. But in my head, I was already working out my battle plan.

"Well," said the corporal, "I like to play this hand game. Maybe you know it?"

He told me to put my palms down. Then he slipped his long, bony fingers under mine, palms facing up.

We had played this game when I was a kid. The idea was for the guy on top to pull his hands away before the guy on bottom could slap them. If the guy on top made the guy on bottom miss, you'd switch places and the guy who had been on top would get to do the smacking.

"Here we go," said the corporal.

Whack! He got me.

Whack! Got me again. The motherfucker was fast.

Whack! No wonder he had called this game.

Whack!

Whack!

Whack!

My hands were turning red and swollen and they hurt like a sonofabitch. Finally, blessedly, I made him miss. We switched places. Now it was my turn and was I ever ready for payback.

Swish!

I hit nothing but air. He was too damned quick for me.

And the serve went right back to the corporal, who continued smacking the tops of my hands, which now felt as big and puffy as catchers' mitts. The fucker was damned near close to drawing blood, and practically creaming his jeans over my obvious pain and suffering.

Just as he started to lift his palms for one more stinging smack, I threw a hard right to his Adam's apple.

Down he went, gasping for air. Straddling his body, I pounded more rights into his face. And there was a distinct change in the sound track:

Pow! Pow! Pow! Pow!

Blood spurted from his nose and mouth. He began to slip into and out of consciousness. I ran to the bathroom, found a towel, and soaked it in cold water. Then I knelt down and put the towel to his face.

When he came to again, I told him, "Forget me. Forget this ever happened. You ever fuck with me or any of my friends again, I will kill you. Understand?"

He got the message.

For several days after, I walked around with my balls in my throat anyway, worrying about possible repercussions. But none came my way. The DI kept silent. I spotted him in the mess hall a couple of times—puffed-up black eye, bandage over the other eye, a big fat lip.

When anyone asked me what had happened, I would simply say, "He fell." I'm pretty sure he was giving out with the same story, although nobody really bought it.

I had not set out to be a troublemaker in the army. If anything, I wanted to avoid fights. But sometimes, to be a peacemaker, you had to be an ass-kicker. And my rep around the base definitely got bumped up a notch, no matter what anyone believed.

ALL DURING BOOT camp, I kept putting in requests to be given tank training and sent to Vietnam where, at this point in history, the Untied States had close to half a million troops. So naturally, after boot camp, I was sent to Fort Knox and given advanced training in communications. Then, instead of being assigned to Vietnam, I was shipped to Germany. When it came to practical thinking, this man's army was really fucked.

After a nine-day Atlantic voyage on an old World War II Liberty ship, crammed in like a sardine with thirty-two hundred other recruits, I arrived in Germany, then boarded a train for my base at Budigen, about thirty kilometers south of Frankfurt.

Tired, ragged, and hungry, I reported to the Bravo Troop

office. Through the door I could see the troop's first sergeant shuffling some papers and talking to another GI. The nameplate on his desk read *Sgt. Horace Brown.*

After my long sea voyage and train ride, I stunk like a bag of onions and was badly in need of a shower. I was desperate for some chow and a bed to bunk out on. I knocked on the office door, asking permission to enter. The sergeant appeared not to hear me. I waited a few moments, then knocked again. He paid me no heed. So finally I just pushed the door open and walked in. As I approached his desk, the sergeant rose up to his full height of six-foot-four and, in a deep, syrupy southern drawl, began to ream me a new one. "Who the hell gave you permission to enter my office, Private?!"

Oh, shit. Here we go again.

"Sergeant," I said apologetically, "I just arrived from the States and am reporting for duty, as instructed, so I just thought—"

The sergeant cut me off. "You *thought*? You *thought*?! Who the hell gave you permission to think, soldier? Shut your dumb Yankee mouth! You will speak when I tell you to speak!"

Well, that did it. By this point in my military career, I had had it up to here with swaggering, bullying shitheads. Dropping my duffel bag, I told the sergeant, "Fuck you, fuck the horse you rode in on, and fuck the entire Confederacy, you lame, redneck, shit-eating motherfucker!"

With that, the sergeant made his move. I quickly backed up and curled my hands into hard fists. Seeing me drop into a serious boxing stance, the sergeant ordered me to drop my fists and stand at attention. Then he commanded one of his clerks, Corporal Burke, to take me to "the dungeon."

Corporal Burke grabbed my duffel bag and led me downstairs into the armory where Bravo Troop stored its weapons.

After throwing my duffel into a cubbyhole, he handed me a large pail of whitewash paint and a large brush.

Swiveling around 360 degrees, he pointed in half a dozen directions. "After you finish that wall, paint *that* wall. Then *that* wall. Then *that* wall. Hop to it, soldier."

I must have stood there for ten minutes after he left, staring at bucket and brush. All these walls? And I was supposed to paint them? He had to be fucking kidding.

I was dirty, exhausted, hungry, and completely disgusted. And here I was, subjected to this at only eighteen years old.

When I finally got a grip, I started to get angry. Which was a good thing. Anger gave me motivation, a sense of purpose, spurring me to exceed my limits. Anger gave me the power to move against anything that was thrown at me. Anger was my biggest ally.

"Fuck it, " I told myself. Just because some guy has stripes on his sleeves doesn't mean I have to bow and scrape. He was no better than those two bull detectives who had roughed me up back in Brooklyn. I didn't cower for those two shitbirds, and I wouldn't cower for these idiots either.

Fueled by rage, I started to paint the wall. For two hours, I kept at it. When I got to the end of the first hallway, I started to turn the corner into the next hallway when . . . *bam!* . . . I bonked into another soldier who also was painting walls. He nearly leaped out of his boots.

"Jesus Christ! Who the fuck are *you*?" he asked.

"I just got here," I answered.

"No shit! Well, you must be a real badass motherfucker to get sent down here your first day."

"That's me," I said. He began to laugh.

The other soldier was a black kid named Robert Hodge, who hailed from New Orleans. We became instant friends.

"Hey, let's get some chow," said Hodge with a killer smile. "Sergeant Dickface has left the base for the day. Besides, I got some guys you need to meet."

After I showered at his barracks, Hodge brought me over to the mess hall and led me to a table where eight guys were shooting the shit. The one at the center of the table was holding court. Dark-haired, dark-complexioned and handsome, his name was Johnny Rosa.

Hodge brought Johnny up to speed on my get-acquainted meeting with Sergeant Dickface Brown. Like me, Johnny and most of the other guys at the table were from the East Coast and had little use for rednecks such as Brown.

From that day on, my army life took a turn for the better. Johnny Rosa was a mover and a shaker on base. As soon as Sergeant Brown went on leave, Johnny persuaded the first sergeant filling in for him to let me bunk in Hodge's billet. He also arranged for me to be reassigned to a tank-training unit. And in a few weeks' time, he got me transferred into Headquarters Troop, which handled all vital services on base—supplies, fuel, vehicle maintenance, the mess hall, the MPs, etc. By bartering favors with the company clerks, Johnny could arrange transfers, finagle sick leave or workday passes, secure mess hall privileges or lighter KP duty, extend loans, and score extra cartons of cigarettes, which could later be resold at top dollar on the black market to the locals. Like a lot of the guys I knew back in Brooklyn, he always had a hustle up his sleeve. If you needed anything, Johnny was the go-to guy.

Three months down the line, when Johnny and most of his crew were due to be discharged, he tapped me to run his operation. Other GIs might have wanted the gig, but Johnny made it clear I was his handpicked choice to fill his shoes. I felt like I had been awarded the Congressional Medal of Honor.

DESPITE MY ELEVATION in status, however, I continued to get into fights. After one particularly nasty altercation with a sergeant, an MP who was a member of my crew tipped me off that the provost marshal—the top cop on base—had initiated an investigation. But it never really went anywhere.

At the base snack bar, when I caught a guy from another unit staring at me, I braced for another brawl. With the rest of my guys protecting my back, I got up and walked over to the table where the ogler was sitting and got up in his face. Leaning my elbows on the table, I looked him in the eye and said,

"You know me. You want to know me. Or you got some kind of a fucking problem?"

"No problem, no," the guy said. "But I *do* know you."

Turned out he was from Brooklyn and he remembered me from a brawl that had erupted during a concert over by the Red Hook piers, when I had hurled some guy headfirst through the band's base drum.

"Yeah, that was me," I said. "So who the fuck are you anyway?"

Next thing I knew, Billy Ellis and I were reminiscing about the good old days in Brooklyn.

Over time, as Billy and I got tighter, he showed me a photo of his girlfriend Gladys. Standing next to Gladys was her sister, Iris. She was a knockout.

"Wow. Is she seeing anybody?" I asked Billy. He said no.

I asked Billy if it would be okay to write to her. After Billy corresponded with Gladys, he gave me the green light. Pretty soon I was exchanging letters with Iris Maldonado, who lived in Hollis, Queens. We wrote back and forth to each other for more than a year, exchanging notes and photos, sharing more and more intimate details about ourselves. Mail call became the most important part of my day. Even though I had never met Iris, I started to have real feelings for her.

Meanwhile, I picked up my boxing gloves again. I landed a spot on the division's boxing team, went on to win the middleweight finals, and snagged a berth on the army's pre-Olympic boxing team. But fate, and my hair-trigger temper, cut short my march to the gold.

In June of 1966, during tank-training exercises about sixty miles from Nuremberg, a bunch of us got a little too rowdy in a local snack bar. Somebody called the base, and before we knew it, two MPs showed up to kick some ass. One of the MPs, a big redneck shitkicker, began poking one of my guys, a black soldier named Mickey Washington, with his baton, taunting him about being a lifer in the army. His racism wasn't even subtle.

I asked him to lay off. Instead, he jabbed Washington even harder in the ribs.

So I leaped up, wrested his baton away, and used it to throw a choke hold on *him*. Gagging, he started to turn blue. His knees buckled and he slumped to the floor. He never had a chance to reach for his .45.

While some of my guys held the second MP at bay, others pulled me off before I could cause any serious harm. But commissioned officers showed up and ordered the MPs to cart me off to the brig, where I spent the night.

Several weeks later, I was brought before a summary court-martial. Other soldiers, including a sergeant, spoke out on my behalf. In the end, I was found guilty of assaulting a military police officer and demoted from specialist fourth class to private first class, which meant a loss of pay. Had the others not spoken on my behalf, the punishment could have been much more severe.

With only six months left until my discharge date, I decided to turn over a new leaf. I simply wanted my pride back. So I cleaned up my act, became less active with my crew, and performed my military duties in an exemplary manner. Knowing how eager I was to get my stripes back, my crew gave me its full support. Two months before my discharge, I was reinstated to specialist fourth class.

And to my great relief, when my time was up, I received an honorable discharge. When my papers finally came through, the guys in my outfit threw me a big party.

At the ripe old age of twenty, I was now a U.S. Army veteran.

A lot of guys like me used to say that if it hadn't been for the army, they probably would have wound up in jail or dead. Owing to the strict code of morality Papa had imparted early on, I don't think I ever would have come to those ends. But there was no question the army had done some good things for me. It had given me a chance to travel and meet people of other ethnic backgrounds and nationalities. It had taught me how to be independent, care for my possessions, manage my money, live on my own. It had given me the chance to go back to college under the GI Bill. And, most important, it had connected me with a beautiful young girl named Iris.

The army also had added one more layer of protective skin to my thickening hide. Over the course of my twenty years, I had tangled with some pretty rough customers: my old man, the nuns at St. Paul's, the thugs and wiseguys of Red Hook, the bulls of the New York City Police Department. And, last but not least, the rednecks and sadists of the U.S. Army.

But all of these encounters would turn out to be useful, since I would soon be going up against the *really bad* bad guys.

CHAPTER FOUR

WHEN I WALKED UP to the nursing residence at Caledonian Hospital in Brooklyn, I could see the venetian blinds up above me flickering. Tipped off that I was coming, the nursing students were giggling and whispering to each other about the soldier who stood below on the front stoop.

"You must be Louis," said the head nurse, who came to the front door when I rang the bell.

"Yes, ma'am," I said, answering in proper military mode. Not only did I sound like a soldier, I still looked like one, too, in my spit-shined boots, pressed army tunic, pressed trousers, medals, ribbons, and beret. A man in uniform was bound to impress the ladies.

"Just a moment," said the head nurse. She picked up the house phone and called upstairs. "She'll be right down."

My heart started to beat like a horse's in full gallop. And then she appeared, walking gracefully down the stairs. Her beauty froze me in my place.

Long auburn hair, plaid pleated skirt, bobby socks, saddle shoes. Iris Maldonado was the most gorgeous woman I had ever seen.

"Hello," I nervously croaked. I extended my hand.

"Hi," she said. She kissed me on the cheek.

I blushed. Never at a loss for words, rough-tough Louie D. was tongue-tied for once.

We held hands as we walked to a nearby Chinese restaurant for lunch. It was the first time I had eaten Chinese food in two years. Hell, it was the first time I had ever been to any restaurant on a date.

We sat down to eat, and I could barely swallow my food. But once I got past my butterflies, we talked, mostly about our letters. I couldn't take my eyes off her face. To me, she seemed like a goddess, the image of perfection. And then asshole Louie nearly spoiled everything by getting in the waiter's face over some perceived slight.

From my letters, Iris already knew about my hair-trigger temper. She suggested, ever so gently, that I might have misunderstood the waiter. Realizing she was right, I apologized and we managed to get things back on track again. After the meal, we took the bus over to my parents' house, where we had dessert and posed for our first photos together. Mama and Papa were bursting with happiness.

Later, we went for a walk along the Brooklyn Heights promenade. Against the backdrop of the Manhattan skyline, just across the East River, I asked her for a kiss. Her lips were soft, sweet, luscious. I was spellbound.

We took the bus back to the nursing school, where I escorted her to the door.

As we said good night, I kissed her again. And again. And again . . .

From that moment on, I couldn't get enough of her.

I was head over heels in love.

EVEN THOUGH I was back from the service, I still needed a job.

The telephone company was hiring, so I snagged a gig as a frame man, connecting, disconnecting, and troubleshooting phone lines inside the central Brooklyn office. My starting salary was eighty-seven bucks a week. Thanks to Papa, I picked up extra work on the weekends as a newspaper mailer, bundling and stacking papers for delivery from the *New York Times* and the *New York Herald Tribune*. After work, I would head over to Queens, where I would eat dinner with Iris's parents.

I also reconnected with a lot of my old Brooklyn pals from elementary and high schools. Returning to St. Francis College, where I had done a year before joining the army, I ran into Johnny Andrejko, with whom I also had gone to Trinity High School. But when Johnny told me he was about to graduate and get his degree, my soul went straight into the shitter. Had I stayed in school instead of joining the army, I, too, would have been graduating this year, then moving on to a good job and a better life. Compared to Johnny, I felt like I had fallen behind a step . . . and I would have to light a fire under my ass to catch up.

Some friends, I was stunned to learn, I would never see again. One had been killed in Vietnam, another had overdosed on heroin, and a third had been whacked by the mob.

But others were still exactly where I had left them before I joined the army. One in particular was hanging out on the same corner with the same bunch of wiseguys, puffing on a Camel cigarette while scanning the streets for friends . . . and foes. The moment Perky saw me, his face lit up.

"Ayyyyyy, look who's back from playin' soldier boy! General Tough Monkey!"

And we instantly went into our shadow-box shuffle, bobbing and weaving and feinting and smacking each other with soft, open hands.

I told Perky I had taken a job with the phone company. But I still had dreams of someday becoming a professional prizefighter.

"C'mon, let's go see Joe's guys," he said.

Joe was "away" upstate, but his crew was still headquartered at Mondo's social club on President Street, the soldiers patrolling the corner, chain smoking. Outside Mondo's, Perky caught the eye of a crew boss who was known as "Punchy" because of all the shots he'd taken to the head in the ring.

"Hey, Punchy," said Perky, "remember this tough monkey, that crazy *espaniole*'s kid?"

Punchy motioned us back inside the club, toward one of the little tables. After we sat down with him, one of his boys brought him an espresso with a slice of lemon rind. Punchy lit up an unfiltered cigarette.

"Kid wants to be a fighter," Perky told him.

Punchy studied me for a moment. Then he said, "I remember you from the Gloves, kid. You handle yourself pretty good. But it takes more than being good, y'know. You gotta take orders, you know what I mean? You know how to take orders, don't you? You learned in the army, right?"

"Sure did," I replied.

"Well, we can bring you along, and maybe give you a shot," Punchy said. And then he gave a twisted little smile. "But you gotta do the right thing."

"I understand," I said. All too well.

Later, when I talked things over with Papa, he quickly put the kibosh on it. He had no use for Joe Gallo or his crew. But I had already decided to pass on Punchy's offer, with or without Papa's blessing. Much as the idea of fighting pro excited me, I wasn't about to take a dive for anybody, not even Crazy Joe Gallo.

Perky was disappointed. But he told me to stay in touch anyway.

It would be a long time, however, before I saw Perky again.

After the fight offer, he seemed to mysteriously vanish. The word on the street was that he'd taken a pinch, probably for dealing stolen guns. He was a connected guy, so a stint or two in the slammer usually went with the territory.

KNOWING I'D HAVE to go back to school if I ever wanted to make something of myself, I enrolled at Kingsborough Community College. It turned out to be bum fit. There I was, freshly minted by the U.S. Army, all decked out in my close-cropped hair, my starched shirts, and my neatly pressed khakis, and with my rigid military bearing. But everyone around me had long or frizzy hair, bell-bottomed jeans, tye-dyed T-shirts, sandals, and love beads. It seemed like every pot-smoking, flower-carrying hippie in New York City was attending Kingsborough. This was a period when LSD was all over the place, the Black Panther party was organizing, and mass protests against the Vietnam War were being staged all across the country. All I could see around me were anti-Vietnam, antiauthoritarian, antigovernment, antieverything, free-loving radicals. They drove me insane, and I always seemed to be getting into pissing matches with one or another of them.

Before long it went beyond arguments. In the second week, I happened to arrive on campus wearing khaki army pants and my dog tags. Suddenly I found myself being shouted down as a fascist. Then I got into a fight with a couple of these clowns and broke one guy's nose. When the cops showed up, they handcuffed me and put me in the back of their squad car, then drove me off campus. Sitting in the back of that police car, an honorably discharged veteran who was now a prisoner of the law, I felt like a social outcast, a freak. It seemed like I didn't belong in my own country anymore.

After driving around for a while, the police car turned down a deserted street and stopped. The cop in the passenger seat swiveled around to face me. "End of the line, kid," he said.

Shit, I thought. *Here we go again.* I had survived the streets of Red Hook and the assholes of the U.S. Army—and now I had to take more crap from the New York City police?

The cop who addressed me got out, then opened the rear door. He motioned me to step out.

"What's up, officer?" I asked, bracing for the beating that was sure to come.

The cop spun me around. He unlocked my cuffs. I could only look at him, baffled.

"Hey, kid," the police officer said, "what you did back there, you did on behalf of every one like us. Now be on your way. There's a train station around the corner."

WHILE WORKING AT the phone company was tolerable, a lot of my old pals were applying for civil service jobs. Good pay, plenty of security, great benefits, solid retirement plan. For blue-collar guys like us, that was the way to go.

So when my childhood buddy Nicky Estavillo came back from the Marines, the two of us decided to take the test for the Police Department. Putting aside my aversion to cops—at least the ones who were brutal, corrupt, and prejudiced—maybe I could be a breed of cop different from the meatheads I had grown up with. Maybe I could even *help* people.

I scored high marks on the NYPD's written exam. And I maxed out on the fitness tests—push-ups, sit-ups, running, jumping, scaling. But the height requirement for the New York City Police Department was five-foot-eight. I was only five-foot-seven.

"Sorry, kid," said the examining doctor when I went for my physical. "You're out."

I couldn't believe it. "I'm out?" I repeated. "For one inch, I'm out?"

He nodded.

"What could be my whole future, and I'm screwed for a lousy fucking inch?"

The doctor shook his head. "Even if it were less than an inch, you'd still be out. Five-foot-eight is the absolute minimum."

"Fuck you!" I screamed at the doctor. At that point, my anger knew no bounds, and scanning all the other applicants in the room, I hollered, "I'll take on any one of you!"

I zeroed in on one large cop already in uniform. "How about you, big guy? You wanna go a few?" Then, looking back at all the others, I bellowed, "I'll beat the piss out of alla yas!"

The room went silent. Everybody put his head down or looked away. I don't think anyone was really afraid. Rather, because I had been found lacking for something over which I had no control, I seemed to have touched their hearts.

As I headed for the door, the big cop in uniform pulled me aside and tipped me that a lot of guys who had flunked the height test were getting themselves stretched out and then making appointments to be remeasured. They would go to chiropractors or sleep all night on wooden boards, then have themselves carried in on those same boards to be retested before their spines contracted. Other guys would actually beat themselves on the head and feet to raise welts, creating just enough swelling to give themselves an extra inch of height for the scales.

But this was complete horseshit. I had served my country and maintained myself in tip-top condition. I wasn't about to stoop to cheap tricks. So back to the phone company I went . . . one motherfucking inch too short.

DESPITE THE KICK in the nuts from the NYPD, I still had it in my head that I could do some good in this world. So I took a civil service test, went for several interviews, and passed a psychological evaluation to land a job as a drug counselor for New York State, landing a gig at a correctional-rehab facility on Manhattan's West Side. Most of the inmates were hard-core addicts, their lives so wretched it was a wonder they hadn't just offed themselves. They might just as well have, since doing drugs was just a slower, costlier, more painful way of committing suicide.

One harrowing story remains with me: a young black kid told me he never knew his father. He had been raised by his mother, who was a dope fiend, and his most vivid childhood memories were of Mom shooting up, being strung out all day, and having all kinds of sex with all kinds of disgusting characters to get money for more drugs. Many of these johns would beat up on her son.

But the worst part was that Mama forced herself on *the kid*, made him have sex with her, and got him hooked on drugs, too.

"She shoulda just flushed me down the toilet when I was born," the kid said. How do you answer something like that?

I TRIED TO put all this ugliness out of mind when I was with Iris, and thanks to the kind of person she was, I generally succeeded. Everybody loved her. Especially Mama and Papa and my Abuelita Adela. Iris had never been with another man, which suited my ego just fine.

And in July 1968, we were married at St. Gerard Majella Catholic Church in Queens, following which there was a big blowout at the Regency House in Jamaica. A hundred and fifty guests had a blast. While the majority were friends and relatives, we also had a couple of "distinguished goodfellas" in attendance, including Joe "Young" Coppolino, who was a made man in the Genovese crime family. Joe's wife, Adela, was my mother's best friend from Spain. Joe and Adela were godparents to my brother Rigel, who would join the U.S. Air Force that winter, eventually to be stationed in Spain and England.

Iris and I moved into a one-bedroom apartment in Queens overlooking Shea Stadium, then home to the New York Mets. The following July Fourth, as fireworks lit up the skies of New York City, Iris went into labor. Ten minutes after midnight, our son, Louis Jr., was born. But he would always be our Yankee Doodle Dandy.

SHORTLY AFTER IRIS and I married, her parents, her sister Gladys, and my old army pal Glady's husband, Billy, moved to Los Angeles. Iris and I began talking about one day moving out west to join them. But we decided to hold off until I could become more established professionally. That fall, I snagged a counselor's job with the city's Addiction Services Agency at the Williamsburg Youth Center in Brooklyn. It paid better than the state job and was closer to my home in Queens.

In my new gig, I would be counseling kids from bad homes about the evils of drugs. The training included behavioral science classes and group therapy sessions with other prospective counselors.

The youth center director, Louie Gonzalez, was a dynamo. He was also smart, articulate, and, to my endless delight, a former agent with the Federal Bureau of Narcotics.

Louie mesmerized me with tales of his undercover work for the federal government, in which his street smarts and bilingual skills enabled him to make big cases. Among the biggest of those cases was a conspiracy in which enormous amounts of heroin from Turkey were smuggled into Marseilles, France, and then into the United States, where the Mafia distributed the stuff on the streets. The caper inspired the Academy Award–winning motion picture *The French Connection*.

But when Louie introduced me to the *real-life* NYPD cops who had made the case—Detective Eddie Egan and Detective Sonny Grosso—it set my soul on fire. I decided on the spot that I wanted to become a narc, just like them.

I immediately applied to the Federal Bureau of Narcotics for a special agent's position in New York. My application moved routinely up the chain of command, heading toward a quick approval.

Until I ran into Erich Leifson.

Unlike the other Federal Narcotics Bureau supervisors with whom I interviewed, Leifson was cool, distant, and remote. When he asked why I wanted to be an agent, I gave him a lengthy and exuberant response. I spoke about my rough-and-tumble beginnings in Red Hook. My fluency in Spanish and my near fluency in Italian, owing to growing up around the wiseguys in Red Hook. My military service in Germany. My continuing college studies. My work with the drug-using kids at the Williamsburg Youth Center. My admiration for Louie Gonzalez.

At the mention of Louie G.'s name, Leifson's eyes went dead.

Oh, shit. Now I've done it, I thought. Was there some history between them?

Leifson went on to ask more questions, each one more brusque than the next. One of them was, "Have you ever smoked marijuana?"

To which I replied: "A couple of times, when I was in the army. But that's all."

Leifson looked at me blankly.

"You are not qualified to be an agent for the Federal Narcotics Bureau," he said. "Good day, Mr. Diaz."

I was shattered.

It was only afterward that I learned from Louie Gonzalez that the pot smoking was bullshit. The real reason Leifson deep-sixed me was that he and Louie had once worked together, and there was bad blood. Because of it, Leifson had screwed me. Simple as that.

In June 1971, I graduated from Queensborough Community College with an Associate in Arts degree and a 3.2 grade-point average. Unlike my final year of high school, when I was barred from graduating with everyone else, I received my diploma along with the rest of my class. Thwarted from becoming a federal drug agent, I took a job as an investigator with the U.S. Equal Employment Opportunity Commission.

Working out of the EEOC office in Newark, New Jersey, I looked into discrimination complaints from people who felt they had been frozen out of jobs or promotions because of their race or their gender. A lot of the complaints were bogus, but I loved going out to interview respondents and witnesses. What's more, the experience might give me a leg up the next time I tried for a criminal investigator's job.

The most memorable moment, however, was neither a case nor a complaint, but our office Christmas party in 1971. Flouting regulations, we sneaked in bottles of booze, and our supervisor, Mr. Lacey, got completely shitfaced. Seeing he was in no condition to drive, I gave him a lift back to his house, which was near my own. But as he stepped out of our government vehicle, Mr. Lacey inadvertently slammed the car door on his own hand. Blood started to drip onto all the gift-wrapped Christmas presents he had brought home for his family. I stepped around to help him, but he waved me off. So I wished him a Merry Christmas and went home.

The following Monday, when I returned to work, I learned that Mr. Lacey was out on sick leave. His secretary told me he had cut off his pinkie finger. Covering his ass, I kept silent about the fact that he'd been three sheets to the wind during this self-mutilation, as well as the fact that it had occurred in a government vehicle. Mr. Lacey later thanked me for keeping it all under the radar.

After the holidays, my EEOC partner Pat Matarazzo and I went to pick up the same government vehicle from the motor pool. A thought struck me. "Hey, Pat," I said. "What if Mr. Lacey's finger is still in the car somewhere?"

"You're out of your fucking mind, Lou," Pat answered.

"No, really," I said. "The car's been parked in the motor pool since the incident, it's been real cold out . . . the finger could still be on ice."

Pat scoffed. "Nah, nah, it had to have fallen in the street when he cut it off."

"Humor me," I said. "Let's toss the car anyway."

So we searched, me in the front, Pat in the back. And, sure enough, there it was, fingernail and all, lodged in the metal rail on which the front passenger seat was mounted. When I picked it up with my handkerchief and held it out to show Pat, he nearly blew his lunch.

We stopped at a nearby deli, bought a jar of pickles, emptied it out, then filled it with rubbing alcohol. Then we dropped the finger inside the alcohol to preserve it. But when we brought the bottled digit back to the office, Mr. Lacey cringed.

"Get that fuckin' thing outta here!" he snapped.

So into the toilet the lonely finger went.

AFTER WE MOVED to our new house in Flushing, Queens, I slowly started to get acquainted with our neighbors, including the one on the corner, Joe Blaise. When he invited me into his home, I immediately caught sight of the framed photos on the wall of him posing with President Nixon. Framed certificates from the U.S. Treasury Department hung near the photos. As it turned out, Joe was a special investigator with the Alcohol, Tobacco, and Firearms Bureau of the Treasury Department. He'd been on loan to the U.S. Secret Service, working in President Nixon's security detail, when the photos were snapped.

"I'm a Treasury agent, Lou," he said.

On hearing those words, my ears perked up. Joe must have seen my reaction because he kept pouring it on thicker with his war stories.

Finally he asked, "You think you might be interested in joining?"

"Sure," I said. "But I carry a little baggage."

I told him about my disastrous interview with Leifson and how I had shot myself in the foot by being too candid about my pot smoking in the army.

Joe laughed. "Half the guys on the job now woulda been shitcanned if they had been completely honest about that kinda crap," he said. "Don't sweat it, Lou. We'll find a way to get you in the door."

With Joe's help, I submitted an application to ATF. After

scoring well on the written test, I was called into the ATF's New York office to interview with a supervisor who had come up from Washington, D.C. Unlike Erich Leifson at the Federal Narcotics Bureau, this ATF supervisor—a buddy of Joe's—was friendly, enthusiastic, and encouraging. I fielded his questions smoothly. He immediately recommended me for an investigator's job.

In January 1972, my dream was finally realized. I, Louie D., was officially sworn in as a G-man.

CHAPTER FIVE

MY FIRST PARTNER IN the ATF, Ray Martinez, had six months seniority on me. That being the case, he delighted in breaking balls.

The first time it was, "Hey Louie, here are the keys. You drive. Carry my briefcase, willya."

The second time it was, "Hey Louie, here are the keys. You drive. Carry my briefcase, willya."

The third time it was, "Hey, Louie, here are the keys. You drive. . . . *Where's my fuckin' briefcase?!*"

To which I replied, "I dunno, Ray. You tell me."

"But you were supposed to carry it!" shouted Ray as he frantically searched the back of our car.

I shrugged. "You may have thought so," I said, "but the fact of the matter is I don't carry briefcases anymore. Maybe you left it at the gun store."

Ray went off like a Roman candle. "Then drive me back there, damn it!"

And, sure enough, that's where it was: in the safekeeping of the gun-store owner we'd visited, just where he had left it.

We had a pretty heated argument about all this, but eventually Ray apologized for the hazing he had subjected me to. What's more, he never pulled that shit on me again.

After that, our partnership and friendship blossomed. A fellow Brooklynite, Ray was a solid agent who would distinguish himself undercover. He would later go on to become an attorney and the resident agent in charge of the San Juan office of ATF.

Ray was my soulmate, my rock, someone I came to feel I could be completely honest with regardless of whether I felt joyful, troubled, or angry. I will never forget him.

All guys remember their first lay or their first love. In addition to all that, I would always remember my very first partner.

THE BUREAU OF Alcohol, Tobacco, and Firearms, created in 1972 by President Richard Nixon, was a misnomer. Alcohol and tobacco were certainly in the title. And cracking down on illicit trafficking in these products was a bureau responsibility.

But it wasn't the primary objective. That would be illegal firearms.

Most of the gun cases we made came off informants. Some were anonymous tipsters, just looking to help the police. Others were "buffs" who wanted to play cops, either because they wanted to be cops or liked hanging out with them.

Some informants were paid, but you had to be extra careful with those. The lure of money was so strong that they might entrap someone into doing a crime that a person never intended to commit. Like the guy who offered to arrange for us to buy a sawed-off shotgun. When I picked him up to take him to the seller's house, I noticed that he had metal filings stuck to his wool coat sleeve. Clearly, he had sawed down the shotgun himself, turning it from a legal into an illegal weapon in hopes of setting up his own buddy for a bust. This was entrapment, pure and simple, and I scuttled the buy.

Finally, there was "the flipper." Arrested for some crime, this informant would provide information in exchange for a break on his own case. For obvious reasons, he was highly motivated. But much like the paid informant, he could be treacherous, ready to sell out his mother if it meant saving his own ass.

Ray and I were introduced to one flipper in 1972 by David Durk, a former police lieutenant who had helped Detective Frank Serpico expose graft and thievery in the NYPD. The informant claimed he could lead us to gunrunners in Harlem who were supplying the Black Panthers.

Led by the informant and backed up by several unmarked ATF surveillance units, Ray and I hit the uptown watering holes frequented by the gunrunners. But each time, we came up empty. Then I began to notice that wherever we went, we were always shadowed . . . by an unmarked van that was *not* one of our surveillance vehicles. Could we be getting set up for a hit?

With the informant in the backseat of our car, I lowered my voice, switched from English to Spanish, and murmured my suspicions to Ray. And we agreed on a plan. I sped up, gave the van the slip, then doubled back around and pulled up behind it. Puzzled by our sudden disappearance, the van had pulled to a stop by the curb. Leaving the informant in the backseat, Ray and I quietly got out.

With guns drawn, we tiptoed up to the rear of the van. I nodded to Ray, and he nodded back. We cocked our guns. At the signal, we yanked open the back doors to find . . . a camera crew?!

While Ray kept them covered, I doubled back to our car, grabbed the informant by the collar, and yanked him out. A quick patdown revealed that he was wearing a wire.

I went crazy. We *had* been set up . . . just not by the bad guys.

As I cuffed the informant, Ray kept his gun on the camera

crew. Once our backup units arrived, they took everyone into custody.

It turned out that David Durk, in cahoots with one of the local TV stations, had hatched a crazy scheme to expose and film the alleged inefficiency of the ATF in dealing with gun violence in New York. And we had been the patsies.

But he'd gone fishing in the wrong pond . . . and gotten skunked. Ray and I were cleared of any wrongdoing.

IN OCTOBER 1972, after I had spent ten months in Manhattan, I transferred to the ATF office in Queens. There, I began mentoring a younger agent named George McNeeney, whom I had helped get on the job. George was married to the sister of Iris's best friend.

George was light-skinned, freckle-faced, and huskily built. With his Irish last name, you would have sworn he'd just come over from County Clare—right up until he opened his mouth and you heard the heavy Cuban accent, since he'd actually been born and raised there.

At one point, George set up a big gun buy. But the suspects screwed everything up by getting themselves arrested before they could deliver the guns to us. The weapons were still in the hands of an associate.

So I decided, what the hell? Let's use a little moxie, call these mooks in prison, and complete the transaction.

Pulling some strings, I was able to reach them by phone at the Brooklyn House of Detention. I told them the guns had been promised to some connected guys in Brooklyn, that I had already taken a down payment on them, and that if the guns were not delivered as promised, we'd *all* get whacked by the wiseguys. The prisoners assured me they would reach out for their associate.

A few days later, they called back and told me to contact their man, who happened to be the chef at a three-star Manhattan restaurant near the World Trade Center. The chef and I made arrangements to meet the following day, during his lunch break.

George and I showed up outside the restaurant in an undercover yellow checker taxicab. I sat in back, in the passenger seat. George was at the wheel, acting as the driver. At the appointed hour, the chef, clad in spanking white cook's attire, an apron, and chef's hat, emerged from his kitchen, carrying a bulky brown shopping bag.

The chef got into the cab with his shopping bag. I introduced him to "my friend" George. Peeking inside the shopping bag, I saw all the guns. I threw a wink at George. He promptly pulled out his own gun and pointed it at the chef.

"Lunch's over, pal, time to settle the bill," I said to the chef. "We're federal agents. And you're under arrest."

IF RAY MARTINEZ was my soulmate and George McNeeney was my acolyte, Tony Gondiosa, whom I partnered up with in 1974, was my straight man.

Tony looked and sounded like he'd come out of central casting. A crew-cut, blond-haired, rugged ex-army MP, he talked through his nose, just like an old boxer whose face has been reconfigured two or three times. When we sparred together at a gym I frequented in South Brooklyn and I tagged him in the head, which was often, he would complain: "Hey, Louie, what the fuck is wrong with you? You wanna give me brain damage or what?"

Tony was a huge hypochondriac, convinced that every little bump, cough, or sniffle would shorten his life span. He'd crack me up.

He'd crack me up all over again with his paranoia about getting jammed up on the job, refusing to talk on the office phone about our cases, never wanting to make a minor left-hand move (like popping a red stoplight or peeking, without authorization, into a suspect's car or property), always looking under the stalls in the office men's room to make certain nobody from ATF could be eavesdropping on our conversation.

Tony was about ten years older than I was, so when we worked together, it was like the old dog trying to keep the rambunctious pup in line. We were like the Odd Couple, but I loved working with him.

Tony was always ready for anything, and to that end, carried two guns, a five-shot Smith & Wesson in his ankle holster and a .357 Magnum in his briefcase, right next to his lunch.

Once, we caught a tip that some guy in Brooklyn was hoarding a bunch of pistols and automatic weapons. After casing his building, we noticed that his apartment abutted the roof of a garage, so we climbed a wall to get onto the roof. From there, we could peek inside the back windows of his apartment, each of us taking one window.

Just as I peered into my window, I heard a loud explosion to the right of me.

"Fuck *me*!" I heard Tony shout.

When I looked over, I saw that a Doberman pinscher, encased in a halo of glass shards, had crashed out through the window and was hurtling through the air over Tony's head. Landing on the roof behind us, the dog wheeled around on its paws and charged us.

"Jesus Christ, Tony!" I shouted.

With the Doberman snapping at our heels, both of us turned and leaped ten feet to the ground and beat feet back to the safety of our car.

WORKING WITH PARTNERS such as Ray, George, and Tony, which I did from 1972 to 1975, challenged me, gave me companionship, and made the job more fun. But for the most part, I preferred to work as a lone wolf.

To that end, I concocted a regular undercover identity, "Louie DelRey," and passed myself off as a mobbed-up trucker and garbage hauler in the employ of a sleazy firm called Tractors Unlimited.

Tractors Unlimited obviously did not exist, and officially any calls for Louie DelRey went directly to a special telephone in the ATF's Queens office. The phone was rigged up to a tape recorder.

Other than me, Filomena, the ATF office secretary, was the only person authorized to answer Mr. DelRey's line. She had all my "personal information" at her fingertips, including my work history, my truck driver's license number, my salary, my previous employers, my bills of lading, my rates, etc. If I was out in the field, Filomena would put the caller through to Kenny Coniglio, the supervising agent in charge of the Queens ATF office, and he would cover for me.

Securing the money so I could make my undercover buys was a pain in the ass. Some guy might be drooling all over himself to sell you guns, but you practically had to do backward flips and pirouettes before the government would agree to fork over the cash to transact the deal. Just making a good connection with the seller wasn't enough. First you had to establish the seller's identity. And not just his street name, but also his *real* identity and his *real* place of residence. This you might do by following him to his home. Then you would attempt to get his name off a mailbox or a utility bill or check with the post office. Next you would have to go over to Police Headquarters to run his name through the NYPD's records to see if the guy had a rap sheet or a criminal history. All of these steps were necessary to open an ATF criminal investigation.

But that was only the first part. Now you would have to start filling out forms, so many forms that you might turn blue in the face. First, a case initiation report. Then a request for advance funds (ATF 28) to justify the withdrawl of the buy money. Once the ATF 28 was signed by your group supervisor and the special agent in charge, you would be issued a receipt (ATF 29). This you would need to bring to the bank and sign before any monies could actually be issued. When you had the money in hand, you could finally make the buy. But as soon as the buy went down, the paperwork would begin all over again. First, a new form explaining your expenditures (ATF 30). Then a new case report detailing what went down during the buy . . . and on and on and on, ad nauseam.

Once I was in the field, things usually went more smoothly. I had no difficulty in convincing gun traffickers that I was a dirtbag ready to purchase illegal weapons. My upbringing in Red Hook, my fluency in Spanish, my familiarity with Italian, and my long-standing friendships with wiseguys all added to my bona fides.

Over time, I added a few extra wrinkles to my act.

For example, if I needed props, I was never at a loss. I still had my equipment from my days with the phone company—belt, tool holster, dial-up, handheld combo phone, clip-on attachment—which came in handy when I wanted to disguise myself as a repairman to slip into and out of buildings without arousing suspicions. Anything else I needed, I'd hit up one of my old pals. A dump truck to prove that I was in the trash-hauling business? I'd borrow one from my next-door neighbor Sonny Perri, who operated a rubbish-removal service, or Ray D'Angelo, who worked for the Sanitation Department. A Con Ed crew, work tarps, and other equipment to conceal an ATF team doing surveillance? Richie Montero, a guy from the old neighborhood, was the ticket. Merchant marine or long-shoreman's ID cards if I was posing as a dockworker? My man George Ripoll, a tough old bird who ran my boxing gym in South Brooklyn, was the go-to guy.

Armed with my props, my looks, my street shtick, and my carefully fashioned character of Louie DelRey, I was locked and loaded.

It was time to go hunting.

CHAPTER SIX

I GOT REAL BUSY ON a bunch of simultaneous hunting expeditions during the summer of 1973. One took me to a luncheonette in the South Bronx.

I had befriended the owner, a hardworking man named Pepe, and the two of us liked to shoot the shit. One day, while we were sipping *café con leche* and chewing the fat, water started cascading down from the ceiling on top of Pepe's head.

I burst into laughter. Pepe went apeshit.

"*¡Hijo de la gran puta!*" he shouted. "Moderfocker! Sonofabitch!"

Reaching under the counter, he came up with a sawed-off double-barreled shotgun and fired a blast into the ceiling.

Jesus Christ!

I dove under a table as Pepe ran out of the store, ranting, eyes bulging, still waving his shotgun, threatening to kill the *moderfockers*.

When he reentered, I crawled out cautiously from my hiding spot. "*¿Qué pasó, Pepe?*"

But Pepe was still on the warpath. "*Hijos de putas*, they steal my pipes!"

The neighborhood dopers and thieves were so desperate for resellable merchandise, he explained, that they'd rip off the copper pipes right over your head—and wouldn't even bother to turn off the water while they were doing it.

I could have had Pepe locked up for having an illegal firearm, and he would have gone down for the rap. But he was just defending his store and his livelihood, so I let it slide. Besides, I didn't want to blow my cover. I wanted to look like a stand-up guy . . . and who knew what bigger game I might flush from the jungle on account of him?

A few days later, I returned to the luncheonette. One of the regulars, a hard-core crook named Tito, walked in and we got to bullshitting about our days as gangbangers—him with Murder Incorporated, me with the Gowanus Dukes. I bought Tito another coffee. Then the two of us stepped outside for a smoke.

I casually mentioned Pepe's shotgun demonstration to Tito. "Yeah," he said, "it's the talk of the whole neighborhood. All the dope fiends and thieves been scared off."

I told Tito I was impressed by Pepe's double-barreled shotgun. Tito volunteered that Pepe bought it from a local dude named Jamal.

Now I was curious. But I didn't want to push it too hard. No sudden moves or inadvertent outbursts. No loud noises. No need to spook the animals before I could line up a clear shot.

Tito, however, happily filled in the blanks, telling me that Jamal was a militant who supplied guns to the neighborhood thugs.

He also trafficked in drugs.

Now Tito *really* had my attention. I took a teeny step forward. "Y'know, I might be interested in doing business with Jamal. I got a lot of outlets for his kinda merchandise."

"Yeah," said Tito, "I figured you for that kinda guy. Be happy to hook you up."

My caution was starting to pay off.

"Muchas gracias, Tito. Hasta luego."

* * *

WITH A FEW more days to kill before meeting up again with Tito, I hopped over to another of my favorite hunting spots.

Williamsburg, Brooklyn.

I knew the area well, since it was the same hood where I had gone to high school. Lately I had been getting cozy with some of the locals. Weather permitting, we'd even play a little stickball in the street. One of the better ballplayers was a sawed-off character who went by the name of L'il Man. His rugged facial features and broken nose gave him an aura of menace.

One day, I impressed the hell out of L'il Man by showing up in a dump truck I had borrowed from my next-door neighbor Sonny. I impressed L'il Man even more by driving him in the dump truck to a work site that Sonny and his crew were in the midst of clearing.

Putting two and two together, L'il Man figured I had to be connected and, therefore, a guy to be reckoned with. So I casually let it drop that I provided firearms to the mob.

Rising to the bait, L'il Man said he knew a lot of guys looking to sell guns and they would give me a good price. In July 1973, he took me to meet one of them—his boy Willie, who lived on the Lower East Side of Manhattan.

Inside his apartment, Willie showed me a sawed-off shotgun. The price tag: seventy-five bucks. I told Willie we were good to go and I would come back in a few days with the cash. "Great," said Willie, adding that he could get a whole lot more shotguns just like this one. All I had to do was come up with the money.

Another trap baited, another target drifting into my sights.

Willie was easy to identify. I could simply lift his name off his mailbox, then check with the utility company to verify it. When I later ran the corroborated name—William Cruz—

through the Police Department's database, it produced a record for possession and sale of narcotics and burglary.

I still didn't know L'il Man's real name. To open an official investigation and get authorization to draw government buy money, I needed to find out. But how could I do it without raising suspicions and blowing my cover?

The next day I picked up L'il Man in my car and we went toodling around Brooklyn.

All of a sudden I began driving like a crazy man, banging into garbage cans, jumping the curb, barely missing other cars, nearly bowling over a couple of pedestrians. I also began drooling like a St. Bernard.

L'il Man went bonkers. "Jesus Christ, Lou, the fuck's wrong with you, man?!" he screamed.

"Ep-lepsy," I muttered as I finally allowed the car to roll to a halt. I gestured feebly toward my chest. "Pocket . . . pocket . . . pocket . . ."

Reaching into my breast pocket, L'il Man found a vial of white pills. He uncapped it and pulled one out. I nodded to him and grunted. He placed it on my tongue. Panting furiously, I swallowed it. Although the pill was just a multivitamin tablet, I made it look like I was starting to recompose myself.

L'il Man was still pretty shaken up. "Man, I ain't lettin' you drive no more, man," he said. "You'll get us both fuckin' killed."

"I'm okay," I insisted. But gasping periodically and rolling my eyes, I deliberately made myself look considerably less than okay.

"Fuck that," said L'il Man, "I'll drive."

"The fuck you will," I shot back.

"No, man, you too sick to drive."

"Fuck you," I said. "You probably ain't even got a driver's license."

L'il Man turned indignant. He pulled out his license and flashed it under my nose. "The fuck you call *that*?"

And there it was, right in plain sight.

I quickly committed the name Antonio Hernandez and his date of birth to memory.

All those years of watching my little brother Alfonsito struggle so valiantly with his epilepsy . . . I could mimic the symptoms to a tee. And I had just given an Academy Award–winning performance.

Once I got back to my office, I ran L'il Man's information through the NYPD. And sure enough, Mr. Antonio Hernandez had done time for drug sales and a whole bunch of other nasty shit.

This meant we were open for business at ATF, and my undercover investigation of L'il Man and Willie could officially start rolling.

BACK UP IN the Bronx at Pepe's luncheonette that same summer, I bumped into Tito and casually inquired about Jamal, the guy who had sold the sawed-off shotgun to Pepe.

A stroke of good luck: Tito had just seen Jamal in a pool hall down the street. He took me over to the pool hall and introduced me to him. Jamal was a rugged-looking black man, smartly dressed in a designer shirt, pressed gabardine slacks, Italian leather shoes, and a panama straw hat.

Jamal challenged me to a game. I impressed him with a few hard bank shots, but I wasn't in his league. In the end, he whipped my ass.

We finally talked a little about Pepe's shotgun incident. "Yeah, I told him to be cool about it," said Jamal. "'Specially since I be the dude sold it to him in the first place."

I told Jamal I myself was interested in that kind of hardware. I had eager buyers. "You hear anything, gimme a holler," I said. I handed him my business card with my undercover phone number on it.

"Right on, my brother," said Jamal, tapping my knuckles with his own.

L'IL MAN AND I returned to the Lower East Side. Up in Willie's apartment, I jokingly asked if the weapon I was about to buy for seventy five bucks actually worked.

Big mistake.

Willie went into another room and came back out with the double-barreled, sawed-off shotgun. Before I could say another word, he swung around and fired deafening blasts from both barrels right out his back window, blowing bricks off the wall off the adjacent building. I ducked down, my heart in my throat.

After a moment of pulling myself together, I handed Willie the money. He gave me the shotgun, along with a promise to sell me as many more as I wanted.

On the drive back to Williamsburg, I handed L'il Man his twenty-dollar commission for setting up the deal.

At this point I had both of them for selling illegal firearms. But I wasn't ready to drop the net just yet.

BACK IN MY office, Jamal had left a message for me on my undercover phone.

"Got something for you," he said. "Get back to me." We arranged to meet at Pepe's the following day.

I showed up in the borrowed dump truck. Jamal walked

me around the corner to his car—business must have been good, since it turned out to be a spanking new Cadillac. In the backseat, under a blanket, lay a double-barreled shotgun.

"Anything you need, my man," he boasted. "My store always be open for business."

I told him I would be back the next day with the cash for the weapon. As we stood by his car, I made a mental note of his license plate.

When I got back to the ATF office, I ran the plate number through the DMV and came up with his full name—Jamal Evans—his home address, and his date of birth. Later I ran him through the NYPD's files and came up with his rap sheet, which included arrests for weapons possession and assault.

Now that I had his complete info, I could open an official investigation on him.

The next day, with $75 in government buy money in my pocket, I met up with him again and bought the shotgun.

AT THE SAME time I was deepening my investigation into Jamal, I was still romancing L'il Man and Willie on the Lower East Side, looking to find even more dirtbags who would sell me guns.

ATF wanted to do surveillance on the sellers to see if they could lead us to their connections. But most of the other agents in the squad stuck out: they all looked like cops. Plus, they all drove unmarked government vehicles that any bad guy with half a noodle could make for a cop's car. So we needed to come up with a different plan.

With my supervisor Kenny Coniglio's approval, I got ahold of a banged-up old Chevy Chevelle. I parked it on the street near the location of each of my prearranged gun buys. As soon as each buy went down, I headed straight for the Chevelle. Once in the car, I reached under the seat, pulled out a long-haired wig I had borrowed from Iris, and plopped it on my head.

Sitting behind the wheel of a piece-of-shit heap that nobody in a million years would ever make for a surveillance vehicle, and looking like some hippie stoner, I waited to catch my subjects in a move. And a couple of times I was able to tail them back to their home bases, noting their addresses.

BACK AT THAT pool hall in the Bronx, Jamal and I cued them up again and talked new business. He had come up with another sawed-off shotgun . . . he had machine guns to peddle . . . and he was pushing heroin.

"Ain't into no street shit sales," he added, meaning that he had no interest in selling glassine envelopes that were good for just one hit.

I told Jamal I would speak to my man about purchasing the dope.

Later, I hooked up with some federal agents in a joint police-federal task force under the Office of Drug Abuse Law Enforcement, the precursor of the Drug Enforcement Agency. One of the federal agents, Cruz Cordero, agreed to play the part of my buyer. Nobody would ever make him for a cop.

In a phone conversation with Jamal—cleanly picked up on the office tape recorder—I told him I had a customer for his dope.

The following day, Cordero and I drove up to the Bronx, where we met up with Jamal. Inside his Caddy, we negotiated the terms—$2,400 for two ounces of heroin. Jamal said he wanted the money up front; then, while we sat in his Caddy with the keys, holding it as collateral, he would go to retrieve the merchandise.

It was against policy to front money for a drug buy without prior approval, but my strong relationship with Jamal and his offer to provide his car as collateral made this appear a pretty safe risk. So I told Jamal we'd go for it. Cordero fronted him the $2,400. I would pay him an additional $75 at a later date for the new shotgun.

While we were doing the deal, a marked NYPD squad car passed us by once, then a second time. Sitting in the backseat was Sergeant Eugene Capp, the supervisor of the federal drug task force that Cordero and I were working with.

Strange as it sounds, sending a marked car to cruise us was actually a smart idea. Police cars patrolling this neighborhood were commonplace. It was the unmarked cars, which thugs such as Jamal could make right away, that posed a greater risk to undercovers like us.

After the squad car disappeared the second time, Jamal got out of the Caddy and went to retrieve the heroin.

Cordero and I waited.

Twenty minutes. A half hour. Forty-five minutes. An hour. And hour and a half. No sign of Jamal.

Finally I drove the Caddy out of the area so we could call our task force base. Had any of our backup units spotted Jamal? The response was not what I wanted to hear: they had lost him.

So I put in several calls to Jamal's residence. No answer. Cordero and I returned to where we originally had met Jamal. Nothing.

I started to think that one of two things had happened: either Jamal had gotten ripped off, or he had fucked us. Not only did this make me look like shit, but it also put Cordero in a worse fix because he had never gotten prior approval from Sergeant Capp to front the money for the buy. He had done it on my word. But in the end, it would be his problem.

As expected, back in the federal task force office, Sergeant Capp reamed us out for losing the government's cash. "You got one day to get it back, kid!" he yelled at me.

With my balls in my hand, I headed back to my ATF office in Brooklyn. At about 7:00 p.m., my undercover phone rang. It was Jamal—*thank God*. But before I could jump down his throat, he told me, "Hey, Lou, *the man* was all over you, my brother."

"What the fuck are you talking about?" I demanded.

"There was a squad car with some old detective in the backseat, hawking on you guys."

After all our clever strategizing, the marked-car ruse had actually backfired. Jamal had made the surveillance. *That's* why he'd never come back with the dope.

We agreed on a new meet to complete the transaction. The next day, Cordero and I headed up to Jamal's Bronx apartment. I drove Jamal's Caddy, and Cordero followed in his undercover car. Inside the apartment, Jamal gave Cordero the two ounces of heroin. I returned the keys to the Caddy and paid Jamal $75 for the new sawed-off shotgun.

Over the next few weeks, Cordero and I made arrangements to do even more business with Jamal. Cordero would purchase half a kilo of heroin, and I would buy another sawed-off shotgun.

On the day of the new buy, Cordero and I went to Jamal's apartment and rang the doorbell. I could hear him peeking through the peephole on the other side. No fool he, he wasn't taking any chances. Recognizing us, he unbolted the locks and swung the door wide open to let us in.

"Hey, my brothers, what's happening?" said Jamal with a great big grin. He was still in his underwear.

Cordero and I stepped to one side.

At that instant, a team of agents from the ATF and the federal drug task force brushed past us and into the apartment to seize the heroin, confiscate the shotgun and other firearms, and take Jamal down once and for all.

STILL LEFT TO deal with were L'il Man, Willie, and the other gun dealers I had met on the Lower East Side.

The U.S. Attorney's office had issued arrest warrants. Willie and the other gun sellers would be easy pickings, since we already knew where they lived. But L'il Man had suddenly dropped out of sight. If I arrested the others before I busted him, he would certainly hear about it, and bolt for good.

For the next week or so, I cruised by all of Li'l Man's regular Brooklyn haunts, hoping to find him. Then, rolling through Williamsburg one morning, *bingo!*—I spotted him walking along the street.

He was surprised to see me, but he willingly got into my car. He apologized for dropping off the radar, explaining that he'd been laying low because he was trying to avoid some shylocks to whom he owed heavy money.

On a dime, I told him I would loan him the cash. But I needed him to do me a solid and accompany me to the Central Post Office. A guy who worked up there had been giving *me* shit on an outstanding loan, and I needed to send him a message. L'il Man, who was a tough-looking customer, would be a real asset. With him at my side, I could be that much more effective in collecting on an outstanding debt and L'il Man, in turn, would be able to settle up on his own debt. Always ready for a good dustup, L'il Man jumped at the opportunity.

Inside the Central Post Office, I took L'il Man to an upper floor. In the elevator, I talked excitedly about what I was gonna do to the guy who'd been holding out on me. Then, as I walked L'il Man down the corridor toward a suite of offices, I got even more jacked up.

"I'm gonna fuck this motherfucker up six ways to Sunday!" I said, pounding my palm with my fist for emphasis.

"Fuckin' A!" L'il Man replied.

L'il Man hung on my every word, his eyes flaring with anticipation. As we entered the suite of offices, I swung my arms around like a man whose hair was on fire, obscuring from L'il Man's view the sign on the entrance door.

Inside the main room in the suite, we passed by several desks. One guy looked up at me blankly. I shot him a hundred winks.

Spotting another desk that was empty, I steered L'il Man toward it.

"Do me a favor," I said to L'il Man. "Sit here for a minute while I go find the motherfucker I need to straighten out."

As I walked away from him, L'il Man picked up a copy of the *Daily News* that was lying atop the desk and began perusing the racing results from Belmont.

Behind him, the guy who had been sitting quietly behind his desk motioned to another guy who had been seated at another desk. Both of them got up slowly. They walked toward L'il Man. Then, standing at either side of him, each flashed something bright and shiny in front of his eyes.

Big metal shields.

"Federal agents," one of them quietly announced. "You're under arrest."

As one slapped the cuffs on, the other began to Mirandize him.

L'il Man looked around in confusion, his eyes practically popping out of his skull. What the hell was going on here?

Returning to the desk where he was being cuffed, I smiled wanly, then shrugged. The door to the office was still open, so I pointed to the stenciled sign on its outside, the one I had concealed with my arm-waving when I had first waltzed L'il Man into this office.

It said:

U.S. Department of the Treasury
Bureau of Alcohol, Tobacco, and Firearms
Brooklyn-Queens Field Office

CHAPTER SEVEN

WITHIN A YEAR OF joining ATF, I became the go-to guy for whatever group I was in. I could pretty much count on my bosses' support in getting whatever I needed to make a case.

I never felt I was better than any of the other agents and I tried not to behave like some prima donna. I simply realized I had a gift for doing undercover work and making cases, and I loved using it.

I always tried to be a team player, respectful of other agents' egos and feelings, not some swaggering asshole always looking to puff himself up and pat himself on the back.

Among all the agents, there was mutual affection and respect. These were the guys I counted on to have my back. And I was the one who generated activity for them—arrests, raids, a chance to taste real action.

In most federal law enforcement agencies, an enforcement group might number ten to twelve agents. Out of that group, there were usually two or three principal casemakers, with the other agents providing support—working surveillance, setting up wiretaps, serving subpoenas, going on raids, and making arrests.

As a casemaker, I was pleased that the bosses would ask me to do things they felt no one else could do or that I could do better. Sometimes it would be a case that was handed down from headquarters, or another agent's case on which I was asked to go undercover. Mostly though, I worked on cases that were self-generated; in other words, my own.

"Diaz?" a supervisor once said. "He's like a Toyota. Tough. Reliable. Gives us a bang for our buck on the mileage."

The truth, however, was that what I did as an undercover and a casemaker I did not do to impress my bosses or anyone else. Rather, I did it to challenge myself. I was always looking to raise the bar, up the ante, push the risks. But this came from a personal need. I craved the danger, the adrenaline, thrived on it. Putting myself in harm's way made me feel whole, alive, like I mattered in this world.

So it was never a contest between me and some other agent. It was always a contest between me and *me.*

OTHER THAN TRUSTED close friends, I never told anyone what I did for a living. Or I would say I was an investigator for the U.S. Department of Labor. My kids, who often saw me toodling around in one of Sonny's big dump trucks, thought I was a truck driver.

While I was doing my thing, Iris was the glue that held our family together. Far more devout than I ever was, she made certain we regularly attended Sunday Mass.

Iris's devotion to the church was not simply a Sunday-only affair. She lived and practiced Christianity every day of her life. She was one of the principal organizers for all the church's bazaars, flea markets, and other charitable events. Her compassion and capacity for forgiveness knew no bounds. She could always find the good in a person. And whenever her hotheaded husband got into a disagreement, which was often, she would bring him to his senses. Her smile and laughter soothed my heart. Her selflessness nourished my soul.

When it came to disciplining Louis Jr. and Maria, I was a benevolent dictator, firm but fair. They were good kids, never gave us much trouble, and both Iris and I felt blessed.

Never did I hit them the way Papa had hit me. The thought of inflicting such brutality on my own flesh and blood repulsed me.

There was one other difference in my style of child rearing versus that of Papa: no matter how angry I got with my kids, I never put them to bed at night without telling them how much I loved them.

IF THERE WAS a source of concern in my family, it was my younger brother Alfonsito.

Alfonsito was still living at home with Mama and Papa, and he could have as many as fifty epileptic attacks a day. Sometimes he would roll his head around while making incoherent sounds, or foam at the mouth, or grab wildly at something or someone. Sometimes he would topple like an oak tree, the back of his head smacking the pavement with a loud crack. It was a terrifying thing to see and hear, and it drove my parents to desperation. Over time, the constant blows to his head and the side effects of his medication combined to severely impede his mental development.

With his terrible temper, Papa had the toughest time of all of us coping. In the spring of 1975, after receiving an emergency message from Iris at my ATF office, I rushed to my parents' house to find four police cars out front and Papa inside—in handcuffs.

"Oh, for the love of Jesus!" I said as I entered the living room. I felt like I was gazing upon a wounded bull. Proud, fierce, but no longer able to raise his head.

Surrounded by cops, Papa was sitting on the sofa, seething, muttering in Spanish. Alfonsito was next to him, looking bewildered and disheveled. Mama was in the kitchen, sobbing, as a female police officer tried to console her.

After suffering a seizure outside a local store, Alfonsito had been accosted and pushed around by a police officer, who interpreted my brother's actions as a drug-induced high. The cop eventually eased up and brought Alfonsito back home. But when Papa saw the condition Alfonsito was in, he flipped out. Because of his volcanic temper and his inability to articulate himself in English, he nearly ripped the officer's head off. So in the end, the cop cuffed Papa and radioed for reinforcements.

Fortunately, I recognized the police sergeant on the scene as an old high school acquaintance and I was able to explain Alfonsito's plight to him. The arresting officer was ordered to uncuff Papa and void the arrest. Gentleman that he was, the sergeant also apologized to my brother, Papa, and Mama.

Over the years, Papa and I would clash endlessly over Alfonsito's care. I felt Alfonsito should receive professional therapy and counseling, even job training. Giving him more freedom and responsibility would be good for him, I reasoned. Papa, insisting he could take care of Alfonsito without help from anyone and fearing that outsiders might put "shit" in Alfonsito's head to encourage him to rebel against Papa's rule, was adamantly opposed to programs of any sort. On this point, he and I were always at odds.

In the end, Papa's pig-headedness just made a bad situation that much worse. By choosing to keep Alfonsito at home, he made himself and Mama slaves to my brother's care. And in so doing, he made Alfonsito weaker, more defenseless, and more dependent than he ever needed to be.

* * *

BEING RATIONAL WHEN discussing possible treatments was one thing. Being rational when Alfonsito was in the throes of a seizure was a whole other.

At those moments, reason went by the wayside. Fear and emotion took over.

Around Christmas of 1975, I drove Alfonsito over to New Jersey to pick up my brother Rigel, who was flying in from England, where he was serving with the U.S. Air Force. Unfortunately, rain began coming down in sheets.

Inside the car, Alfonsito started to get fidgety. The downpour got so bad on the Jersey Turnpike that I could barely see through the front windshield. The poor visibility made Alfonsito even more nervous.

Then he suffered a seizure.

Unable to control his psychomotor reactions, he began to flail, contort, and gyrate. Thrashing about in his seat, he began tearing at his seat belt. He grabbed at my arm and began to pull on it as I tried to keep the car moving straight ahead on the rain-slicked road.

I shouted at him to stop, tried to swat him away, but he either couldn't or wouldn't hear me. Worrying that we might get into an accident, I started to pull the car off to the side of the road. But I couldn't really see who was behind me in the outer lane, so I steered it back to the center lane and tried to keep us on course.

But Alfonsito's movements became even more violent. For whatever reason, he tried to wrench the steering wheel away from me.

I slapped him away again with one hand, struggling to keep the car from swerving.

Alfonsito grabbed again for the wheel, and I panicked. Convinced he was about to kill us both, I pulled my gun out, put it to his head, and told him I would put a bullet in his brain if he didn't stop.

In the next instant, I went cold. My finger actually started to pull the trigger.

As if by divine intervention, Alfonsito suddenly went calm. The thrashing stopped. He sank back into his seat again, dazed but at rest. He was finally, blessedly, coming out of it.

I quickly put my gun away and thanked God in heaven that I had not used it.

"Why are you crying, Louie?" Alfonsito asked.

I fought back my tears. "I'm crying because . . . because . . . because all three of the Diaz brothers will be together for Christmas. And that makes me very happy."

Alfonsito smiled blissfully, as innocent as a puppy. He knew he had suffered an attack. But he had no recollection of the details.

Sometimes, however, Alfonsito's seizures drove me completely over the edge. Without even realizing it, I'd revert to my undercover character of Louie DelRey. And my behavior could be downright terrifying.

One day, Alfonsito suffered a grand mal seizure. When Mama phoned me at my ATF office, frantic with the news, I dropped everything I was doing, dashed out the door, threw a flashing red light on the roof of my car, flipped on my siren, and buck-assed straight to my parents' home in Brooklyn. Then I put Alfonsito in my car and raced to the emergency room at Kings County Hospital.

When I got there, one of the doctors asked me what the problem was. Pumped with adrenaline and fear, I excitedly blurted, "Listen, doc, he's a grand mal epileptic."

The doctor immediately challenged me. "What do you know about epilepsy? Are you a doctor? Who are you to tell me he's a grand mal epileptic?"

Already hot from the breakneck race to the emergency room, I went off on him.

"Because, motherfucker," I answered, "this is my brother! And I know him since he's a baby. And I cared for him his whole life. Does that answer your fuckin' question?!"

The doctor got up on his high horse. "Are you threatening me?" he demanded.

"Why?" I fired back. "Does it sound like I'm threatening you, motherfucker?"

"Are you threatening me?!" he demanded again, only this time in a louder, more indignant tone.

And that did it. My temperature shot straight up, from hot to molten. I tore into him as if he were some punk-ass wiseguy who was scamming me on a gun and dope deal.

Grabbing the doctor by the throat, I slammed him up against the wall. Then I pulled out my gun and put the barrel up his nostril.

"I tell you what, man," I said. "How about I blow your fuckin' head off, huh, cocksucker? Now take care of my brother, like you're supposed to."

The doctor began screaming, and security guards came running. As I saw them coming toward us, I quickly tucked my gun away and said to the doctor, "You just keep your fuckin' mouth shut. This never happened."

When the guards arrived, the doctor got his balls back. "He attacked me with a gun!" he began shouting at them.

I showed the guards my ATF shield. Then I said, "Listen, guys, not for nuthin', I'm on the job. My brother here is a grand mal epileptic. I just came off a case. He was with my mother and she called me from home when he started to have a real bad seizure. I mean, it coulda killed him, for chrissakes."

"You gotta be here?" one guard asked.

"Yeah, I gotta be here," I said. Then I gestured at the doctor. "But not with *that* dick-in-the-ear. Just take us somewhere else, willya?"

"Okay, but how about I hold your gun while you're here?" the guard asked.

"Fine," I said. "That'll work for me." I handed him my weapon.

The guards started to lead us toward another room, where a different doctor would examine Alfonsito. But just before we left, I turned back to eyeball the doctor. Raising my hand to my head, I curled my knuckles into the shape of a handgun and pointed my index finger at my temple. Then, twitching my thumb as if I were pulling the trigger, I murmured, "You talk, you *go*. You hear me? I'll blow your fuckin' brains out."

Yeah, I could be Papa's son, all right. Straight out of the same gene pool.

When I felt disrespected or put down, my rage could boil over and singe whoever was in proximity. Throughout my life, I would struggle mightily to control it. And when it got the best of me, I often felt upset afterward.

Still, I could be one scary, crazy, off-the-wall motherfucker.

CHAPTER EIGHT

YES, LOUIS, THE U.S. Drug Enforcement Agency is the unequivocal fucking premier, fucking paramount agency in law enforcement. When it comes to protecting the citizenry from the fucking cocksuckers, the shitbirds, and the dirtbags, DEA is the last fucking bulwark of a democratic, progressive, and enlightened society."

Jim Hunt, the associate regional director of the New York Field Division of the DEA, was the agency's master articulator. Steeped in Ph.D.-sounding eloquence spiced with colloquialisms and peppered with unbridled vulgarity, his manner of speaking was like nothing I'd ever heard before. It was as if William F. Buckley Jr. had been crossed with Bugsy Moran. The man had invented his own language.

"Sit down, Louis," Hunt said to me during the summer of 1975.

Dressed in my street attire—combat boots, dungarees, and army fatigue jacket, I took the chair across from Hunt's desk.

Bespectacled, barrel-chested, whitish-haired, Hunt looked like an aging fullback. An ex-army boxer, he was celebrated for knocking out crooks with a single punch, leaving them convulsing and pissing their pants as they lay writhing on the pavement. In the DEA, Jim Hunt was a living legend.

Hunt told me that he had heard all about me from some

other agents who had come over from ATF, as well as from my former mentor Louie Gonzalez.

Studying my résumé, Hunt leaned back and started to murmur.

"Hmmm . . . let's see now . . . pugilist, military veteran, ATF experience, college degree," said Hunt. "You'd be a genuine asset to us here in drug enforcement. Plus, you're a minority, and minorities are very much in demand under our current hiring guidelines. You shouldn't have any fucking trouble at all securing this position."

I leaped from my chair. "Excuse me, Mr. Hunt," I said. "I appreciate all that you just said. But if that's the way this is playing out, I gotta tell you, it's most definitely *not* because I'm a minority. It's because I'm well qualified to do the job."

Hunt rose slowly from his own chair, seemingly growing bigger and angrier by the second. I was certain he was about to reach across his desk and strangle me for my insolence. Jowls aquiver, Hunt glanced at the other agents who had brought me up to his office to make certain they had heard what he had heard.

Then he looked at me and said, "I want this kid on the fucking job as expeditiously as possible. If not today, then tomorrow. Prioritize Mr. Diaz's hiring ASAP. Good day, gentlemen. Now all-a-yas, get the fuck outta my office so I can get some goddamn work done."

The other DEA agents who had brought me up to meet Hunt choked back their laughter.

That year, 1975, had been a harrowing one for federal law enforcement agents. Patty Hearst had been kidnapped and turned into an urban guerrilla by the Symbionese Liberation Army. Terrorist groups had set off bombs in Manhattan and at

LaGuardia Airport, causing multiple deaths and many injuries. The need for seasoned personnel was pressing.

And by midsummer, I was a U.S. Drug Enforcement Administration agent.

I HAD WANTED to transfer into the DEA for several reasons.

First, the pay and advancement opportunities were better than at ATF. Second, there was less paperwork. If you ever wanted to know the real meaning of the expression "Don't make a federal case out of it," it was ATF in a nutshell. When it came to generating paperwork, ATF was the undisputed champ. Third, making cases for ATF was difficult. There were no major gun cartels or gun gangs. Most of the weapons we scooped up had been stolen in residential robberies or rip-offs of public carrier shipments. They were resold one at a time, making the investigations tedious and time-consuming. The sellers were small fry and so were the cases, with gun buys often set up by rats looking to incriminate their own buddies.

Unlike weapons, which were tough to find, drugs were all over the damned place. Hell, this was the '70s, and it was a bazaar out there—heroin, cocaine, LSD, pills, and marijuana wherever you looked. Major drug-running organizations had been set up—and that made the cases, the investigations, and the potential consequences of successful investigations that much grander.

During the twenty-one years I would work in DEA, from August 1975 through February 1996, drugs were where the action was. I was always looking for bigger and more challenging game, and in this particular neck of the jungle, the trophies were everywhere.

On a personal level, I had developed a real hatred for hard-core drug use. I'd seen its ravages firsthand as a drug counselor for the state and the city. And decent guys I had grown up with had gotten hooked on junk, overdosed, and died. Someone needed to put a stop to the slaughter.

There was, however, one thing I needed to go back to school to learn: chemistry.

If I was going to make drug buys, I would have to be able to differentiate a righteous product from a bad product, known on the streets as "turkey." So shortly after hiring on, I began to hang out in the DEA's lab, where I put myself under the tutelage of one of the technicians.

After every heroin or cocaine buy I made, I would bring the stuff up to my lab buddy for an "expedient field test" to determine its purity. For heroin, the purity could range from 0.4 to 3 percent for street-level dope and up to 98 percent for wholesale, pure dope. The purity on cocaine normally ran from 25 to 98 percent, depending on whether the coke was street-level or wholesale. After the techie determined the purity, I would examine the powder or granules carefully. Taking a pinch in my hand, I would roll it between my fingers, get a feel for it, smell it, even taste it. Then I'd take another pinch and smear it on a small piece of glass. Using a small penknife, I would move the granules back and forth on the glass. The purer the product, the less it would smudge. The less it smudged, the less it had been cut with dilutants such as mannite, lactose, or baking powder.

Out in the field, I carried around an old coin bag that contained my personal testing kit: an ivory-handled penknife, a tiny mirror, Marqui test tubes, and several vials of testing reagents—sulfuric acid and formaldehyde, which turned blue to dark blue to near purple in the presence of heroin, and nitric acid, which turned light blue in the presence of cocaine.

By doing my tests, I would get a good sense for whether a seller had sold me good dope or turkey. And if I was planning to meet up again with the same seller for an even bigger buy, I'd know if I needed to be on the lookout for a rip-off or a hit.

There was one more difference between working ATF and working DEA: the targets. No small fry in this jungle; DEA targets were top-tier players—high rollers, big hoods, and often, stone cold killers.

SOMETIMES THE TARGETS were celebrities.

In 1980, when an Argentine informant set up a buy from a high-priced call girl who funneled cocaine to stars, Case Agent John Tully busted her. She immediately flipped like a pancake and agreed to lure some of her A-list customers into incriminating phone conversations for the express benefit of our tape recorder.

At one point, Agent Chris Eagan and I glanced at the call girl's phone book . . . and came across James Caan's name.

I was a big fan, and I wasn't about to let him go down. So I tore out the telltale page, crumpled it up, and tossed it away. For all we knew, Caan's name could have been there simply because he was an aquaintance. There were a lot bigger fish to fry.

Like Robert Evans, the one-time head of Paramount Pictures. Evans had produced *The Godfather, Rosemary's Baby*, *Love Story*, *Chinatown*, *Marathon Man*, and *Urban Cowboy*. He, too, was listed in the call girl's phone book.

After Tully and Group Supervisor Jeff Hall attached a recorder, the call girl phoned Evans and lured him into conversations about past drug deals. Then she suggested a new deal.

Evans told her to contact his brother, Charlie, to work out the details on a fresh batch of blow.

To facilitate the sting, Chris Eagan pulled off the coup of the century by flim-flamming the New Jersey–based pharmaceutical giant Merck & Co. into loaning him eleven pounds of pharmaceutical cocaine for show and tell.

In the company of the call girl, Chris, John Tully, and I showed up at Charlie Evans's midtown Manhattan office, where the call girl introduced us to Charlie and his brother-in-law, touting us as connected wiseguys who trafficked in stolen jewelry, guns, narcotics, anything we could peddle for a fast buck.

When Chris flashed the eleven pounds of coke, Charlie and his brother-in-law practically drooled down their ties. The price tag, Chris told them, was $150,000. Charlie immediately phoned his brother Robert, who agreed to pony up the cash.

The next day, we returned to Charlie's office. Chris handed over the coke. Charlie and his brother-in-law passed back the money. The instant the exchange was completed, we busted them both.

As we escorted them out of the building, preparing to cart them off to the DEA's midtown office, Charlie got a glimpse of Chris's banged-up Plymouth Fury.

"Not that car," he said to Chris. He nodded toward a sleek black limo parked by the curb. "*That* one."

Charlie insisted that his chauffeur be allowed to drive him downtown to DEA headquarters.

Chris studied the limo. Then he looked back at Charlie. "How much cash you got on you?" he asked.

Charlie fished around in his pockets. "Five hundred bucks."

"Lemme see it," said Chris.

"Here."

Taking the cash, Chris walked over to the waiting chauffeur and piled it in his palm. "Take the day off, pal. He won't be needing you."

Hustling Charlie and his brother-in-law into the back of Chris's banged-up heap, we drove the two suspects to the DEA office to be processed and fingerprinted.

Indicted for conspiracy to purchase and possess narcotics, Robert Evans also surrendered to the DEA. Ever the showman, he appeared in federal court after donning a swirling black cape and a large, black, broad-brimmed hat for his date with justice. And ever the impresario, he began ordering everyone around like they were members of his production crew—his attorneys, the prosecutors, the court officers, etc. Right up until U.S. Magistrate Vincent Broderick got in his face and told him to sit down and shut up.

Back at the DEA lockup, Chris told me that when Chris described what could happen to high rollers like him in jail, Robert Evans lost it and started blurting out some A-list names, perhaps in his panic thinking he could make a deal.

Robert Evans ended up pleading guilty to conspiring to purchase and distribute cocaine. He was sentenced by Judge Broderick to one year of probation, provided he finance and produce a film on the evils of drug abuse. He did just that, and even enticed many of his celebrity pals to make cameos.

The film was called *Get High on Yourself.*

More celebrities came into our sites. Such as Vitas Gerulaitis.

Gerulaitis was a flamboyant party animal who drove a yellow Rolls-Royce, hung out at Studio 54, dated actresses and models, and played in a rock band.

He was also the world's fifth-ranked tennis player. And with his shoulder-length blond locks, his wild-catting ways, and his natural charisma, he was considered one of the sports world's biggest personalities.

In 1982, when Agent Tully's Argentine informant tipped him that Gerulaitis had arranged to receive two kilos of cocaine worth $80,000 from a pair of Cuban drug dealers, we set up surveillance on Gerulaitis's Manhattan apartment. Canvassing the streets, we spotted a parked car matching the description of one we knew was being used by the Cubans. Under the backseat I could see a brown paper bag containing a partially visible white plastic package.

The package was in open view. Time was of the essence. Ordinarily, if there had been enough time, we would have gotten a search warrant. But we were operating in an emergency situation or, in legal terminology, under "exigent circumstances." We didn't have enough manpower to sit on the car, and there was the distinct possibility that the Cubans might bolt with the drugs. That being the case, under federal statutes we were permitted to do a search without a warrant. So I smashed the rear passenger window with a tire iron. Sure enough, the bag contained cocaine.

Meanwhile, Gerulaitis was playing Ivan Lendl in the Volvo Masters Tournament at Madison Square Garden. While other agents kept up the surveillance on his apartment, I played backup and went with Tully, Agent Chris Eagan, and our group supervisor, Jeff Hall, over to the Garden. For fear of sparking a fan riot, we decided to hold off on busting Gerulaitis till his match against Lendl had ended.

Standing just off to the side of the court, we watched Gerulaitis and Lendl volleying back and forth. Suddenly I felt a tap on my shoulder. When I turned to face the tapper, the tapper practically jabbed his finger into my eyeball.

"You!" he said. "You! You! You!"

There in front of me stood the most celebrated and notorious attorney in the City of New York: David Breitbart, defender of celebrities, sports figures, and some of the biggest alleged mobsters and suspected narcotics traffickers in town. Because I was a prominent regular in federal court, having brought in many important drug cases for trial, he was well aware of who I was. And because I had gone head-to-head with him on one of his own big cases, I was even more visible on his radar. As it turned out, Breitbart also was the attorney for Vitas Gerulaitis.

Breitbart gave me the fisheye. "What brings you here, Louie?" he asked.

"I'm here to see the match. Just like you."

"Yeah, sure," he said. He knew I was full of shit.

I managed to escape Breitbart's clutches, regroup with the rest of my team, and set up again on Gerulaitis, who eventually lost his match to Lendl. Once it ended, we trailed him back to his apartment. Just before he walked inside, we arrested him on federal drug charges.

Even though the arrest made headline news, the case turned out to be a dud. Given that we'd never caught him with the drugs in his possession and there was no other direct evidence, Gerulaitis was never indicted.

Ultimately he came to a tragic end of a different sort. At age forty, and apparently in good health, he was found dead in a Long Island guest cottage. While drugs were initially suspected, it was later determined that a malfunctioning heating system caused poisonous carbon monoxide gas to seep into Gerulaitis's sleeping quarters.

It was the gas, not drugs, that had killed him.

* * *

SOMETIMES THE TARGETS were people you assumed you could place your trust in. Such as physicians.

When the DEA learned in the fall of 1985 that a fly-by-night health clinic in the Bronx was dispensing narcotic prescriptions to all comers, without ever bothering to do examinations, I was one of several agents to go undercover.

Most of the clinic's clients were pushers, who would use the prescriptions to buy drugs and then resell them on the street, or users who just wanted to get high.

Posing as various street scum, my fellow agents and I wouldn't even bother with the required questionnaires or physical examinations when we came into the clinic. Whenever the doctors went through the motions of asking how we felt, we would simply say, "Hey, doc, let's skip the bullshit. Just give me the usual fifty-six, twenty-eight, fifty-six." This was street code for an illegal transaction: fifty-six units of 50 mg tablets of Elavil, twenty-eight units of 200 mg tablets of Tuinol, and fifty-six units of 10 mg tablets of Valium.

Without blinking, the doctor would immediately write a scrip. The undercover, in turn, would fork over thirty bucks, which the doctor would pocket.

Down the line, we arrested all these shitbags with stethoscopes and closed the clinic down for good.

SOMETIMES THE TARGETS were borderline crazy. Such as the homicidal Italian and the gang of Russians with whom Agent George Pantoniou and I negotiated to buy five kilos of cocaine.

The middleman was a Colombian kid, a cartel wannabe. The price tag per kilo was $55,000. Our plan was to buy one kilo, then set up the purchase of the other four for a bust.

Unfortunately, because the DEA cashier was short of funds on the day scheduled for the buy, we were only able to come up with $30,000 for show-and-tell. The DEA bosses, both in New York and Washington, were often stingy with the cash we needed to do our jobs. They wanted field agents like us to look good in the cheapest of suits. Plus, George and I were trying to score cocaine, and the higher-ups felt that the lion's share of the cash earmarked for drug buys should be reserved for heroin.

When George and I finally secured the $30,000, it was all in $50 bills, and this posed another problem. Only "the man" gave out big bills like fifties. So over to the bank we traipsed, where we swapped the $30,000 in fifties for $30,000 in fives, tens, and twenties. Hopefully, the increased number of bundles would conceal the shortfall in the total dollar amount.

But when we met up with the Colombian at a city-owned parking lot, he knew right away we were short. So I went into my street dance and jumped in George's face about the missing money. Not missing a beat, George swore on his grandmother's grave that he had put all the money in the bag. Together, George and I could have taken this terrific act on the road.

"Does that look like all the money to you?" I screamed at George. "You fucking idiot!"

"Holy shit, Louie, I fucked up. This is the thirty grand for *that other thing* we were supposed to do. I took *the wrong bag*."

"Listen, my man," I told the kid, "we fucked up here. You gotta believe we weren't looking to short-change you. We want your product, no bullshit. But I can't blame you if you want to call this whole deal off. Fuck it, I sure as hell would."

The Colombian told us we were still good to go. He liked us . . . but we'd have to prove to the Russians we had the full amount. So we had to go back to the DEA cashier again and initiate a brand-new request for the entire $55,000. This time, fortunately, he had all the cash. And a week later, with the full amount in hand, we met up with the Colombian kid and his Russian overlords in an office in Manhattan's Diamond District.

First things first: the Russians insisting on frisking us. To accommodate them, I spread the flaps of my cabretta leather jacket outward and upward. The Russian doing the patdown went directly to my armpits and my waist, nicely missing the concealed mini-tape recorder I had concealed in the jacket's inside breast pocket.

Also on the guest list for the meet was an Italian, whom I immediately sized up as the big kahuna of the bunch. By way of cozying up to him, I threw a few phrases in Italian his way. Delighted to hear his native tongue spoken, he responded in kind. But this sent the head of the Russian gang into a paranoid, screaming hissy fit. It took us a long time to get the negotiations back on track.

Finally, we flashed the fifty-five grand. Using a scale to weigh all our cash, the Russian leader grunted his seal of approval. Given that each bill weighed a gram, he'd worked out a system to calculate the total dollar value of all the bills based on their combined weights. A stack of one hundred-dollar bills weighing five hundred grams would consist of five hundred hundred-dollar bills, or $50,000. A stack of twenty-dollar bills weighing a thousand grams would consist of 1,000 twenty-dollar bills, or $20,000.

With that, I told the Italian in his native language that I was going to the bathroom, and that he should come in right after me. Then I barked out in English, "Where's the fucking can around here? I gotta go."

The Russian leader got pissed off all over again that I had switched back into Italian. "Hey, it's a sign of respect!" I snapped at him. "Now cut the shit. Where's the bathroom?"

Still suspicious, he ordered one of the other Russians to escort me. When I stepped into the men's room stall, he actually tried to walk in right behind me.

I bristled. "Hey, you fucking mind, *gumba*?" I said. "I gotta take a shit!"

Then I slammed the door in his face. Inside the stall, squatting on the throne and making grunting noises, I pulled out a pen, took an old business card out of my wallet, and wrote my undercover phone number on it.

When I came back out again, my Russian guard was still waiting and watching like a hawk. He began leading me back down the corridor toward the office when Georgie, who really *did* have to use the bathroom, came walking toward me. Suddenly here comes the Italian, barreling up behind Georgie and shoving him out of the way.

"I gotta go, I gotta go," the Italian said. And right then and there, I knew he'd picked up on my play. As he hurried past, I tucked my business card into his palm. None of the Russians noticed.

Later that day, once I was back in my office, the Italian called me on my undercover phone. He wanted to meet me the next day at Ali Baba, a sleazy nightclub and notorious mob hangout on Manhattan's East Side. I readily agreed.

Georgie and the Colombian kid were at the sit-down. The Colombian raised a toast, saluting my clever play. Although he couldn't cut the Russians out of the coke deal, he was thrilled that *we* had. They'd been driving him nuts.

The Italian had brought a small sample of the cocaine. Together, he and I slipped away to the bathroom so I could test it.

Once inside, I turned to bolt the door behind us when I heard the distinct sound of a gun slide chambering a round.

"You better not be a fucking cop," the Italian said, pushing the barrel into my temple.

For an instant, I went cold. Although my street instincts were firing on all cylinders, this was something I had never expected. But then anger, always my biggest ally, kicked in. And with my anger came focus. Clarity.

"What are you, fucking out of your mind?" I snapped. "You think I'm a cop? Go ahead then, motherfucker. You think I'm a cop, *just shoot me*."

The whole world seemed to freeze around us. I waited for what seemed like an eternity.

The Italian pulled back his piece, tucked it in his waistband, and put his hands to his face. "Man, I'm really sorry," he said. "I been under a lotta pressure lately. One of my boys just got taken down behind this, and I ain't been right since. I'm really sorry."

I took several deep breaths to calm my own jangled nerves. Then I took his sample and performed my field test. The stuff was shiny, white, and had the consistency of small fish scales, all positive indicators. It tested nicely with the reagent. I even took a taste. Within a minute, the shit hit home. Dynamite. We shook hands, cementing the deal for me to receive the rest of the coke a few days later.

After the deal was consummated and we had scored the drugs, our DEA backups locked up the Italian, the Colombian, and all those crazy Russians.

Case closed.

SOMETIMES THE TARGETS were people you knew but didn't want to know.

A guard at the Brooklyn House of Detention tipped me that an inmate was offering information on a major Brooklyn gun and drug runner. The prison was just a few blocks from where I had grown up in Red Hook.

The guard introduced me and George to the inmate, who began to describe the gun and drug dealer in detail. Five minutes into the conversation, I got a hot flash. The guy he was describing was someone I recognized.

But after two more minutes, I shut down cold. Long ago, I had made a vow that I would never betray my job . . . but I would never look to bust a friend either.

A year or so later, I happened to stop by at a bar in Brooklyn. And who did I chance to run into? The very same friend that prison snitch had tried to set up for a bust. The two of us got to talking about the good old days—pulling that fire alarm and running like hell, the wiseguys on the corner, the fistfights down at the schoolyard.

But my old buddy pulled me up short when he said he thought I had been one of the feds working with Donnie Brasco, aka FBI agent Joe Pistone, who had gone undercover to infiltrate the Bonanno and Colombo crime families, and whose story later became a best-selling book and acclaimed movie.

"Nah, no way," I assured him. "Not me. Even though some of Brasco's targets were targets of mine, too. But I gotta tell you something else. Something that may come as a shock you. I covered your ass on something *you* coulda gone down for."

I told him about the snitch in the Brooklyn House of Detention who'd been bartering for a break by trying to drop a dime on him, and how I had nipped the whole thing in the bud. When I finished my tale, my friend threw his arms around me and hugged me.

"You always was one tough monkey," he said.

And so it was, after all those years, that Perky and I reconnected. He'd gained a few inches in his pants size, lost a little hair, developed a couple of crow's-feet around his eyes, but it was still the same old Perky.

"By the way," Perky told me, "that snitch? He ain't doin' no snitchin' no more."

"Oh?" I said.

"R.I.P.," sniffed Perky.

End of story.

SOMETIMES THE TARGETS were monsters.

Like "El Viejo," an older pusher in the East Bronx.

When I met up with him, he flashed me two ounces of Mexican brown. I ran my field test, which indicated the stuff was legit. But eager to show me it was top quality, El Viejo summoned his personal heroin tester—a skeevy, sore-covered, emaciated Hispanic guy—to give me a demo.

Right there in front of us, the tester used a cigarette lighter to melt some heroin in a spoon, drew the liquefied heroin into a syringe, cinched up an elastic band around his left bicep, and mainlined a vein in his forearm. Suddenly the vein exploded, spurting blood all over him . . . and me. Wiping the blood from my face, it was all I could do to keep from putting the deal down, let alone vomit. Undeterred, the tester gave it another try, this time finding a sturdier vein. Then, as he untied the elastic band from his bicep, his eyes rolled up into his head.

"You see? You see?" said El Viejo with a big, toothless grin. "Dat's some good shit, no?"

That it was, as our DEA lab guy later verified. Sixty-five percent pure.

Then there was Sylvia, a coke and smack dealer who

worked for Colombian and Dominican drug lords and made her prospective smugglers, all of them females, pass a hideous endurance test before hiring them as mules.

While in my presence, she grabbed a pound of large white grapes and counted them. Each grape, she explained, represented a single plastic capsule of cocaine being smuggled into the States. Then she made the prospective candidate slowly swallow the entire pound of grapes *without chewing them*. After sitting quietly for five minutes, the girl was ordered to jump up and dance around. She promptly vomited the grapes into a bucket.

The girl was immediately disqualified for mule duty. To pass muster, a candidate had to keep all the grapes down for a fixed period of time, notwithstanding the jump-and-dance test. If she did, Sylvia would personally drive her to the airport and put her on a plane to Colombia or the Dominican Republic.

For each pound of cocaine that girl successfully smuggled back into the States, she would be paid $2,500.

Monsters, each and every one of them.

WORKING THESE CASES and others like them helped me to hone my instincts, sharpen my senses, raise my game. They prepared me to take on even more challenging undercover investigations, the cases that would *really* make the headlines.

Which was how I came to take on the biggest, baddest drug dealer of them all.

CHAPTER NINE

As a teenager, Leroy "Nicky" Barnes was just circling the porcelain, about to go down the drain.

Raised in the tenements of Harlem, he'd played basketball on Eighth Avenue between 113th and 116th streets. Heroin was all around in those days, in every alley and on every stoop and every corner, and he couldn't help but notice. The first heroin he sold belonged to his own father, who was holding for a street dealer. Eventually Nicky became a pusher in his own right for a mobbed-up distributor named Fat Herbie, who taught him how to cut the powder and make the drops. Fat Herbie also introduced Nicky to Matty Madonna, who was plugged into the Lucchese crime family.

Many of Nicky's drug sales took place in local pool halls. But then he started to use himself—small amounts of heroin, coke, speedballs. By age fourteen, he was a full-fledged junkie runaway. He got busted a bunch of times for possession of a hypodermic needle, possession of burglary tools, breaking into parked cars. In prison, he went cold turkey and kicked his habit. Then he found religion, vowing never to touch junk, take a drink, or even smoke a cigarette ever again.

Out of jail and back on the streets, he apprenticed with Harlem's most notorious heroin dealer, William "Goldfinger" Terrell, and became a midlevel dealer, relying on a Dominican connection for product. He tried to build a drug empire of his own by recruiting other peddlers with names such as "Big

Robbie," "Hollywood," "Mustache Bobby," and "Movie Star." But his organizing efforts never got off the ground. So he decided to go it alone.

Still in his early twenties, he was busted again on a narcotics rap and packed off to Greenhaven Prison to serve a sentence of twenty-five to life. It looked like his grand plan for becoming New York City's top-dog drug kingpin was kaput. And, for all intents and purposes, he was, too.

But then a strange thing happened. Behind bars, his luck turned.

He now had plenty of time to think. And to read. He began devouring everything he could get his hands on. He was highly intelligent, tackling Machiavelli's *The Prince*, books on history and culture, treatises by black scholars, the teachings of the Black Muslim founder Elijah Muhammad. He subscribed to thirty-seven different legal journals. He read the Bible. He embraced Islam.

In prison he also reunited with Matty Madonna, who was doing twenty to life for murder. Madonna taught Nicky how to play chess and educated him about the workings of the Mafia.

But his biggest mentor was the one and only "Crazy Joe" Gallo, the notorious Brooklyn mob boss from back home, who was doing five to fifteen at Greenhaven for extortion.

Joey G. didn't give a shit whether an inmate was black, white, Hispanic, or Norwegian. He was connected to all the big Mafia families, and everyone in the joint knew it. Cliques and gangs didn't frighten him. Chin out, balls big as grapefruits, he'd strut around the prison yard, stopping to talk with anyone he damn pleased. Beautiful women came to visit him—and service him—on a regular basis. He read Sartre, Kafka, Camus, Dumas, Hugo, and Tolstoy. He took up painting and produced watercolors. If he perceived a fellow inmate to be a threat, he would politely invite him into his cell and serve him a plate of antipasto laced with strychnine.

Nobody fucked with Joey G. He got respect.

Gallo immediately recognized Nicky's intelligence, as well as his potential usefulness for the future. Joey always rooted for the underdog (although his fondness for and association with the black community eventually fueled a war with the Profaci-Gambino family, which was depicted in the movie *The Godfather*). In Nicky he saw ambition and talent, but recognized that it had been thwarted by society's bigoted attitude toward the color of his skin. So he took him under his wing.

They played chess, talked politics, art, and philosophy. They discussed the operations of the Mafia, and one day Joey shocked the shit out of Nicky when he said, "Nick, you coloreds oughta show the mob who's boss."

Joey went on to talk about the difference between *white* kilos (heroin dealt by whites) and *black* kilos (heroin dealt by blacks), which were considerably inferior. Perceiving the blacks to be weak and powerless, the Mafia had no qualms about selling them inferior product.

Joey said that after the Mafia had grown fat and lazy out in Vegas, it had recruited the blacks to do all its dirty work and take the risks, while the capos sat back in their social clubs, smoked their fat cigars, and sipped their cappuccino. He proposed they team up—Nicky Barnes in Harlem, Joe Gallo in Brooklyn—to take back the streets and the drug trade from the old-time wiseguys. Together, he said, they'd make a fucking mint.

Nicky was keen to learn, so Joey took him to school.

He talked about importing pure heroin from Southeast Asia, through Italian middlemen. The pure heroin could be cut down, or diluted, many times before it was actually put out on the streets for the junkies, and this was a way to significantly multiply the profits. Hell, fifty kilos of 90 percent pure heroin, cut thirty times, with either quinine or milk powder or a cheap laxative called mannite, could generate $280 million in cash.

Joey taught Nicky how to set up a tightly knit organization, centralizing all the key components—importing, wholesaling, and retailing—under one roof. The organization would need a clearly delineated hierarchy and specific job titles, much like the Mafia had its *capo de tutti capi, capo regime,* consigliere, captains, lieutenants, soldiers, associates, and button men.

A few years down the line, Joey did something else for Nicky. As soon as Joey got out of jail, he hooked Nicky up with a top-flight attorney to handle his appeal.

When the testimony that led to Nicky's conviction was reexamined, discrepancies were noted. Tape recordings of wiretapped conversations were replayed, but portions appeared to have been mysteriously erased. Other, unerased portions strongly suggested that Nicky had been framed. As a result, he won a new trial.

In 1969, after four years behind bars, Nicky Barnes's original conviction was reversed, and he was cut loose. Undeterred, and fortified by the lessons he'd learned at the knee of Joey G., Nicky returned to the streets with a vengeance. Only this time he was wilier and a whole lot stronger. "Goldfinger" Terrell had landed in jail. Brimming with piss and vinegar, Nicky corralled his network of suppliers and went into the drug business on a grand scale.

With the help of Frank and Matty Madonna, Nicky began importing pure heroin from abroad. At home he set up an operation to control both the mills and the deliveries, doing trade not just in Harlem but also in upstate New York, Pennsylvania, and Canada, with outposts in Chicago, Arizona, and other parts of the country. In so doing, he pushed aside the old-time Italians who, for so many years, had monopolized the drug trade and sold him smack when he was a kid. The payback could not have been sweeter.

Fearing that male workers would waste time by drinking, smoking weed, and watching TV, Nicky staffed his cutting mills with young women who wore surgical masks and were required to work naked. Their jobs were highly specialized—baggers, spooners, and tapers—and they were always under the watchful eye of a shotgun-toting lieutenant. The thinking was that, without clothes, the women would be motivated to do their work more quickly and efficiently and not try to steal any of the product. For sixteen hours of labor, the women would be paid $500 to $1,000 apiece.

After the heroin was cut—or turned into "scrambled eggs"—it would be placed in glassine envelopes, given to "salesmen" or "jobbers," transported in gypsy cabs to local candy stores, bars, luncheonettes, and other outlets, and finally sold to the junkies who were pining for their fix.

Nicky recruited subordinates with nicknames such as "Brother," "Gaps," "Sugar Pie Guy," "Jazz," "Radio," "Bat," "Frank Nitti," "Chico Bob," "Farmer Brown," "Wop," and "Fat Stevie." The top tier of the organization—which was comprised of Nicky and six lieutenants—decided to call themselves "the Council." Even though they were all Black Muslims, they modeled their operation around La Cosa Nostra, the syndicate of Mafia crime families. They parceled out territory and promised to respect each other's boundaries. They cultivated contacts in the judiciary and the Police Department. One of the Council members had a brother who was a cop. This inside man agreed to funnel to the Council the names of snitches, find weapons, and give members martial arts training. Other cops would be bribed as much as $5,000 not to patrol the blocks where the Council's street vendors were plying their trade. Nicky had it all figured out.

To cement their bond, the Council members duplicated the Mafia's code of silence, *omertà*. They held their arms across their chests, took each other's hands, and swore an oath of loyalty.

Treat my brother as I treat myself.

To make sure the Council's members never lost their edge, Nicky forbade them from using heroin, speed, angel dust, and marijuana. The only drug he tolerated was cocaine, because he felt it heightened a person's mental sharpness. To keep himself fit, both physically and mentally, he worked out with weights every day.

As far as the coke itself, he'd never go near it, nor would he personally handle the cash it generated. And, for fear of being wiretapped, he would never talk on the phone. This way, he could never be directly linked to the illicit business he was masterminding. It was a brilliant scheme, guaranteed to make him arrest-proof. Instead, the drugs and the cash were handled by midlevel distributors and street vendors, who would yell "Black Tape!" to alert their customers that it was time to line up to get their fixes.

The results of Nicky's careful planning and extra precautions were nothing short of spectacular. As he would write in his 2007 memoir *Mr. Untouchable*, "After years of plotting and waiting, I pulled off the boldest score in the underworld—seizing the distribution of heroin on the streets of New York City."

He added, "And they say crime doesn't pay. The only question was—what were we gonna do with all that money?"

At one point, his organization was grossing several million dollars a month, with Nicky netting a sizable chunk of the take. By the early 1970s, authorities had determined that he was the largest, richest, and most powerful drug dealer on the Eastern Seaboard.

Nicky knew the cops would follow him and even bug him, but he was already one step ahead. Obtaining copies of transcripts from recent drug trials, which included detailed testimony about police surveillance methods, Nicky handed them out to his lieutenants so they could be prepared. As further protection from the long arm of the law, he also made them file regular tax returns. He even gave them introductions to a Detroit accounting firm that specialized in providing tax shelters for doctors and lawyers.

According to a November 1978 article by Blake Fleetwood in *High Times Magazine*, by the mid-1970s Nicky was reporting miscellanous annual income to the IRS of more than $250,000, much of which he wrote off against his investment in a $7 million Detroit housing project. His other investments were in travel agencies, car washes, and gas stations.

Besides the steady inflow of cash, there were other rewards, Fleetwood wrote. Four high-rise, high-rent apartments. A fleet of luxury cars, including several Mercedes-Benzes, a Thunderbird, a Lincoln Continental, a Volvo station wagon, and a Citroën Maserati. And a wardrobe that positively dazzled—more than fifty leather coats, three hundred custom-designed suits, twenty-five color-coordinated hats, and one hundred pairs of shoes and boots. With his broad shoulders, his handsome, sharply chiseled features, and his trademark tinted, gogglelike Gucci eyeglasses, he could have passed for a Hollywood actor or a fashion model.

On the streets, Nicky became a legend. He was balls, he

was flash, he was verve. Dressed to the nines, surrounded by his bodyguards and his women, he was the Al Capone of Harlem. Whenever he walked into a club such as the Gold Lounge or the Shalimar or Small's Paradise, which was frequented by jazz musicians, politicians, and superstar athletes, the crowds would part to let him pass, bowing in respect but never, ever touching.

In the community, he was a regular Santa Claus. He gave out a thousand turkeys for Christmas, bought ice cream for little kids, helped pay rent, handed out cash to buy gifts for Mother's Day. Unlike other black men who had achieved fame and financial success, then fled the ghetto for greener—and whiter—pastures, he had stayed behind and, because of that, he'd become a local hero. Whenever he appeared in public, a crowd would gather around in awe and adoration.

For more than a decade, Nicky Barnes was labeled a major narcotics violator by city, state, and federal law enforcement agencies. But whenever the cops hassled him, he refused to bow and scrape. Arrested in 1976 for drug and weapons possession, he had to make an appearance in Manhattan Criminal Court. During an adjournment in the proceedings, he went into the men's room, where he bumped into two narcotics detectives he knew.

In his June 5, 1977, cover story in the *New York Times Magazine*, writer Fred Ferretti described what followed: After washing his hands, Nicky lifted them up to the mirror, appeared to inspect them closely, and said aloud, just so the detectives could hear, "I need a handkerchief. Let's see, is this a handkerchief?"

Reaching into a side pocket, he pulled out a fat wad of fifty-dollar bills. "Oops," he said, "that ain't no handkerchief, is it?"

Reaching into his other side pocket, he asked aloud, "Is this a handkerchief here?" Then he pulled out a matching roll of fifties. "No, that ain't no handkerchief either, is it?" he said.

Tucking the two rolls of bills back into his pockets, he looked into the mirror and grinned broadly at the two detectives. Then he shook his hands dry and walked out.

Often the cops would tail him. In fact, during one seven-month stretch, they kept him under surveillance twenty-four hours a day. Nicky knew they were following him, so just to piss them off, he would play a game of cat and mouse. Sometimes a car would pull out of the garage of his building with his wife, Thelma, at the wheel and Nicky lying flat on the backseat. Heading over to the West Side Highway, it would hit speeds of 100 mph, then simply return to the garage, where Nicky and his wife would walk nonchalantly back into their apartment. The cops never issued tickets because they were more interested in seeing where he was going than tagging him for speeding. In the end, it turned out that he was going absolutely nowhere . . . and, much to their disgust, so were the detectives who had been following him.

At other times his car would head over to Brooklyn, where Nicky would get out, walk into a building, come outside, shoot a hard stare at the surveillance vehicle, then get back in his car. On the return trip to Manhattan, the car would make endless and pointless U-turns before bringing Nicky back to his apartment. Or it would kill its lights and pull off the road, into the brush, allowing the police surveillance vehicle to pass by. Pulling back onto the road again, Nicky would turn on his lights and pull up behind the cops, blowing his horn loudly to scare the shit out of them.

But to really fuck with them, Nicky came up with an extra-delicious kind of torture. Driven up to Harlem, he'd stop at a hundred different locations, forcing his police tail to pull to the curb, then watch, wait, and wonder about what was going down at each and every one . . . which again turned out to be absolutely nothing at all.

There were would-be rivals, such as Frank Lucas, the murderous drug dealer so flamboyantly portrayed by Denzel Washington in the movie *American Gangster*. Frank, who came from North Carolina, had his own crime crew, "the Country Boys." He did a brisk trade in heroin, some of which he smuggled into the States from Southeast Asia by getting U.S. soldiers to stash it inside the their baggage, their furniture, and other personal possessions they were shipping back to the States, since they were rarely subject to inspections. It also was sneaked in by U.S. Air Force flight personnel.

Like Nicky, Frank was a high roller. According to a story in 2000 by Mark Jacobson in *New York Magazine*, Frank lived in a suite at the Regency Hotel and palled around with celebrities such as Muhammed Ali, James Brown, Berry Gordy, Diana Ross, and Sammy Davis Jr. He screwed lots of good-looking women. He favored mink and chinchilla coats and cruised the city in his Rolls-Royce, his Mercedes, or his Corvette Stingray. On the streets, Frank was known as "Superfly."

Frank and Nicky staked out their territories and respected each other's corners. But in the overall scheme of things, Frank was small potatoes—according to Nicky, he was a guy who wildly exaggerated his own accomplishments, especially his Southeast Asian heroin-in-the-furniture scam.

Frank also was an intellectual and cultural inferior to the highly intelligent and self-educated Nicky, a country "bumpkin from the word go, just like the rest of his bumpkin gang," as Nicky would write in his 2007 memoir. "They [the Country Boys] all had some vague blood link, so you could technically call them brothers, but I called them a pack of clowns who'd throw a rock at a baby carriage for a dollar."

Still, Frank had an understanding with Nicky, one that let him continue doing business and coexist in peace. There were others circling around in Nicky's galaxy, however—liars, schemers, welchers, short-changers, and rats—who did not fare so well. With them, Nicky's vengeance and brutality knew no limits.

Guys who thought about short-changing Nicky were given a quick education. Once hung over the side of the George Washington Bridge, so terrified that they would crap their pants, then forced to eat their own shit, they'd get the message loud and clear.

When a dude named Billings was thought to have become a snitch for the DEA, the Council ordered a hit on him. Billings was shot three times, half his face blown off. Incredibly, he survived and, from his hospital bed, blamed Nicky Barnes for the assassination attempt. So Nicky sent an emissary to his room with $10,000 in cash in a brown paper bag to keep him silent. The police quickly placed Billings into protective custody . . . but Nicky's boys tracked him down again and upped the bribe to $20,000. When the case finally went to trial, Billings suffered a mysterious lapse of memory about the shooting and who had ordered it. After that, he was never seen again.

Others were the victims of more finite fates. Reggie Isaacs, a lieutenant suspected of holding out on Nicky in a heroin deal, was an avid golfer. The cops found him dead on the eighteenth hole of the Mosholu Golf Course in the Bronx. Stanley Morgan, another apparent short-changer, was shot eight times, his corpse left lying just a few doors down from a police station.

One woman accused Nicky of personally stabbing her husband to death with a penknife. During the court proceedings, $100,000 bail was posted for Nicky by a Harlem minister. The bail was rejected by the judge, who felt the minister's money probably came from Nicky's drug dealings. So instead Nicky put up the collateral with his equity from a $4.6 million Detroit housing project backed by the federal government. Ultimately, the whole case just fizzled dead. Like so many others, the bereaved widow who had brought the original murder charge against Nicky had a sudden and mysterious memory lapse—once she got up on the witness stand, she couldn't remember a blessed thing.

Amnesia was a common affliction among those called to testify against Nicky. In fact, it was damn near epidemic.

Nicky would later implicate himself in eight murders. But law enforcement people suspected that the actual total was even greater. In addition to murder, he was arrested for bribery, gun possession, drug possession, and drug dealing. Few of the charges ever stuck, and he spent only minimal amounts of time behind bars. Police and prosecutorial improprieties had a way of cropping up in court proceedings. Evidence against him had a tendency to fall apart. Witnesses had a habit of disappearing.

Things got so bad that on June 5, 1977, the *New York Times Magazine* did a full-cover story about Nicky Barnes. The cover photo showed him defiant, posing with hands crossed, in his best threads, wearing dark Gucci sunglasses. On his face was an expression that basically said, "Fuck all of you."

The headline read, *"Mister Untouchable."*

The subhead below that said, *"This is Nicky Barnes. The Police Say He May Be Harlem's Biggest Drug Dealer. But Can They Prove It?"*

A lot of people had tried in the past, and failed. They had waltzed around Nicky, attempted to get close, and gotten burned . . . some of them so badly that they were never seen or heard from again. Meanwhile, his perpetuation of mind-poisoning, soul-sapping, body-destroying drugs was running like wildfire in New York.

Nicky Barnes was pure, unadulterated evil. And now it was up to me, Louie D., to ask this devil to dance.

CHAPTER TEN

GETTING NICKY BARNES ON a hand-to-hand buy was impossible. Too shrewd to handle the drugs himself, he always left the dirty work to his lieutenants and distributors.

The only hope of ever touching Mister Untouchable and bringing him to justice would be to mount an undercover operation, then gather enough evidence to indict him under the federal Racketeer Influenced and Corrupt Organizations Act (RICO) for conspiracy to sell and distribute narcotics.

But *how*?

Given that the Police Department and the city's courts leaked like sieves, Nicky sometimes got wind of new investigations before they were even up and running. Informants who tried to get close to Nicky had a way of disappearing . . . usually forever. Some other way needed to be found.

In the summer of 1976, the DEA found it.

A twenty-four-year-old hood named Robert Geronimo got himself busted by the FBI for selling $25,000 worth of nonexistent television sets and stolen cars. In addition to peddling swag, Geronimo was a loan shark and ran numbers.

Once in custody, Geronimo quickly let it be known he was ready to deal, although he refused to give up any of his fellow Italians. Nevertheless, he still claimed to have something worth dealing:

Nicky Barnes.

After FBI agent Ford Cole alerted Don Ferrarone, the

head of the Southern District Conspiracy Group in the DEA's Manhattan office, Cole and Ferrarone jointly debriefed Geronimo.

Geronimo was mobbed up. His uncle was a made guy from Pleasant Avenue in the Bronx. As a kid, Geronimo had run with a black guy named Wally Fisher. Wally's brother, Guy Fisher, had been Nicky Barnes's top lieutenant until he was jailed for driving without a license and attempting to bribe a cop, who, upon searching Fisher's car, discovered $103,000 in the trunk.

With big brother Guy now cooling his heels in the slammer, little brother Wally decided it was time to step up himself. Tired of living in Guy's shadow and being little more than a gofer, Wally was eager to jump off the bench and into Nicky's game. He was hungry—and being hungry meant he might be the weak link that could be exploited by the DEA.

Geronimo claimed to have run scams for both Guy and Wally Fisher. He said the brothers had tried to hire him for ten grand to whack a guy who had assaulted their sister. After Geronimo had declined the contract, Nicky Barnes himself had agreed to step in as his replacement killer, and the cops were tipped off to the plan. They caught Nicky and two of his lieutenants with $10,000 in cash and two loaded guns.

Because his tip had panned out, Geronimo's stock as a government informant had skyrocketed. Indeed, after several hours of grilling, Agent Ferrarone was convinced that Geronimo could take the DEA straight into the belly of the beast.

The most plausible strategy would have been to send black informants and cops up to Harlem to try to get the goods on Nicky. But over the years, those who tried to get close to him had gotten burned. So what if the DEA resorted to a little reverse psychology and did the opposite of what was expected?

What if the federal government came at Nicky with a white man? It was a notion totally off the wall . . . and, therefore, it just might fly.

But Geronimo was a con man, not a drug dealer. So the DEA would need someone else, someone with experience around drugs, to chaperone Geronimo when he tried to make inroads with Nicky's organization. A "handler" of sorts. A deep cover agent who could pose as a drug dealer and pull off the ruse convincingly.

Which is why Agent Ferrarone thought of me—because of my experience, my upbringing, and my wiseguy street shtick, Ferrarone felt that Geronimo and I would fit like hand in glove.

A meeting was arranged.

THE DAY OF the meet, I showed up wearing my gray checkered Carnaby cap, my army fatigue jacket, my hooded blue sweatshirt, blue jeans, and combat boots. I wanted to make certain that Geronimo knew from the get-go that I was not your run-of-the-mill, deskbound, suit-and-tie Fed.

My partner during this period, Bobby Nieves, joined us at the table.

Tall, big-boned, a ruggedly handsome-looking kid with a beard, muscles, and slicked-back hair, Geronimo was street-smart, quick on his feet, brash, and funny. After I was able to take the measure of the man I said: "G, I got a good feeling about you. You remind me of a guy I grew up with. But there are some things we need to go over. So when these two guys Ferrarone and Bobby Nieves are gone, me and you are gonna go have a couple of drinks together."

"Great," said Geronimo. "Uncle Sam buyin'?"

Wiseass. But I let it slide. I liked the kid.

Later, over a round of beers, I laid it down to him: "G, this is a partnership, a brotherhood. My life will be in your hands. Your life will be in my hands. You gotta be straight with me at all times. If you can't do that, it won't work. You understand?"

"I hear you, Louie," Geronimo said.

I went on. "Now, there are some things we're gonna have to do, some left-handed things that only you and me are gonna know about. But I'll tell you one thing: If you fuck me, I'll fuck you back twice as bad. You screw me, you better cover your asshole, plain and simple."

Geronimo grinned. "Okay," he said. "But on one condition."

"What's that?"

"I don't work with nobody but you, Louie."

"Deal."

Over the next few days, Bobby Nieves and I continued to debrief Geronimo. We also compared notes with Detective Larry Gierholdt of the DEA-NYPD Joint Task Force, who was extremely knowledgeable about Nicky's organization. In the fall of 1977, Gierholdt and his team had pulled off a bold coup when Nicky celebrated his 40th birthday at the Playboy Club in Manhattan. Staffing the joint with undercover cops posing as waiters, busboys, and valets, the task force had scored surveillance photos of Nicky's inner circle, which allowed us to put names to the faces of Nicky's top lieutenants.

With the surveillance photos in hand and Geronimo now under wing, we began to map out a plan.

The key would be to come up with a foolproof story, one that would convince Nicky and his boys that we had to be anything *but* cops.

Geronimo was already covered. He already knew Wally

and Guy Fisher, was acquainted with Nicky and his lieutenants, was mobbed-up in his own right, and had a criminal rap sheet. To save Geronimo from testifying and preserve his role as an informant, the DEA persuaded the Bronx DA to drop the gun charge against Nicky stemming from the attempted hit on the assailant who had roughed up the Fisher brothers' sister. This cleared the way for Geronimo to become the DEA's Trojan horse.

But I would need a credible story of my own. So here's what I cooked up: I was a connected Mafia guy who peddled dope and hired myself out as a professional hit man. Not a made man, but a freelance operator. I had dealt with all the major crime families, but I was so insane that the mob guys were reluctant to do business with me anymore, 'cause they didn't know where my allegiances lay. At one point I had gotten too hot—my problem being that I enjoyed killing too much—so they had packed me off to California to cool off. But now I was back in town and itching to get into the game once more. I couldn't go back to the Italians, having burned that bridge. So I needed to find a new source of product, and a new playing field, which was why I had hooked up with "my cousin," Geronimo, who had uptown connections to the movers and shakers who ruled the roost in those parts.

So hello, Harlem and hello, Nicky Barnes.

There were other good undercovers working out of the DEA's New York office, all of us sporting big, fat, egos that needed to be massaged, all of us competing to see who was the toughest, who would command the most respect, who could make the most cases, the best cases, the most arrests. When Don Ferrarone gave me the nod to team up with Geronimo and take on Nicky Barnes, I felt honored. While it was never promised, I knew that once this case concluded, a promotion would be forthcoming. I could sense the jealousy of my colleagues, but it went with the territory.

Putting aside my personal agenda, I knew I would have to be extra-convincing, extra-sharp, extra-vigilant. As an undercover, I had been good. But now I would have to be *better* than good.

I would need to give an Academy Award performance. Anything short of that could cost me my life.

ON A CHILLY November night in Harlem, I was introduced to Wally Fisher.

He was perched on the corner of Adam Clayton Powell Boulevard, warming his hands over a garbage can fire, when Geronimo and I pulled up. The average price on a GM car in 1976 was $6,000, but Wally was in possession of a $15,000 Corvette Stingray that sat nearby.

Geronimo had set up the meet, talking me up ahead of time as a connected guy, and I came dressed for my star billing. Camel hair coat, cashmere scarf, black silk shirt, expensive Italian shoes, plenty of shiny bling dangling from my neck, wrists, and fingers, the whole nine yards.

I also had allowed my mustache and beard to grow out, keeping them neatly trimmed. The facial hair buttressed my cover story. Wiseguy Italians frowned on mustaches and beards, but since I was purporting to be a renegade on the outs with the local crime families—one of which might be looking to whack me—it made sense for me to have come back to town in disguise.

I also was driving a set of fuck-you wheels, a brontosaurus-size, canary yellow Cadillac Coupe de Ville plucked from the DEA's stable of seized vehicles.

The moment I stepped out of the Caddy, I could see that Wally was excited. Wally looked about twenty-one, had sharp, angular features, a short black Afro, prescription eyeglasses, a small black mustache, and a goatee. He was dressed in a dark wool overcoat, cashmere sweater, and expensive boots, and he was grinning from ear to ear.

Two mob guys coming up to Harlem to talk business with *him*? The kid was ready to cream in his jeans. So I went into my street dance and milked it to the max.

"Howya doin', my man?" I said, sounding like Joe Bag-a-Donuts from Bensonhurst as I gave him a real man's man's, knuckle-cruncher of a handshake. "Yeah, I heard a lot about you. It's nice to finally meet you."

"How *you* doin', man?" asked Wally.

Geronimo briefly spelled out my checkered past with the mob. Then I went into my sales pitch: "Wally, lemme just lay this down to you. I know G already has laid it out to you, but I'm not lookin' to fuckin' scramble. I'm not lookin' to fuckin' get taken from one end of Harlem to the other. I'm lookin' for a steady source. And I need a reliable product. I got my people waitin', but before I can open the door, I need a steady source. You hear what I'm sayin'?"

"I hear you, brother," Wally gushed.

I continued, "Now if you can't do that for me, then fuck off. But this is what I'm lookin' for. Now, obviously, you know I'm G's cousin. I stand where I stand. But we could do a lotta things together. Not only this, but there may come a time where you can come in with us as a full partner if this thing takes off."

Geronimo, quick-witted street guy that he was, immediately backed me to the hilt on my spiel.

By now Wally's eyes were practically spinning in their orbits. He slapped his hands together and said, “Say no more, brother. I’m in.”

We proceeded to set a time and date for my very first buy of Nicky Barnes’s heroin.

TEN DAYS LATER, Geronimo and I met up with Wally at the Kingdom Garage in the Bronx, one of Nicky Barnes’s car depots around the city. I had brought $8,000 with me to make a buy.

Wally, ever hungry to make his breakthrough into Nicky’s inner sanctum, ballyhooed his connections. “See that yellow Volvo over there?” he asked as he excitedly pointed to one corner of the garage. “And the Cadillac? And the Mercedes? And that other Mercedes right behind it? All of ’em belong to Nicky Barnes.”

“Nicky Barnes, eh?” I said, sliding into my dumb and dumber act. “Yeah, I heard of this Nicky Barnes. You know, I think Nicky Barnes and I could help each other. Do a little business, even. Matter of fact, I’d like to meet him someday.”

“Well, fuck it, Louie, I’m the man to make that happen!” Wally bragged.

“I’ll just bet you are, kid,” I said.

Later that night, at the Two Cousins Lounge in the Bronx, a deal finally went down. From my Caddy, Geronimo, Wally, and I watched as one of Nicky’s boys, Petey Rollock, walked inside. I then shuttled Wally and Geronimo back and forth between my car and the lounge to negotiate an eighth-of-a-kilo buy for my eight grand. Once they were certain Petey had the package with him, Geronimo was to bring him a $4,000 down payment. When I was satisfied that the package was righteous, I would give G the other $4,000 to bring to Petey.

After several trips into the lounge—where two black DEA agents, working undercover, sat at the bar, observing—Geronimo and Wally came back to my Caddy with a clear plastic bag.

I told G to get behind the wheel and drive the three of us around the block. After we parked in an alley, I told Wally to reach behind the seat belt retainer on the driver's side and pull out the cigarette pack containing my Marquis field-testing kit.

"Fuck it, I'm not gonna get stuck with no lame shit," I sniffed. "I ain't goin' back to my people with fuckin' turkey."

While Wally groped around for my kit, I shot a quick glance into the rearview mirror. The unmarked DEA surveillance car that had been tailing us rolled to a stop up the block. I knew that my partner, Bobby Nieves, was inside the car, watching my back.

Luckily, Wally hadn't spotted anybody. "Here you go, Louie," he said, handing me the cigarette pack.

Poking a hole in the plastic package with my penknife, I extracted a small sample. I felt it, smelled it, tasted it. Then I put a pinch on a small glass side and proceeded to do my abracadabra act with my eyedropper and my chemical reagents.

"Holy shit!" Wally blurted out as the brown heroin, tinged with a tiny droplet of sulfuric acid, turned bright purple.

"Dy-no-mite!" I said, smiling. "She's righteous, kid." We slapped high fives.

Then Geronimo pulled a boner.

Totally by accident, he hit the Caddy's flashers—the prearranged signal to my DEA backups that we had either been made or were being ripped off.

Suddenly Bobby jumped out of the DEA surveillance car and came running toward the Caddy. In one hand he held a brown paper bag, which concealed the .38-caliber revolver he held in the other hand.

But Bobby played it just right. Seeing nothing amiss inside the Caddy, he just kept on running, *right past us*, and back around the corner. Wally, who was still gaga over my razzle-dazzle smack-testing display, didn't even see him go by.

Once things calmed down again, Geronimo drove the car back around to the Two Cousins Lounge, where I dropped off Wally with the other $4,000, plus $300 extra for his commission. Wally walked back inside to complete the transaction with Petey.

Later that night, at the DEA's offices, I removed the two guns I had been concealing, pulled out the Kel transmitter taped to my groin, and liberated the Nagra recorder taped to my back. I extracted the tape from the Nagra, initialed and dated it, then sealed it in a plastic evidence envelope.

Exhibit no. 1 (the heroin) and exhibit letter A (the tape recording) were prima facia evidence in the U.S. government's investigation of Mister Untouchable, Leroy "Nicky" Barnes, and they were now in DEA custody.

WHEN THE LAB results came back, I was not a happy camper.

The heroin Petey had sold us turned out to be considerably less pure than I originally thought. So I went back and bitched to Wally.

"What the fuck we doin' here, Wally? You're talking about *your man* being this, *your man* being that. I can't open my fucking store with this crap. This is bullshit."

Up at Bubba Jean's Emporium on West 125th Street, Wally and Geronimo then bitched to Joseph "Jazz" Hayden, Nicky's top deputy, about Petey Rollock's less-than-stellar package. And during the conversation, Nicky himself showed up—a DEA surveillance team observed him walking into Bubba Jean's.

When Nicky appeared, Wally began to lobby him about providing me with a better-grade product. Geronimo later told me about their conversation:

"Look, you wanna fuckin' do this?" Nicky had said to Wally.

"Damn right I do," Wally had answered.

"Well, I usually don't deal for anything less than fifty g's," Nicky had said.

Wally replied, "Hey, let us go for a little less on this first round, then we'll start moving heavy. My man is hungry and righteous, Nicky. He's lookin' to do some serious business with us."

Nicky then had said, "All right, you wanna fuckin' deal? You wanna do this right? Then go see Fat Stevie." "Fat Stevie" Monsanto was an important heroin distributor for Nicky.

Geronimo's account of this conversation was tantalizing. It clearly incriminated Nicky in a heroin distribution network . . . but I wanted to hear it straight from one more horse's mouth. So a day or so later, when G and I met up again with Wally, I managed to draw Wally into a friendly chat inside my car. Then, all of sudden, I dropped it on him: "Hey, Wally, not for nuthin', what's this conversation I hear you had with Nicky? How the fuck you know Nicky?"

"Shit, Louie," Wally told me. "I told you. Nicky is my brother's boss. He's the man. He's the guy you're gonna meet."

Geronimo then tried to vouch for Wally's bona fides.

"Shut your fuckin' mouth!" I snapped at G., adding a little polish to my act. "This is not your conversation. I'm talkin' to Wally here, *capiche*?"

Wally, God bless him, then spit out every last detail of his conversation with Nicky at Bubba Jean's Emporium and Nicky's instructions to see Fat Stevie Monsanto for a new package of heroin.

Fantastic. It corroborated everything Geronimo had told me. More important, it added a solid piece of evidence to our budding case, given that I had gotten the entire conversation about Wally's meet with Jazz and Nicky on tape.

JAZZ HAYDEN WANTED $30,000 in drug money washed.

The purpose of such "washes" was to exchange small-denomination bills—ones, fives, tens, and twenties that Nicky's and Jazz's dealers might have unwittingly gotten from undercover cops—for larger bills that came from banks, car dealerships, or other legit businesses.

Geronimo and Wally sold Jazz on the idea that I was the man for the job, especially since I purportedly had a crooked banker in my back pocket. I was hot to trot to make it happen, since Jazz's involvement in a drug-money wash would be further evidence against Nicky in the overall conspiracy case.

Using Wally as a messenger, Jazz sent word that he wanted to do a trial run. A courier would bring me $10,000 to wash. If everything went smoothly, a lot more money would be coming my way.

Over by the West Side Highway, just north of the newly built World Trade Center, I met up with the courier, Wayne. When he pulled up in his burnt orange Chevy Malibu, his wife, Brenda, was by his side. Also in the car was Geronimo, who had driven down from Harlem with them.

Inside the car, Brenda handed me a small brown shoulder

bag containing neatly bound packets of tens and twenties—the proceeds of some of Jazz's and Nicky's drug sales.

I tried to push Wayne on a heroin deal with Jazz, but he sidestepped the subject and limited the chitchat to the money wash. So, easing off, I nodded over my shoulder, in the direction of the Woolworth Building. "My banker's in there right now, waiting on me," I told them. "He's ready to do the deal."

Then I added, "I'm gonna throw my own money in your bag. I've got 10 g's of my own I want to clean, as well." No doubt Wayne would report this move back to Jazz and Nicky as proof of my criminal bona fides.

Inside a restaurant in the Woolworth Building, I met up with my "crooked banker"—DEA group supervisor Joe Braddock. I passed Joe the bag of money. In return, he handed me two white envelopes emblazoned with the logo of Irving Trust Company and containing the "clean" $20,000.

Exiting the Woolworth Building, I walked back to Wayne's car and got inside. Wayne counted the fresh bills, then handed me the hundred bucks I had been promised as commission. "Jazz gonna have some more for you," he offered.

"How much more?" I asked.

"A hundred grand."

"Fucking beautiful," I said. "Might take me a few days to set it up, deal of that size."

"That's cool," said Wayne.

I decided to push him again on a new heroin deal. And this time I hit pay dirt. "Don't worry, man," said Wayne, "Jazz be good for his word. He gonna have a package for you real soon."

We parted company. Then Wayne headed back up to Harlem with Jazz's and Nicky's clean money, unaware that the serial numbers on all the bills had been prerecorded at DEA headquarters.

* * *

PERIODICALLY, WHEN WE met up at bars, restaurants, or in my car, I made it a point to bitch to Wally about having to deal with underlings such as Petey Rollock and Wayne.

"I don't wanna deal with no scrubs," I told Wally. "I want to deal directly with the big man," which, of course, meant Nicky.

"Nicky don't sell like that," Wally chided. "Nobody big-time like that selling." To reassure me, he added, "Dealing with Jazz is like dealing with Nicky direct. Jazz is Nicky's right-hand man. Took over for my brother Guy while he's doing his time in the joint. Don't worry about it, Louie. The stuff we be getting is top-grade. And Nicky's behind it. It's from the same spaghetti. Blessed by God Himself."

SQUIRED AROUND BY Wally, who touted me as his "personal" Italian wiseguy, I began to burnish my rep in Harlem.

I made the rounds of the jazz lounges, the nightclubs, the cabarets, and the after-hours joints, places such as the Cotton Club, the Hubba Hubba, the Scales Social Club, Club 83, Ja Gazze's, the Two Cousins Lounge. Most of the time Geronimo and I would do this without DEA surveillance on us, without prior DEA approval. It was one of those little left-hand turns I had run by G when we first met up, one of those unsanctioned maneuvers I said we'd need to make now and then. Not having surveillance on us made it easier for us to move around unhindered. Plus, I hated putting surveillance agents on a baby-sitting gig, leaving them to pull their puds while G and I bounced around uptown.

The clubs we hit were watering holes that regularly drew Harlem society but were rarely visited by white men. But thanks to my colorful and dangerous Mafia backstory, I was considered a special guest and always rewarded with my own table close to the stage.

If anyone frisked me, I was ready for 'im.

"Whoa, take it easy pal!" I'd say. "This is what you're looking for, right?" Then I'd pull out the 9mm pistol I had tucked in the back of my pants and present it to the security guard.

"Why don't you hold the clip?" I'd suggest. And I'd make a show of dropping the clip into the security guy's open palm to demonstrate that my gun was no longer loaded.

"Mind if I keep the piece?" I'd ask.

"No problem, buddy. Everybody up here need a gun, right?"

"Ain't *that* the truth," I'd quip, tucking my piece back into my pants while knowing full well that I still had one bullet left in the chamber.

Meanwhile, by presenting my 9mm pistol for full inspection, I had defused the necessity for any further searching, which undoubtedly would have revealed the .25-caliber pistol still in my jacket and the Nagra tape recorder fixed to the small of my back, as well.

On other occasions, when some hired muscle moved in to pat me down, I'd whip my coat flaps open wide. Then, as I extended the edges of my coat upward and outward like wings, I'd let him poke around my chest, underarms, back and waistline.

"Go ahead, you're okay," the guy would eventually say, waving me past the security cordon.

Making a show of pressing my coat flaps back into place and smoothing them over, I'd march inside, secure in the knowledge of my old trick that, by facilitating the full body search, I had conned the security guard into bypassing the handgun and the tape recorder that had been hidden in the inside pockets of my coat flaps all along.

Once I gained entry, I'd often look to embellish my pedigree as a Mafioso hothead by deliberately provoking fights with the clientele. First I'd feign the perception of some personal slight or muttered insult. Then, mimicking my brother Alfonsito, I'd go into flailing epileptic fits. A couple of times I actually came close to duking it out with some prick, but I let Geronimo pull me back.

Once, after walking into a Queens diner with Wally and G, I happened to spot Gary "Bat" Saunders, another one of Nicky's underlings whom I had been trying to romance into a drug deal. "Bat" had gotten his nickname because of his absurdly tiny, batlike ears. After we sat down, Wally got up and walked over to Bat. Wally was sent back with a message that Bat was still interested in dealing.

While we waited for our food, a couple of white wiseguy wannabes started giving us hard stares. I let it slide while we ate, but later realized that this presented a golden opportunity for me to further burnish my rep. So when we got up to leave, I stopped at the punks' table. Knowing that Bat was eyeballing me, I stepped up to one of them, pulled my pearl-handled .25-caliber pistol from my outside coat pocket, and screwed it into his ear while locking eyes with his pals.

"Anybody here got a problem?"

"No, sir!" they all snapped with schoolboy deference.

Then, without another word, I turned and followed G and Wally out. Bat saw the whole show and would undoubtedly report the incident to Nicky. And I was confident I had added one more star to my rep.

Plenty of people saw and heard me pull this kind of shit. And after a while they began to say, "This dude Louie . . . he's a nice enough guy, but don't mess with him. If you do, you're nuts. Because *he's* nuts."

Pretty soon the locals began to size me up as a walking time bomb, a real Jekyll and Hyde . . . which was exactly what I wanted them to believe.

Guys now started coming to me with all kinds of deals. Gun deals. Swag deals. Dope deals. But none of them were in the lineup I was looking at. None of them were Nicky's guys, and my bottom line was to get dope off Nicky's guys. Doing deals with competitors or wannabes or two-bit freelancers would not serve my purpose. I was up here for one thing and one thing alone: to make buys off the upper-echelon guys working for Nicky and Jazz and link them all back to Nicky.

Throughout all of my bobbing and weaving, Nicky remained the primary target, the grand prize, the holy grail. And with the help of Geronimo and, albeit unwittingly, Wally, I saw myself as the white knight who was on a quest to topple him.

At one point I was offered a partnership in the Scales Social Club in the Bronx, where I had scored several coke samples from Nicky's other dealers. The joint was a real vipers' pit, an after-hours watering hole for pimps, drug dealers, loan sharks, fences, and assorted other shitbirds.

Spruce the place up, rig it with concealed cameras and tape recorders, put undercover agents behind the bar or in waitress uniforms, and it would have been like shooting fish in a barrel.

Unfortunately, the DEA wouldn't spring for the $10,000 down payment. And my vivid fantasies of busting a bunch of lowlifes in one fell swoop—and becoming a late-nightclub impresario—went up in smoke.

* * *

IN THE RUN-UP to the new heroin buy from Fat Stevie, Geronimo and I spent a lot of time riding around uptown with Wally. Wally was a car nut and liked to show off his wheels, so he would take me for a spin in his Stingray while G waited for us.

Usually, DEA surveillance cars would follow us. Wally was much better at spotting them than we were. And just to bust their balls, he'd take his Corvette up to 105 miles per hour on the Major Deegan Expressway, then swerve suddenly off the exit ramp doing 80, leaving the government tails eating his dust.

At other times, when the three of us would toodle around in my yellow Caddy, the DEA agents would get so far up our asses they probably should have proposed marriage. One night they came up so close that we could have been towing them. Wally got upset. And that worried me.

"Cazzo!" I cursed in Italian. Big, white guys with sunglasses driving big black sedans? Get the fuck outta here! *"Un catz a gol! Vaffanculo!"*

I figured I had do something or the whole operation could unravel. So when Wally stopped at a bar to make a phone call inquiring about the heroin deal with Fat Stevie, I reached under the seat of my Caddy and grabbed for my portable.

"Whiskey's made you," I whispered into the radio, using Wally's code name. "Toss us. And make it look good."

While Wally watched from the bar, the DEA guys pulled their cars around my parked Caddy. Then, swarming our vehicle, they rousted me and Geronimo. They took pains to make it look like we were the targets of their interest, not Wally. Yanking me and G out of the Caddy, they threw us roughly up against the hood, made us put our hands on our heads, kicked our feet apart, and patted us down. After a few minutes, they kicked us loose and took off.

When Wally came back out of the bar, he was convinced that Geronimo and I had been the targets. But he still wondered how the agents had missed my .9mm. I lied, saying that I had tossed it under my seat but they had neglected to search the car.

Meanwhile, given what had just happened, I said we would have to postpone the deal with Fat Stevie. "It's no good, my brother," I said to him. "The street's too hot. The shit's down for tonight. Let's back it up and wait it out till things cool off a little."

My note of caution saved the day. As far as Wally was concerned, we were still good to go . . . just a few days later than originally planned.

Still, I had to keep in mind that Wally was no dummy. He had his antenna up just like everyone else out on the street. One time he insinuated that Geronimo was asking too many questions, especially about Nicky—where he parked, why he parked there, what was he up to, that kind of shit.

"You're one nosey motherfucker, y'know that?" Wally said to G. "Why the fuck you askin' so many questions?"

But Geronimo, God bless him, didn't even skip a beat. " 'Cause I'm working for the government," he shot back. "I gotta find out everything I can. What do you want me to do? A half-assed job for Uncle Sam?"

Wally and I nearly bust a nut laughing.

But then came an even closer call.

Wally, Geronimo, and I were riding around one night in my Caddy, just shooting the shit. The transmitter under my car dashboard was relaying the entire conversation back to the DEA agents who were following us. Everything was going great . . . until, without warning, the car radio went haywire.

It started spitting conversations *back. The transmissions between the DEA agents who were tailing us.*

"Holy shit!" I heard myself saying as G turned white as a ghost.

I quickly turned off the car radio, then started banging on it. "What the fuck is going on?!" I screamed.

If Wally put two and two together, Geronimo and I were toast—the both of us would get blown away this very night.

So I started screaming as a cover: "Fuck this! I've had it!" In a fit of rage, I sped up, then turned the car into a darkened side street. Then I spun around on Wally and G. "All right, both of you, outta the fucking car! *Now!*"

They protested loudly. But I jabbed my finger in their faces and screamed at them: "If you guys are hot, I don't want you near me!"

Once they were outside the car, I made a show of patting each of them down for concealed wires. When I came up empty-handed, I upped the ante. Whipping out my 9mm pistol, I jacked in a round.

"That does it!" I said, looking around for the DEA surveillance cars. "I'm gonna waste these motherfuckers once and for all!"

Wally nearly shit his pants. "O my God!" he said with a gasp. "O my God! Louie, what the fuck you doin', man?!"

"I'm gonna blow their fuckin' brains out, that's what I'm doing!" I announced. My eyeballs were popping outta my skull. I must have looked like I'd lost my mind. I ended up pushing both Wally and Geronimo back into the car.

"Lemme outta here!" Wally screamed.

"Fuck that shit!" I fired back, flecks of spittle bubbling up at the corners of my mouth. "You guys stay here till it's done, you hear me?"

G lunged frantically for my arm. "Take it easy, Lou! Take it easy! You can't just whack these guys!"

"The fuck I can't!" I snapped back, slapping his arm away. By now, the veins were bulging purple in my neck, and I truly resembled the lunatic, out-of-control, bloodthirsty Mafia hit man I purported to be.

Wally began to plead with me. "Calm down, man! You'll get us all killed!"

But I was a powder keg, ready to detonate. By all appearances, the urge to pull that trigger, to take scalps, to blow everyone and his mother to kingdom come was just too overpowering for me to control.

By now, Wally truly thought I was about to start massacring federal agents.

"Easy, Lou!" yelled G. "Easy, for chrissakes!"

Slowly, reluctantly, I started to ease up on the gas. And appeared to hear what both of them were trying to tell me.

Wally and Geronimo suggested we come up with an alternate plan. I stood silently for a few moments, my eyes and nostrils flaring, "motherfucking" my furious refrain over again. But eventually I tucked my piece away. And made it seem as though they had finally gotten through to me. By all appearances, I was finally managing to rein in the raging beast that was Louie D.

Wally let a deep breath out, his body finally starting to relax. G made a show of wiping his forehead with his hand. Both of them sensed that the danger had passed.

And I silently thanked God that another Oscar-winning performance had gone down convincingly, no doubt saving my life for one more day in the process.

CHAPTER ELEVEN

GERONIMO WASN'T SUPPOSED TO carry a gun.

Yet there were times when G was packing; I knew it and so did he. But even though it was against DEA policy, I wasn't about to stop it. This man's life was in as much danger as mine, so I let it slide. As a matter of fact, when he wasn't carrying, I'd loan him a gun of my own.

"You got Baby Jesus with you?" I'd ask, using the nickname we'd agreed on for a handgun.

"Nah," he'd say. "Not today."

"Then *here,* take my Baby Jesus."

And he would . . . but for the record, I didn't want anyone else to know. Not even the good guys.

WORKING THE NICKY Barnes case was like playing chess against a grand master. To make a federal conspiracy case, all the pieces had to be moved with great calculation over time, with patience and cunning.

The next gambit would be the heroin buy from Fat Stevie Monsanto, scheduled to take place shortly before Christmas 1976. I tried to speed up the buy. Wally complained that there were too many cops on the street to do the transaction, but I pushed back hard to make it happen.

"Fuck that. Go back to Fat Stevie, get a sample from him," I insisted. "And if you have to, get it right under the cops' noses. They'd never expect anyone to have that kinda balls."

Although Wally and G conferred with Nicky's people and Fat Stevie, they came back empty-handed. Naturally I threw a hissy fit. "Listen, you two better get your fuckin' act together. You can't come back to me with that sample, then forget about doin' any business at all till after the New Year. The store will be closed for the holidays."

Just after Christmas, Wally and Geronimo tried again, and went to see Nicky Barnes at Bubba Jean's Emporium on 125th Street.

Across the street, at the elevated train station, DEA agents had erected a makeshift wooden shack from which they could train their surveillance cameras on Bubba Jean's. Unfortunately for the agents, some of the locals greeted the new structure by turning it into a public outhouse, regularly spreading yuletide cheer by pissing on its roof and exterior walls, sometimes while the agents were inside. Happy holidays.

Inside Bubba Jean's, Nicky gave Wally and Geronimo the green light to move forward with Fat Stevie. The deal would go down that very night.

Later that evening, I drove G and Wally over to the the Harlem River Motors garage on West 145th Street, which was another limo and leased-car depot that Nicky owned.

By leasing his cars out to others, Nicky was cleverly shielding himself. Under the law, if Nicky owned a car outright and it was caught carrying dope, the government could seize the car, compel its forfeiture, and bring drug charges against Nicky. But if Nicky had previously *leased* that same car to a second party, who then used it to facilitate the drug deal, Nicky was insulated from arrest. Although the vehicle might be seized, it would eventually be returned rather than forfeited, and Nicky would not be held liable for the drugs.

Another nifty trick Nicky had learned in prison from his mentor Crazy Joe Gallo.

Fat Stevie pulled up to the garage in a white Cadillac Seville. While I stayed behind in my own Caddy, Wally and Geronimo went into the garage. Inside the garage office, they saw what must have been fifty kilos of heroin. Worth a few million wholesale, that kind of weight might fetch $280 million after it was cut and resold on the streets. There was more than $100,000 in cash spread out on the office desk.

Fat Stevie handed one of his crew members a white shopping bag containing plastic packages stuffed with heroin. The packages were then handed off to other crew guys, who stashed them under the seats of Nicky's leased cars—the delivery fleet, just like UPS.

Fat Stevie told Wally and Geronimo he wouldn't be able to deal them a package till later that night. So, leaving Wally behind at the garage, I took G in my car and went looking for a landline to alert my DEA base.

Unfortunately, cruising through the no-man's-land of the South Bronx, the first five phones I stopped at were broken. It wasn't until we pulled up to a bodega near Yankee Stadium that we found one still in service.

Once I finally got through to my DEA superiors, I gave them the makes and partial plate numbers on Nicky's cars.

"When you toss 'em, make it look like routine traffic stops," I said. "That way, you score any of Nicky's dope, it doesn't come back to Harlem River Motors. And I can keep doin' my thing up here."

Other DEA teams went ahead and intercepted several of the cars. But Nicky had been a step ahead of them from the get-go. It turned out the dope had been switched to different cars—the ones I had seen pulling out of the garage were just decoys. The cars actually containing the dope had slipped through our dragnet earlier and dropped off the heroin with Nicky's distributors.

We drove back to 145th Street and parked in the Getty gas station directly across the street from Harlem River Motors. Geronimo got out and walked back inside the garage, where he rejoined Wally and Fat Stevie.

A few minutes later, G returned with a message from Fat Stevie: he would let Geronimo show me a sample of the heroin if I paid half the purchase price up front. If I was not satisfied with the product, my money would be refunded in full.

Fat Stevie had actually wanted me to come into the garage myself, but I told Geronimo to go it alone. As a "mob boss," I didn't want to come across too down or too eager to stick my nose in the middle of Nicky's shit—it would look pushy and amateurish and could raise eyebrows.

I handed Geronimo $10,000 in cash. "Make sure you give Fat Stevie the money out in the open, so our surveillance can get it on camera."

Poor G was nervous. Who could blame him, when we were all playing with our lives?

"You got your Baby Jesus with you?" I asked.

"No."

I handed him my backup .38-caliber snub-nose revolver. "Then take mine."

Once he realized I had his back, Geronimo got his nerve back. Returning to the garage, he passed the 10 g's to Fat Stevie . . . in full view of our surveillance. When he came back out again to the car, he was carying a brown paper bag containing half a kilo of heroin.

I broke the seal, cut a slit with my penknife, and removed a sampling. The grains were fine, like sand. The granules had a sour, vinegary smell. And they tasted bitter, which was good. The bitterer the taste, the purer the product.

When I did my Marquis field test, the results confirmed what I already knew. Merry Christmas and Happy New Year, too. Yesiree, this was some damn fine shit.

I sent Geronimo back into the garage with the rest of the money, and he was to relay my compliments to Nicky himself through Fat Stevie.

But it was one of our other DEA observation teams, operating from a post they had set up in an apartment building across the street, that snagged the *real* brass ring this night. Using a telephoto lens, they caught Nicky walking out of the garage right after the deal had gone down—and throwing Fat Stevie a big old bear hug. It was the moment everyone had been waiting for.

SOMETIMES THINGS DID not go according to plan, and we had to scramble to make up for missed opportunities.

Hoping to get Nicky on tape corroborating that he had engineered our deal with Fat Stevie, Geronimo and Wally met up with him at the Hubba Hubba Club on West 117th Street. Our surveillance was later able to put G, Wally, Nicky, and Jazz inside the club at the same time, which further bulked up the conspiracy case.

Inside the club, Geronimo brazenly complained to Nicky that the package we'd gotten from Fat Stevie was "fucked." Nicky was not happy to be dressed down by a lowlife like G.

At this meeting, G wore a cast on one leg and supported himself with a black cane; his backstory was that he'd gone away skiing over New Year's and busted his ankle. It was the perfect ruse to conceal the Kel transmitter inside his cane.

Unfortunately, because of all the loud music and background noise, the transmitter did not clearly pick up Nicky's conversation. Back at DEA headquarters, we tried every piece of electronic wizardry known to law enforcement to clean up the tape and filter out the extraneous noise. But in the end, it was all for naught—G's tape was garbage.

Hoping to salvage the whole thing, I met up with Wally the next day. Inside my car, Wally angrily told me that after the meet at the Hubba Hubba, he'd ripped Geronimo a new one for having the balls to come down on the man himself, Nicky Barnes.

"Lou," he told me, "this fuckin' boy of yours, he's about to mess up everything."

I played dumb. "Whattya talkin' about, Wally?"

"I'll tell you what I'm talkin' about, man. Fuckin' asshole, he gets right up in Nicky's face. Goes into the Hubba Hubba with his fuckin' broken ankle and goes off on Nicky about the fuckin' package we got from Fat Stevie."

"Fuck that shit!" I said. "You never told me nuthin' about that, Wally!" Furious, I banged my fist on the dash of my Caddy. "That fuckin' asshole! I'll cut his fuckin' balls off! You and me, we're tryin' to do some serious business up here. I gotta straighten G out, and now . . . I won't put up with that kinda bullshit rudeness. Nicky is the capo, the boss. No shitbird underling, whether he's a made man or not, ever confronts a boss!"

By complaining to me about Geronimo, Wally neatly corroborated everything G had said about his testy tête-à-tête with Nicky Barnes. And unlike the noise-marred tape Geronimo had made inside the Hubba Hubba, the tape I made of Wally was crystal clear, free of any interference or background noise.

* * *

WHEN JAZZ SENT word through Wally that he needed another $100,000 washed, I jumped at the opportunity, knowing it would provide one more piece of evidence for the conspiracy case.

After securing $100,000 in government funds, Bobby Nieves and I made photocopies of all the $100 and $50 bills. The bills were then bundled in stacks of $10,000 each and bound with rubber bands.

On January 19, 1977, I drove up to see Jazz at the Club 83, a place that Jazz and Nicky co-owned on Lenox Avenue. To buttress my cover story about being a Mafia big shot, I pulled out all the stops and all the props. I wore my slickest, most expensive wiseguy attire, arriving with Geronimo in the backseat of a black Lincoln Continental limo driven by my personal chauffeur and muscleman, who was actually Mike Levine, another well-respected DEA undercover agent and friend.

I left Mike with the money when we got out. As G and I walked toward the club's entrance, I noticed a Con Ed repair truck and a delivery van parked along the street. A yellow taxicab cruised by. I smiled to myself—all of these vehicles were manned by DEA backup agents.

Inside the club, the clientele gave us the hairy eyeball, and why wouldn't they? This was the first time any of them had seen a white guy inside the club. And *this* white guy was reputed to be an honored guest—a dope-dealing, loose-cannon, homicidal, organized-crime associate.

My transmitter was concealed in my crotch, taped above my genitals. It was a compact device, smaller than a cigarette pack, from which a wire protruded straight up, under my pants and my undershirt. I also wore a band around my waist to keep it in place. The mike itself was fastened under one of the buttonholes in my shirt.

Given that I was also packing a 9mm Smith & Wesson in the small of my back, a .25-caliber Baretta in one of my inside breast pockets, and a .38-caliber snub-nosed revolver in one of my outside coat pockets, I felt secure. Which was why I didn't just walk into the club . . .

I *strutted* in—the street was my stage, and it was showtime.

As we moved toward the stairs, a very large, muscular black man stepped in front of us. "Got to pat you down, bro."

Oh, shit. I hadn't expected this. Given that I already had been vouched for by both Geronimo and Wally and previously been accepted by Jazz for the underworld figure I purported to be, I had assumed that I would not have to submit to the indignity of a search.

Now, my guns were one thing—given my street rep, I could come up with a plausible explanation for those. But if this goon found the wire . . . *I was dog meat.*

Geronimo saved the day, jumping in front of me, right into the bouncer's face. "Wait a second! You got any fucking idea of who we are? Or maybe you didn't get the word?"

The bouncer hesitated.

"Call up to Jazz," G demanded.

Using the intercom, the bouncer did just that. "Hey, boss," he told Jazz, "two guinea white boys down here to see you. What's up?"

"My dick up your ass if you don't let them up right now," Jazz snapped back over the intercom.

The bouncer let us pass.

Up on the next floor, we were greeted by a gang of Jazz's henchmen, along with Jazz himself.

If I had thought I was the cat's meow, Jazz put me to shame. He was decked out in a tan suede Carnaby cap, tan suede three-quarter-length jacket, dark pants, tan wool turtleneck sweater, gold-rimmed glasses, gold chain . . . and a big gold medallion that hung from the chain like a boulder. The medallion was studded with small diamonds that spelled out "JAZZ."

Playing the role of consigliere, Geronimo introduced us.

"Yeah, we been on you, Louie," Jazz replied. "Your shit is lookin' good. You all right, man."

I extended my hand. With a collegial grin, Jazz shook it.

As Jazz's bodyguards kept a watchful eye on us, G and I sat at a table. Jazz stepped behind the bar to fix us each a drink. Then we got down to business.

One of Jazz's gofers—a skinny guy with big teeth whom we later nicknamed "Bucky Beaver"—passed me a long flower box containing stacks of tens and twenties bound with rubber bands. I counted the bills. They added up to only $47,000.

"I thought we were doing a hundred g's," I said to Jazz.

Jazz apologized. "I know, Louie, but this is what it came down to."

I was disappointed, but I tried to sound accommodating. "Yeah, it's okay. Whattya gonna do, right? That's the way it is."

I sent Geronimo downstairs to get Agent Mike Levine, who came back up the stairs carrying the flight bag of money. I extracted $47,000 and passed it to Jazz—he immediately began to count it himself to make certain it was all there.

While he was doing that, he asked, "What about your fee?"

"What about it?"

"One percent is the going rate."

"Well, that *is* what I got on the last wash. But since I been at this a long time, lemme set you straight, my friend. Truth is, these kinds of deals, the 'vig' could be anywhere from one to ten percent." I paused for effect. "Then again—who knows?—maybe I can do better than that. A whole lot better."

That got Jazz's attention. "Oh?"

"You give me a break on the price of a new package, maybe I don't need to charge my usual fee. Maybe I don't need to charge any fee at all."

Jazz studied me. "I'll consider it," he said.

And there it was. The opening I'd been waiting for.

I turned to Geronimo and Mike. "The two of you, beat it. Wait for me outside."

Left alone, Jazz and I let our hair down and had a heart-to-heart about race relations, law enforcement, and the economics of the drug business. I hadn't planned to come up here for a sociological discussion, but now that I found myself in the middle of one, I went with the flow. Besides, I was enjoying the drift and Jazz's keen perceptions on these things.

"Hell, we *are* capitalists!" Jazz said at one point. "What we doing is the same thing as the Rockefellers and the Vanderbilts."

I chimed in, "Except, bein' up here, we don't have the same shot they had." Then I took a big, fat chance and rolled the dice. "Listen, Jazz, up till now, I've done some things with you people, but the shit hasn't come back right. I did an eighth with Petey for eight grand, fuckin' shit sucked. I did a money wash with you for ten g's, your boy Wayne was supposed to come back to me on a package from you. So I do a deal with Fat Stevie for half a key, and it comes back shit, terrible."

Now it was my turn to look him in the eye. "So what the hell we doin' here? Huh? I mean, level with me, Jazz. Out of respect, at least gimme that much."

Now all Jazz had to say was, *What the fuck are you talking about, Louie? I don't know anything about that.* And it would have been over, end of story, right then and there.

But that's not what he said at all. Instead he took the bait and offered, "Well, you know I was busy, Louie. I'm trying to remodel my club. Not only that, I got my boss, too, so I just can't move so freely."

So I was still at the table, still in the game. And Jazz kept the hand going. "Man, you just establishing yourself, Louie. And, quite frankly, your people—the Mafia—they ain't looked so good in the past."

I scoffed, waving my hand in disgust. "Well, fuck that, man. I've had my problems with them, too. *Hell, that's why I'm here, right?*"

Then I handed him a load of 99 and 44/100 percent pure bullshit. "Look," I said, "I used to be somebody with them. But when I wanted to hire young blacks to run the numbers and other things, they didn't like it. So they pushed me out. That's why I had to go out to the West Coast, stay on the bench till I could get myself back in the game. You think I enjoyed being on the sidelines?"

I kept giving it the gas, waxing rhapsodic about things such as trust and loyalty, pride and professionalism. Hell, even I started to believe what I was saying. So much so that, at the end of the night, Jazz not only went for it . . . he went for it in a big way.

My patience had paid off. Jazz agreed to a new deal. Five kilos of heroin . . . which, if the quality was right, would go for $250,000.

MEANWHILE, RUMORS THAT could put us in real danger were swirling. Among them:

Carmine Galante, the capo de tutti capi of all the Mafia families, wanted to take back the heroin trade from the blacks and the Hispanics. A dozen hit men had been recruited to whack Nicky and his lieutenants.

Articles cropped up in the *Amsterdam News* to the effect that the mob was looking to make a move on Nicky.

Although we didn't know it at the time, two of Nicky's guys had killed an Italian mobster named Carmine Puglise over a drug deal gone sour. In fact, they had shot him so many times at close range that his shirt had caught fire. Now they worried that the mob was looking for revenge.

So having brazenly advertised ourselves as seasoned Italian wiseguys, Geronimo and I were now under the microscope. Terrific.

A week or so after our $47,000 money wash, Jazz invited me, Geronimo, and Wally to Club 83 for drinks.

I kept pushing for the five-kilo buy Jazz had promised, but Jazz steered the conversation back to a new money wash, this one for $50,000. When it came to the five-ki buy, he was suddenly evasive. "Hey, if it was up to me, there'd be no problem," he explained. "But it's not up to me alone. I have a boss I got to answer to."

Sweet. It was the second time he had mentioned his "boss."

Suddenly Jazz asked me about the rumors that the mob was looking to put a hit on Nicky.

Sweeter *still*. He had just tied himself and his boss, Nicky, to all our drug dealings.

"I've heard 'em, too," I told him, trying to stifle my excitement. I said I had heard from some police sources that the hit would likely come from Frank Lucas and his Country Boys, not the Italians Jazz suspected. At the mention of Lucas, Jazz sneered. "Just a buncha backyard coons looking to go Beverly Hills. Like in that TV show *The Beverly Hillbillies*."

Then he added, "You shoulda come to me sooner on this

shit, Louie. A man of your stature oughta be dealin' with people on my level."

"Hey, man," I explained, "I'm not into that kinda shit. I'm beyond ego trips. I don't wanna be that out front on these things anyway. I gotta be careful up here."

I kept bobbing and weaving, feinting and lunging, allowing Jazz to become entangled even more in Nicky's spidery web. Again, I made a point of bringing up my heroin buys from Petey Rollack and Fat Stevie Monsanto, my money wash for Wayne and his wife, and Jazz freely corroborated his own role in all of these deals.

Ciao, baby, I thought. *You're going down even deeper.*

NICKY WAS A fox, constantly on the alert for possible threats. His eyes were always scanning the horizon, his ears always facing into the wind to pick up distant sounds.

Early on, some of our guys planted a bug in the Harlem River Motors garage office. Using my intel about the layout, a dozen DEA agents dressed in black wool caps, black pants, and black turtlenecks shimmied down ropes from the garage skylight to plant the listening device.

Neither Nicky nor his boys ever found the bug. Nevertheless, they still managed to learn that the garage was under surveillance.

An old man who lived nearby tipped him that DEA agents were taking photos with a telescopic lens. Bo Hatcher, the manager of Harlem River Motors and another of Nicky's lieutenants, actually blamed me for bringing the heat down. And Jazz himself worried that the clash of color schemes—two suspicious-looking white dudes seen in the company of all these black Harlem gangsters—might be the cause.

Wally, bless his soul, kept us in the game by reassuring both Bo and Jazz that we were "stand-up people."

One night in early February 1977, Wally told me that the deal for the five kilos of heroin was finally going down.

Unfortunately, when I communicated this to DEA headquarters, they kept me on the string about the $250,000 purchase price, ultimately failing to approve the expenditure. Was this another instance of the bosses wanting to get off as cheaply as possible while preserving the cash for other cases? Was politics involved? Did New York not have enough pull with Washington, D.C., to get what it needed? If so, it was lunacy. This was one of the biggest and most important drug cases in DEA history.

True, $250,000 would have been an unprecedented drug purchase by the DEA. And buying drugs for a lesser amount would have generated just as much evidence in court. But I was so crazed with enthusiasm for the bigger buy, I couldn't see that part of the picture.

"What the fuck is going on here!" I shouted at Don Ferrarone. "How the fuck could you not get this done? We're putting it on the line here, doing backflips to get the most we can out of this case, and you guys can't get a simple approval?"

"Louie," said Ferrarone, "we did all we could, but headquarters has us on a tight leash."

Sadly, I knew it was the truth. But I also knew that my failure to come up with the cash would make me look terrible with Jazz and Nicky, an already suspect white guy who shot off his mouth and now was unable to deliver the goods.

So I radioed my DEA partner, Bobby Nieves, who was tailing us at a distance. "G and Wally and me are supposed to meet up at Harlem River Motors in twenty minutes to finalize the five-ki deal," I told him. "Put some fuckin' heat on us. All the heat you can."

Pretty soon half of Harlem was crawling with federal agents in readily identifiable surveillance cars, many of them wielding big binoculars and cameras with telescopic lenses.

When I reconnected with Wally, I warned him off. "Tell your people to forget about it. Too much fuckin' heat out here. Whether it's on me or whether it's on you, it's not safe. I'm outta here."

Wally later told me I had pulled a cool move by putting the deal off. And I quietly thanked the Lord that everything had turned out the way it had. I kept on thanking Him, too, right up until I learned that, with the exception of a tiny handful of DEA people, virtually all of the other agents who had been prowling around our set were not DEA agents at all—Jazz and Nicky found out they were IRS agents doing surveillance on an illegal gambling den up the block from the Harlem River Motors garage. The gambling den had nothing whatsoever to do with Nicky's operation, and the IRS surveillance had nothing to do with what DEA was doing.

It was only a coincidence that the IRS agents happened by when I needed an excuse to kill the five-ki deal. They had no idea we were out here doing our thing—it was dumb luck that they got me off the hook, but Nicky and his crew now knew that the heat hadn't been coming from me.

STILL, THE CHANCES of us being exposed were increasing every day. Jazz seemed to have pulled out again on our new heroin deal. Nonetheless, I kept pushing for one more buy. With Jazz on the sidelines, Wally went fishing for one of Nicky's other dealers.

He came back to me with the news that Stevie Baker, another heavy hitter on Nicky's team, was ready to deal to us. "He just got rid of twenty-five kilos of righteous white," Wally told me over the phone. "And his shit can take a nine-cut." I picked up this conversation clearly on my tape recorder.

I immediately went into my refrain of not wanting to go scrambling from one guy to another to come up with a package. Zeroing in on Jazz for pulling out on us at the last minute, I told Wally, "I'm tired of jumping through hoops."

"No hoops, Louie," Wally insisted. "It's just that Jazz has his fingers in a lot of pies. He's got his club, the gambling, his store, his investments. Whereas Stevie, he's just into the devil's white, you understand what I'm sayin'? You deal with Stevie Baker, you dealin' with Nicky. Just like I said before, it's from the same spaghetti."

Toward the end of February, we arranged to buy a full kilo of Stevie Baker's product for $55,000. Like before, the deal would go down inside the Harlem River Motors garage.

I had the cash with me when I pulled up to the garage one chilly February night. Geronimo and Wally met me outside.

Wally was freaking out. "Jesus Christ, Louie!" he blurted out. "Nicky himself is in there. His bodyguards are all around. Look for yourself."

When I looked over, I couldn't make out Nicky. But I sure as hell could see the half-dozen tall, heavily muscled black males milling outside the entrance. Grouped together, they looked like the offensive line for the New York Giants.

"What the hell is Nicky doing here?" I asked.

"What do you think?" Wally fired back. "Something heavy's going down."

While we sat talking, a familiar black-and-silver Cadillac

limousine pulled into the garage—one of the decoy delivery vehicles that had been loaded up with Nicky's heroin, then off-loaded at another location before our guys could catch the batch.

I told Wally and Geronimo to stick by the garage and work out the new deal for Stevie Baker's drugs, while I drove over to a nearby restaurant to catch a bite.

A little before 9:00 p.m., Wally and G showed up at the restaurant, and the news was not good. The deal was off—Nicky himself had put the kibosh on it. Too many cops and agents had been circling the garage.

Another fucking setback, and my patience was wearing thin. And my confidence as well. I started to wonder . . . could Nicky and his crew just be pulling our chain? Were they about to flush us down the drain?

WHILE WE WAITED, Stevie Baker sold us out to a higher bidder and a better offer. I was disappointed, but I could understand it. Business was business.

It wasn't until March that Wally arranged another deal, this one with Bo Hatcher, another of Nicky's top lieutenants.

Given all the street heat and the bullshit we had been through, we decided it should be for a smaller package, half a kilo. Bo Hatcher insisted that all the money—$35,000—be paid up front.

But this posed a problem. DEA policy was never to front the money. On the other hand, I didn't want to kill the buy, especially since it would again play out at the Harlem River Motors garage, Nicky's inner sanctum.

Since we already had blown deals with Jazz and Steve Baker, I told Wally to set up the meet anyway, figuring I could smooth things over with my DEA bosses as we got closer and closer to the actual handoff.

ON MARCH 11, 1977, my partner, Bobby Nieves, was able to withdraw $35,000 from the DEA cashier. That night, Bobby and I met up at my favorite Bronx restaurant, where he handed me the money in a brown paper bag. The cash had been bundled in stacks of twenties and fifties, all the serial numbers prerecorded at DEA headquarters.

But I still needed an official green light from the DEA brass downtown before I could actually fork it over. Bobby, who would be watching my back from his surveillance car, said he'd give me a heads-up as soon as the word came over his radio.

After Bobby and I finished our meal, Geronimo came by in a silver-gray Buick. Bobby left the restaurant. A little while later, a Kawasaki 2000 motorcycle zoomed up. The driver was wearing a red, white, and black jumpsuit, dark sunglasses, and a helmet. When he took the helmet off, we could see it was Wally.

Wally told us that Bo Hatcher had the heroin waiting for us at the garage. He reiterated that the full 35 g's needed to be paid up front. But I still hadn't gotten clearance on the deal from Bobby. So I stalled Wally by haggling him on the price.

"Bo tries to beat us, I'll personally shoot the motherfucker myself," Wally boasted.

Still looking to buy time, I demanded that Bo give us a sample. Wally said the chances were slim. "Well," I said, "did you make it clear to your man that this is just the trial run? That if this half ki is righteous, I expect to buy another two kis before the month is up?"

"Bo will have the other two kis for you next Tuesday," Wally said.

"Okay, then," I said. "But I'd still appreciate it if you could get me a sample and ask him to do better on the price. Business is business."

Wally grunted, then jumped on his Kawasaki and zoomed off. Meanwhile, I kept looking around for Bobby. If Bobby didn't come by soon to give me the okay on the 35 g payoff, this whole deal would turn to shit.

About twenty minutes later, Wally roared back on his motorcycle. He had an answer from Bo: "No deal on the price. Or the sample."

Shit. Where was Bobby?

Just then, I spotted a yellow taxicab coming toward us. About a hundred yards away from us, the driver flashed his high beams. And at that moment I knew I had the go-ahead to proceed with the buy.

It was Bobby, behind the wheel of the cab, giving me the agreed-upon signal that the DEA had consented for me to front the entire $35,000. Or so I thought. Turned out that Bobby had never gotten their approval—he just signaled me that he had. He made that decision on his own balls.

I let the cab pass by us. Then I turned to Wally and said, "I tell ya what, kid. I'm gonna trust you on this one. Just as long as I can hand Bo the money myself. And he hands me back the drugs."

"You crazy, Lou," Wally said. "You don't need to take that kinda risk. You best let me do it."

"Sorry, kid," I said, "but I gotta insist."

"Man," said Wally, "you don't know what you're sayin' here. Ain't safe for you to walk in there, especially with all that money on you. They got a lotta muscle down there."

"I can handle it, Wally."

"Maybe so, Lou, but don't look right for the main man to be goin' in with the money. Should be me doin' that. Otherwise they gonna lose respect for you, you bein' a boss and all. And that just ain't good, man. That ain't good."

Wally had a point. "All right, fuck it."

I reached into my glove compartment, where I had stashed the $35,000 in government buy money. "Wally," I said, "you and me, we're family, right?"

"Lou," he said, "I got your back."

I handed him the cash. "I know it, kid."

Once he had passed the money to Bo Hatcher, the plan was for him to put the half ki of heroin in the backseat of his Corvette. I insisted that I be the one to drive the Vette out.

Stuffing the cash inside his jumpsuit, Wally put his helmet back on, jumped on his bike, and took off over the East River. Geronimo and I followed behind in my Caddy.

On 145th Street, Wally pulled into the Harlem River Motors garage and parked his motorcycle next to the interior office. G and I parked across the street, at the Getty gas station. Then we waited for Wally's signal.

Inside the garage, we could see Wally talking with the usual contingent of musclebound bodyguards. With the big men enveloping him, he suddenly disappeared from sight.

Several moments later he reappeared, walking back toward the front with a guy who looked like Sasquatch. About six-foot-two and 270 pounds, this man's hair was cropped short and it had thinned to leave a bald spot at the front of his forehead. His nose was broad and below it was a thick mustache. He was dressed in a waist-length blue jacket, yellow polo shirt, and blue jeans.

It was Bo Hatcher. Bo led Wally into the garage office.

A minute later, Wally came out of the office and looked across the street, in my direction. He crooked his finger, signaling me to come across the street.

I turned to Geronimo. "Time to dance, G," I said.

Leaving my car, I began walking slowly toward the garage. I tried to make myself appear calm, but I'm not certain how well I succeeded. After all, I was walking straight into the devil's lair.

The journey across 145th Street took only seconds, but to me it felt like a lifetime, as though everything had downshifted into slow motion. My heart was pounding, my legs felt like jelly, my feet seemed to get sucked into the pavement with every step.

As I neared the garage, I could see at least seven oversized black men forming up a line outside, glaring at me. Their eyes bore into me like red-hot pokers. Focusing on them, I knew that every one of these motherfuckers had to be packing a gun or a knife. Or, more than likely, one of each.

No, I usually didn't go into a fight thinking what some other guy could do to me, only what I could do to him. It was the psych-out factor, like Mike Tyson—the other guy was beat before he even got into the ring.

But this time something was different. This time I actually felt scared. I had a .25-caliber pistol inside my coat pocket and my 9mm in the back of my pants, but sooner or later, every man has his Waterloo. Could this be mine?

Nearing the line of muscular, murderous giants, I made a move to step between two of them. Unbelievably, the line separted to let me pass and I went inside. It was like the parting of the Red Sea.

The garage was a pretty standard affair, two rolling doors, an entrance wide enough for three cars, concrete columns separating the parking spaces, a caged office in the middle. Wally's Corvette was sitting in one of the spaces. When I stepped into the garage, he motioned me toward it.

As I walked toward the car, I happened to glance into the caged office. Bo Hatcher was standing inside, his eyes fixed on me. But some other guy was in there, too, giving me a scalding stare.

Trim, fit, and muscular, he was dressed casually but tastefully. Suede, waist-length suburban jacket, open-collared shirt, tailored jeans. He wore expensive, sporty Gucci sunglasses that were lightly tinted.

He slowly removed the sunglasses to get a better look at me. And when he did, I felt something icy and viselike curl around my heart. His skin was smooth and clear. His cheekbones were high and chiseled. But it was the eyes that told the real story. They were black. Cold. Lifeless as a shark's. And they were following my every step.

Nobody in the garage breathed a word.

I got into the driver's seat of the Corvette. The keys were already in the ignition. Outside the office, Wally jumped back on his Kawasaki, flipped on the ignition, and peeled out. I turned on the Vette's engine, backed out of the garage, and spun out behind him.

Across the street, Geronimo revved up my Caddy, raced out of the Getty station, and joined up with our little parade. Then all three of us headed over the Third Avenue Bridge across the East River, back into the Bronx.

I got to the rendezvous point first, a darkened alley at East 153d Street and Gerard Avenue. G came in right behind me. Wally must have turned down a side street and taken a different route—he had disappeared. I figured he must have taken a back way to shake any tails.

While we waited for him, I started rummaging around in the trunk of the Vette for the drugs. And felt . . . nothing. My gut did a somersault. I slammed the trunk shut.

Red-faced, I turned and shouted at Geronimo, "There's no junk!"

"What do you mean, there's no junk!?"

"I mean there's no motherfucking junk! This kid just beat us for the thirty-five g's!"

I pictured Wally tear-assing through Queens on his motorcycle, on his way to Kennedy International Airport and a red-eye to Brazil. One second later, I also pictured my career and entire future going up in smoke.

I was on the verge of losing it completely when Wally roared up behind us. The moment he jumped off his motorcycle, I grabbed him by the lapels and threw him roughly up against the Vette.

"Motherfucker!" I said with a snarl, ready to rip both his lungs out.

"Calm down, Lou!" Wally said. "Just calm down! It's there."

I let him down slowly, then watched warily as he walked around back and popped the Vette's trunk. From somewhere in the back, he pulled out a shoebox. The dope was inside, hermetically sealed in a clear plastic bag placed in a brown paper bag. Along the border of the plastic bag, the letters "BO" had been printed in blue ink. It was concealed so well I could have gone over it five times and never spotted the package.

I relaxed. Grinned. And tapped Wally sweetly on one cheek, goombah-style. "My man," I said to him.

Then I took the dope back to my own car, reached into my coat pocket, and pulled out the crinkly leather coin bag with a drawstring attached—my test kit.

The stuff looked good. It smelled good. And it tasted good. By my estimate, it was 60 percent pure.

But just to be certain I hadn't just plunked down thirty-five grand in government money for a slice of turkey, I ran the full Marquis field test on it. No worries.

"Dy-no-*mite,*" I said aloud. "This shit is righteous."

Stepping out of the car, I high-fived Wally. "You're beautiful, kid."

Wally and I made plans to meet the following Tuesday for another heroin deal. I got back into my car and drove off with Geronimo. After I had dropped him off, I drove back down to the DEA's office. During the trip downtown, I had a chance to reflect on the events of the evening.

What kept popping back into my head was that second guy in the office. The one standing next to Bo Hatcher. The one with those tinted Gucci sunglasses.

No question about it, this was a guy who commanded respect. And those cold, sharklike eyes told me right away that he also was a killer—not some cat burgler or junkie thief who killed when he needed money, or killed in a panic, or killed because he got off on it.

This was the kind of person who would take action only when absolutely necessary. But when that moment came, God help you, because he wouldn't hesitate. Not even for a second.

He was a stone-cold killer. A *righteous* killer.

But what else would you expect from Mister Untouchable, Mister Leroy "Nicky" Barnes?

CHAPTER TWELVE

I LIVED IN FEAR THAT Nicky Barnes might have me followed, make me for a cop, target me for an ambush . . . or try to kill my family.

So I took precautions.

If I needed to go to the DEA's office in Manhattan, I would take indirect, roundabout routes, approaching it from directions nobody else took. If I came in on a day off, I would dress down—stevedore cap on my head, sunglasses, dungarees, army fatigue jacket, hood of my sweatshirt draped over my jacket collar. In that getup, nobody in a million years could have made me for my uptown persona of Mister Dapper High-Rolling Mobster, Louie D.

I would always make a couple of passes before driving into the DEA's parking garage, checking for any suspicious-looking characters who might be loitering outside. Once I parked, I would never walk straight into the building. Instead, I'd duck across the street to buy a cup of coffee and a buttered roll, then trot over to the Mobil gas station on the opposite corner, where I would have my breakfast and gossip with the workers before making my move into the DEA building. While breaking bread, I would do visual scans of the streets outside my office.

Driving home at night, I would always keep my 9mm by my side. And I would constantly change cars. Usually I'd start in a big Buick Electra, borrowed from the DEA's motor pool of seized vehicles and outfitted with fake license plates. Halfway home, I'd detour and park the Buick in some other neighborhood, then switch to either my yellow Cadillac Coupe DeVille or a light blue and white AMC Matador belonging to my partner, Bobby Nieves. Sometimes I'd ditch the second car for the third car. The next day I would reverse the process. Before getting inside any of my cars, I'd look for the Scotch tape I had placed on my car doors, hood, and trunk to see if any of it had been smudged, torn, or removed by intruders.

My drive home at night would always be circuitous. Cruising along steadily on the expressway, as if heading for the distant reaches of eastern Long Island, I'd speed up, slow down, speed up again, then suddenly swerve into the right lane and zip off an exit ramp, barely making the turnoff.

Turning down a local street, I would park and kill the lights. Then I would sit for several minutes, watching to see who, if anyone, might have been following me. Once certain I had not been tailed, I'd start the engine up again, drive to where I had parked one of my other cars, and change horses.

At stoplights, I would maneuver to be first in line. If I could not be first, I'd leave space between my car and the car in front of me, giving myself plenty of room to make a quick getaway if I needed to make one. If there were two lanes leading up to the stoplight, I'd try to straddle both of them to make it difficult for another car to pull up on my left. If someone did manage to roll alongside, I'd watch him from the corner of my eye while pretending to fixate on the stoplight. Casually sucking on a filtered cigarette with my left hand, I would tighten the grip on the 9mm in my right, and slowly roll down my window to get a clear shot.

Sometimes, instead of going straight home, I'd drive into Brooklyn to give the appearance that I still lived there. I had access to a couple of big apartment complexes in Brooklyn—I knew the keypunch code to the electronic garage door at one, the maze of entrances and exits at the other—so I'd walk in one way, then dart out another to frustrate any would-be followers.

To make it look like I actually lived in Brooklyn, I carried around phony registration cards and driver's licenses listing one or another apartment complex as my address. I also wrote my undercover names—Louis DelRey and Louie D. Canelda (a slight variation on Canellada, which was part of my father's formal last name in Spanish)—on labels and inserted the labels into the name-tag slots on empty mailboxes at both complexes. On several occasions, when Wally and Geronimo accompanied me, I would drive to one of the complexes on the pretense of needing to pick up something from my supposed residence. Disappearing inside a building, I'd linger for ten or fifteen minutes before coming back out again. It was all part of my elaborate plan to convince Wally, and the rest of Nicky's boys, that this was where I hung my hat.

At the end of the night, when I *finally* arrived at my real home, I'd take a few spins around the block before pulling into my driveway, checking to see if anyone suspicious-looking was parked near my house.

Once I was inside, the first thing I would do was shower. In my mind, the filth and contamination of the drug underworld still clung to me, and I needed to scrub them out of my pores and hose myself down before touching Iris or the kids. After checking on my sleeping kids, I would head into the master bedroom. But before getting into bed, I'd take one last peek through the blinds, checking the street for funny business. In the mornings, I'd check again.

When I was on the job, I could control my fears. But after

hours, it was a different story. And at night, when I slept, my subconscious would awaken with full fury. *You know what, Louie?* it would say to me. *You're* supposed *to be afraid, so fuck you. I'm this little guy who lives inside you, and you're always scaring the shit out of me.*

I slept with a loaded handgun under my pillow, but I often fell victim to gruesome nightmares . . . large men invading my house, violating my wife, and making me and my kids watch . . . grinning, faceless assailants pointing their guns at me while I futilely tried to squeeze off a round in self-defense but couldn't make my frozen fingers function.

Many times, I'd wake up in a cold sweat, yelling aloud and lunging for my gun. My outbursts would startle Iris awake. Apologizing, I would soothe her back to sleep, then try, usually without success, to catch a few more winks of my own.

I never told Iris what my nightmares were about.

I ALSO NEVER told Iris what I was actually doing for the DEA. As far Louis Jr. and Maria were concerned, I still drove a truck for a living.

At home, I tried to maintain a semblance of normalcy. But when the Barnes investigation heated up, and I sensed it would be wise to lower my profile, I stepped aside on my familial responsibilities.

There were times, though, when the investigation intruded more directly in my home life. Especially around the holidays.

Bad guys knew that cops and agents liked to scale back around the holidays, because they all wanted to be home with their families. So the scumbags would be ratcheting up, moving their biggest shipments, doing their biggest deals, pulling off their biggest scams and heists because they knew there was less heat on the street. To make sure we wouldn't lose a step on Nicky, my team and I worked around the clock, right up till Thanksgiving Day, Christmas Day, and New Year's Eve.

THERE CAME A point where I needed to take certain precautions with my family.

I warned my kids to be wary of strangers and, should they ever feel menaced, to run to a neighbor or into a local store where they knew the proprietor. I told Iris that if she ever thought she was being followed, she should park her car near a busy intersection, make a beeline for a public phone to call for help, and make certain that whoever was watching saw her make the call.

Finally, there was Lady. Black and tan, big-boned, powerful, and weighing 110 pounds by age two, she was the most magnificent German shepherd you'd ever seen.

After Lady learned the basic commands, I began taking her for walks in rougher neighborhoods, keeping my eye peeled for people who looked threatening. Pulling on Lady's collar, I would tell her, "Watch 'im, Lady!" which would prompt her to utter a low growl and brace for attack. When the hairs on her neck bristled in readiness, I would praise her.

At home, I would show my gun to Lady and try different things to piss her off so that eventually she came to associate a gun, or anything ominous in a person's hand, as a threat. Outside, when she started barking, I quieted her if it was a blowing leaf or a darting squirrel, but praised her effusively if it was a stranger.

And then came Lady's baptism under fire. I took her to the training compound of the NYPD's Canine Unit.

Holding Lady leashed by my side, I walked her into a fenced-in pen. Then a very large cop in heavy protective gear began to wave his arms, yell and scream, and make lunging, threatening gestures.

The hair on Lady's neck and back bristled. She began to growl.

"Watch 'im, Lady!" I commanded. She became even more agitated. I unfastened the leash. "Get 'im, Lady!"

Lady tore into that poor cop like a bat out of hell, knocking him off his feet and chomping ferociously on his padded arm. I ran over to pry her loose, hugging and praising her like a proud papa. Lady was now a full-fledged guard dog.

Even though the only person she ever ended up attacking was our mailman—who teased her once too often and paid the price when she took a chunk out of his butt—Lady gave me peace of mind. (Thankfully, the mailman was a neighborhood friend who declined to bring legal action.)

I knew that Lady could be counted on to safeguard my family.

WHILE I WOULD never tell my brothers exactly what I was doing in the Barnes case, I knew they were both very proud of me for being a federal agent. At times, when my brother Rigel, who was in the air force and stationed in England, came home on leave, he and I would talk about our jobs. Alfonsito, still living at home with my parents, always wanted to hold my shield and my DEA credentials.

Papa, as had been his custom, never showed much interest at all in my work, which only made me hunger for his approval that much more. If only I could do something that would make him respect me, make him proud of me. . . .

If only I could do something that would finally make him love me.

Mama assured me that Papa was impressed by what I was doing, but most of the time I suspected she was just paying lip service so that my feelings wouldn't be hurt. Given my history with the man—the insults, the abuse, the endless beatings—I often felt that Papa didn't give a damn about anything that happened in my life.

CHAPTER THIRTEEN

A FINE MARCH DRIZZLE PISSED across my windshield as Geronimo and I sat parked near Yankee Stadium. The Yankees were down at spring training in Florida, but later that year—1977—they would defeat the L.A. Dodgers in six games to win the World Series. At this moment, however, we were killing time by the empty stadium, waiting to connect with Wally on a new deal for a full kilo of heroin.

Suddenly the portable radio under my seat crackled to life. "This is thirteen-oh-one. We're going in."

So this was it. The final act.

A few minutes later, Wally was rapping his knuckles on my car window. When I stepped outside to talk to him, I could see he was nervous.

"Lou, something's goin' down," he said, glancing around nervously. "I can't contact nobody. We can't do anything tonight."

"Fuck," I said softly, slowly raising the hood on my sweatshirt up over my head, which was the prearranged signal. Despite the scumbags we were about to take down, for some reason I felt like Judas.

Out of the corner of my eye, I saw Agents Dwight Raab and Sammy Blackburn, having picked up on my sweatshirt signal, get out of their unmarked van and start moving toward us. In his hand, Dwight held a silver .357 Magnum.

For a split second I imagined myself stepping out of character and blowing him away.

"Motherfuckers!" Dwight screamed, sticking his gun to the back of Wally's head. "DEA! Get down! Get down! You're all under arrest!"

I shoved past Dwight as he threw Wally to the sidewalk and Sammy rushed in to cuff him, giving me just enough time to jump back into my Caddy. Once I slammed the door behind me, Geronimo floored the gas and the two of us made our getaway, just as it all had been planned. We needed to remain out on the streets, just in case.

A few hours later, when I showed up at DEA headquarters, Wally figured they must have collared me, too.

Looking up from the desk where he was being grilled by other agents, he beamed at the sight of my face. But then his expression changed to something else. It was simultaneously ironic and unbearable. Wally was worrying that I must be blaming him for bringing the feds down on us.

"Lou," he said, "I didn't tell 'em shit. You gotta believe me."

"Wally . . ." I started to say, nearly choking on my words. My heart ached for what I was about to do to this kid.

"Nuthin', Lou, absolutely nuthin'. I swear to God."

"Wally . . . I *am* the fucking man."

Wally's head snapped back. He looked like he'd just taken a dropkick to the balls. "What?"

"Wally," I repeated, this time long and slow. "I . . . am . . . the . . . man."

Like a pane of freshly shattered glass, Wally's face started to come apart at the seams, all the pieces threatening to fall out at once. "No, man. *No.*"

"Wally," I said one more time. "I am the man."

He put his hands to his eyes and began to cry. "Oh, fuck, man. *The fuckin' man.*"

* * *

NICKY BARNES WAS cruising around uptown in one of his luxury cars when they dropped the net on him.

As a dozen cars full of DEA agents and New York City cops surrounded him and a NYPD helicopter swooped down from overhead, an official on a bullhorn bellowed, "This is the police! Bring your car to a halt! Step out with your hands up!"

He gave up without a fight.

Elsewhere, a joint federal-city task force of agents and cops armed with shotguns and riot gear rounded up Jazz Hayden, Guy Fisher, Chico Bob, Bo Hatcher, Stevie Baker, Scraps, Petey Rollock, and a bunch of Nicky's middlemen. The next morning, the New York *Daily News* bannered the whole business across its front page: *200M DOPE RING IS SMASHED; GRAB THE KING AND 24 KNIGHTS.*

When they locked up Wayne, they found $220,000 in cash in his apartment, including $35,000 in marked bills that I had used for my last heroin buy, plus five pistols and ledgers detailing the workings of the entire operation. Two of the ledger pages showed a fraction of the monthly transactions handled by Jazz Hayden's distributors. If the pages were accurate indicators, Nicky was hauling down at least $84 million a year.

At Stevie Baker's pad, they came up with $180,000, pistols, four kilos of smack, two kilos of coke, and fifteen thousand glassine envelopes.

The most damning evidence against Nicky Barnes and his crew, however, would ultimately come from me and Geronimo. We had personally bought $64,000 of Nicky's heroin and could tie him directly to the sales. Through Jazz Hayden and others, we had laundered tens of thousands of drug dollars on Nicky's behalf. We had incriminating audio and videotapes of him and his lieutenants. We would bring in other witnesses who could connect him to the product.

When the case finally did come to trial, it would be a historic occasion. President Jimmy Carter himself had ordered attorney General Griffin Bell to oversee the prosecution. At the behest of Bell, the U.S. attorney for the Southern District, Robert Fiske Jr., announced that he would personally prosecute the case in federal court.

The government was bringing out its big guns, and Geronimo and I would be their silver bullets.

IT WAS ONE thing to be out on the street, doing my dance with the devil. It was a whole other to be held accountable in court for what I had done.

In a way, you could liken it to fishing. You might have hooked the fish on your line, but you had to be extra careful bringing it in. You didn't want to lose it, or the line to split, or the fish to spit out the hook. You still had to get him into the boat.

So, in the interests of securing my catch, I spent countless weeks relistening to all my tapes, went over all my reports to make sure I had gotten everything right, worked with the prosecutors to prepare for the day I would be called to the witness stand to tell my story. Transcribing all the undercover tapes took hours upon hours. To break the monotony of all this work, Bobby Nieves, Don Ferrarone, and I would mimic the distinctly uptown voices we heard on the recordings. Then we'd try to mimic their body language, pimp stroll, everything. Finally, when we heard background music on the tapes, usually from one of the clubs Geronimo or I had visited to grease a deal, we'd trio up and start disco dancing or harmonizing like the Temptations. Thanks to the electronics expert who came in daily to help us enhance the sound quality and always brought bags of doughnuts, potato chips, and pretzels with him, I gained an extra ten pounds.

DURING THE SPRING months of pretrial prep, when I would spend my days inside the downtown offices of the U.S. attorney, I would take my lunch in the courtyard outside, where a bunch of Italian food vendors had set up their carts.

It was ironic. Here were guys who had come over from Little Italy to peddle their pizza, fried calamari, sausages, provalone and prosciutto heros, and gelato. No doubt, their bosses had the blessing of the mob. Yet they were operating within a stone's throw of the offices of the U.S. attorney, the FBI, the New York City Police Department, and all the major state and federal courthouses. I couldn't help but wonder which politicians had put together that deal.

After I bought my lunch, I would walk across the street and eat it on the benches facing the U.S. District Courthouse, where I would soon be testifying. One day, a woman sat down near me—she was Latina, one of the most gorgeous I had ever seen, with a body that could stop traffic. She gave me a friendly, come-hither smile.

For several days after, I continued to run into her at lunchtime, and the looks she gave me advanced beyond just casual. So I finally made a move and started to chat her up.

She took my move in stride. Easily. A little *too* easily.

Suddenly it hit me.

I was a nice-looking guy and liked to flirt, but I was also happily married. Could this be a setup?

After lunch, back in the U.S. attorney's office, I ran it by the prosecutors. They brought me up to speed in a hurry. There was talk that Nicky Barnes was trying to orchestrate the murders of witnesses. Geronimo was now stashed safely away in the Federal Witness Protection Program, but there were rumors of poisoning the water pitcher from which G would take drinks when he was on the stand. Or bribing, threatening, kidnapping, or even killing G's mother to keep him from testifying. Another rumor had it that Nicky was trying to bribe cops and witnesses with money . . . or with beautiful women who would seduce and compromise them.

So from that day on, whenever I caught sight of this Latina babe, I backed away from her like a man from a rattlesnake. I grew eyes in the back of my head, took no one for granted.

As one of the government's star witnesses, I was not about to get caught with my pants down, one way or another.

WHEN THE TRIAL started in September 1977, throngs of reporters, photographers, TV anchors, and cameramen crowded the courthouse steps and corridors, shoving room only. Beefy U.S. marshals, tripled in number from their usual quota, patrolled the corridors and security checkpoints, using metal detectors to search for concealed weapons and explosives.

The front rows were reserved for royalty—state and federal prosecutors, police chiefs, FBI and DEA brass, and the cream of the press corps (Jimmy Breslin, Dan Rather, etc.). Behind them sat cops, detectives, and agents who had worked on the case. And behind them, the wives, girlfriends, relatives, and friends of the fifteen defendants.

For their own protection, the jurors were never publicly identified in court. It was the first time in federal court history that a jury was selected anonymously.

The judge, the Honorable Henry F. Werker, was a large,

heavyset man who was known as "Speedy" for the pace at which he tried cases.

Facing him on the left were the prosecutors, Robert Fiske Jr. and his two assistant prosecutors, Thomas Sear and Bobby Mazur.

Facing him on the right were the attorneys for the defendants, led by the ever-pugnacious David Breitbart. With his thick, perfectly styled hair and Mediterranean complexion, Breitbart could have passed for a Hollywood actor or a professional football quarterback.

Notorious, contemptuous, irrepressible, headline-grabbing, and brilliant, David Breitbart was a formidable foe. Even before the trial started, he and his fourteen associates had been able to chip way at the evidence, trying to convince the court that the money, drugs, ledgers, and pistols recovered from the homes of Wayne and Stevie Baker should not be admitted because they had been seized without proper warrants.

FIRST ON THE witness stand was Robert Geronimo, aka G, the slick-talking, badass-walking, sharp-dressing, wiseguy-scheming informant.

Dressed in a pressed suit and dark tie, his hair neatly trimmed for his court appearance, G was a piece of work. Led through his testimony by U.S. Attorney Robert Fiske Jr., he gave crisp, confident answers seasoned with a saucy Pier 6 Brooklyn accent. Day after day, he mesmerized the courtroom, enjoying the hell out of himself and delighting the spectators. The papers gave ample space to the colorful descriptions he gave of his exploits in the investigation. And the prosecutors were confident he would win them round one.

Even before the prosecutor sat down, however, you could

sense Breitbart ready to counterpunch. G, sensing that he was in for a thrashing, began twisting and fidgeting in his seat.

As soon as the bell sounded for round two, Breitbart led off with a thunderous right that landed flush on G's most delicate and vulnerable part: his truthfulness.

Mr. Geronimo, in an interview with the DEA, you said that you and Wally Fisher traveled to Baltimore during the weekend of December 10, 11, and 12 in order to purchase two pounds of angel dust for a person named "Jap."

Yes, that's correct.

But, Mr. Geronimo, isn't it true that on those dates, you and Wally Fisher had actually taken two women to the Sheraton Pocano in Stroudsburg, Pennsylvania?

Well, I . . .

Geronimo's knees started to buckle. Breitbart followed with a flurry of punishing body shots. Hadn't G been arrested for loan-sharking? Numbers-running? Swindling? Wasn't he being paid a lump sum of $25,000 by the government for his work as an informant? Plus $350 a week in expenses? Wasn't he simply getting paid to *lie*?

The jury was confused. The spectators began shaking their heads. And Nicky Barnes and his boys sat up a little taller in their seats as their battered Judas began to bleed all over himself.

Afterward, in the offices of the U.S. attorney, we heard Fiske, until this point a model of decorum and professionalism, utter something completely out of character. "Shit! Shit! Shit!" he barked as he walked back in with his team of assistants.

Worried that his case had just been torpedoed, Fiske directed Bobby Nieves and me to drive down to Baltimore

ASAP to check the records of the hotel where Geronimo claimed to have stayed on the dates in question. No meal, no suitcase, no change of clothes, no toothbrush . . . *just go*.

What choice did we have? We spent all night in this dark and dingy Baltimore hotel basement, working under a jerry-rigged light fashioned from a single fifty-watt bulb and some electrical tape, turning the place topsy-turvy to search through hundreds of stacked-up boxes in hopes of finding something, anything, that could corroborate G's story.

But there was nothing.

Back in court the next morning, Fiske did a good job of shoring up G's initial testimony on redirect, but his credibility remained bruised.

Meanwhile, I sat waiting my turn.

Camped out in a heavily guarded witness room at the far end of the corridor, still sleep-deprived from my futile shlep down to Baltimore, I stretched my legs, flexed my muscles, cracked the bones in my neck. I kept glancing over at Flip, the big U.S. marshal who was watching over me and would give me the nod when my time came.

While I waited, my brain started to play nasty tricks on me. I went from confident to scared, hot to cold. All the facts, dates, words, and names started to collide and congeal into a murky, gelatinous blob, and I began to feel like my head would explode. I fought down a growing panic attack.

Then, all of a sudden, Flip turned to me and nodded. More marshals stepped into the room behind him.

I looked back at Flip dumbly. I felt like I was in a dream state, everything moving with the speed of molasses, funny faces peering back at me like when I was a kid wiggling my ears and grimacing in front of those fun house mirrors at Coney Island. I felt myself rise, surrounded by strong, tight-lipped men with starched white shirts and handguns dangling from their belts. Big men with big mustaches and big badges.

In the next instant, we were moving down the long corridor, me in the middle, all of us walking in cadence with a soft, quick-time shuffle, like a fighter being escorted by his entourage into the ring for the championship bout.

At the entrance to the courtroom, just outside the huge oak doors, we came to a halt. And then, all was still. And silent.

Standing with my nose barely a few inches from those massive doors, I listened to the drumlike pounding of my heart in my ears. Da-*dum*, Da-*dum*, Da-*dum* . . .

Suddenly the massive doors swung open. And I was facing the arena.

Enter Louie the Kid, the Brando-De Niro-Marciano wannabe, the walking, talking, woulda-shoulda-coulda-been-champ, the frustrated mob guy, G's wacky, out-of-control Italian cousin, DEA special agent Louie Diaz.

All eyes were fixed on me. Especially the eyes of the fifteen defendants, dead as the peepers you'd see on corpses.

As I got up on the stand, I made a point of looking right back at them, especially Nicky Barnes. But I avoided eye contact with their attorneys. The message in my body language was simple: If you're one of the bad guys, you don't frighten me. If you're one of their pinstriped mouthpieces, go fuck yourself. You're not even worth my time.

As I stayed focused on Nicky, the court clerk swore me in. Assistant U.S. Attorney Bobby Mazur bid me a polite good morning. Then the two of us did the usual Q and A, the traditional formality of introducing a law enforcement agent on the witness stand.

Agent Diaz, would you kindly spell your name for the record. Thank you. By whom are you employed? How long and in what capacity? Please, can you tell us what is a special agent for the Drug Enforcement Administration? What do you do? What is an undercover agent? Could you explain please? Thank you. Directing your attention to November 15, 1976, could you please tell the court . . .

I proceeded to identify each of the defendants for the record with the utmost deference and respect.

Agent Diaz, do you see Mr. Barnes present in this court?

Yes, sir.

Would you please point him out?

Yes, sir. The gentleman to the left of Mr. Breitbart, dressed in the fashionable, cream-colored mohair suit and silk tie, well-groomed, rough-looking, muscular build . . .

Nicky beamed.

Mr. Diaz, could you identify Joseph Hayden?

Yes, sir, he's the distinguished-looking gentleman with the neatly trimmed salt-and-pepper beard, dressed in the English gray tweed sports jacket.

With pride and the bearing of a blueblood, Jazz began to straighten his tie, a gesture that prompted some of his less dapper cohorts to cover their mouths as they snickered.

Now, Mr. Diaz, could you please identify Wally Fisher?

An eerie silence spilled over the courtroom. Everyone knew this would be the toughest one of all for me. As I proceeded to give his description, Wally cringed in his chair, as if saying, *Please, Louie, please make believe I'm not here.*

I felt like shit. But I forged on.

After that came moments of levity.

When I was asked to identify Gary "Bat" Saunders, I

replied that he was "the gentleman with the angular features" and the dark sunglasses. His attorney jumped all over me with objections, no doubt hoping to suggest to the jury that my remarks bordered on racist.

Agent Diaz, just what do you mean when you say Mr. Saunders has "angular features"?

I looked over at the defense table to see that one of Bat's pals, anticipating what I was being pushed into saying, was already grinning.

Well, sir, he's known as "Bat" because of his tiny ears that jut out like little bat ears.

The courtroom promptly exploded, everybody going nuts. And Judge Werker, himself the bearer of a nickname, wisely let it laugh out, knowing that all of us needed a break from the tension.

But then, just as I was asked to identify Wayne, the guy did something totally unscripted. In full view of everyone, he shot me his middle finger.

To save time, I simply stated for the record, "Your Honor, that man is the gentleman who just gave me the finger."

"Objection!" shouted his attorney.

"Overruled," said Judge Werker. "Agent Diaz gave an appropriate answer. I'll let it stand."

Once we got through the roll call of the defendants, Assistant U.S. Attorney Mazur brought me through all the dates, names, and events of the case.

Having been through this drill many times before as a government witness, I made it a point to look directly at the jurors as I gave my answers, knowing it was the best way to build a rapport with them.

* * *

When the defense got its turn, it immediately brought out the bats and chains.

The fiercest gladiator, of course, was David Breitbart. He may have had the look of somebody important, but he was probably netting a million or two off Nicky for defending him, so in my mind he was just one more dirtbag with a briefcase.

At first, in deference to my long experience working undercover and testifying as an expert government witness, he was respectful. But, as his confidence built, off came the kid gloves and he came at me with everything he had.

His strategy was to try to push me into agreeing with him that Wally was nothing but a stupid, silly kid looking to make a rep for himself, and therefore his statements about being tight with Nicky Barnes were complete and utter fabrications. Moreover, Breitbart suggested, when Wally met up with me, he was so bowled over by my manufactured Mafia billing that he began to believe his own lies and his own self-inflated sense of importance. But in the scheme of things, Breitbart asserted, Wally was of no more consequence than a mosquito on Nicky's ass.

Breitbart was good, probably the best I had ever squared off against. But I wouldn't let him take me down this path. And once he realized that, he did what every other defense attorney does once he starts to flounder: grasp at straws.

Agent Diaz, did he give you the dope with his left hand or his right hand? How far were you from the corner? What kind of day was it? What were the denominations of the currency you paid him in?

Total bullshit.

After Breitbart took his shots, the other attorneys had a go at me. No matter how much they tried to discredit me, I stood firm on my story, knowing I held the moral high road as I was telling the truth.

Bobby Mazur got to question me again, on redirect, and it was all going smoothly. As I looked out over the courtroom, I recognized the faces of the regulars who had been in the courtroom each day since I had begun my testimony. But then I noticed someone new, someone who was not a regular. A real gangster puss on him. He clearly didn't belong. And my imagination went into high gear:

He reaches into his jacket and pulls a Roscoe . . . first he drops a couple of marshals, who tumble backward over their chairs . . . then splinters of wood and bone fly up as his bullets smack into the tables and the witness stand . . . a couple of the defendants take rounds to the backs of their heads, their brains splattering across the $500 Italian suits of their attorneys . . . the attorneys dive for cover under the defense table . . . then the gunman turns and trains his pistol on me . . . he steadies his aim . . . squeezes the trigger and . . .

After I wrapped up my testimony, I pulled Flip, the chief marshal, aside and told him about my suspicions. Within seconds, he and some of his guys rousted the unfamiliar spectator, hustling him downstairs for a little hard-nosed Q and A. Sure enough, he was a made guy who was out on parole. He claimed to know G's uncle.

He was not permitted to return to the courtroom.

THERE WERE TIMES I felt I was getting more consideration from the defendants and their attorneys than I was from my own people.

After I finished my testimony, one of the prosecutors asked me to retrieve a law book from his office. But by the time I came back with the book, the courtroom had filled to capacity and a big, unruly crowd in the hallway outside was being kept at bay by the marshals.

A new deputy marshal, a rookie, was at the door. When I flashed my badge and announced my identity, he sniffed, "I don't care who you are. Nobody else gets in, nobody. Those are my orders."

Whereupon someone standing a few shoulders away from me shouted, "Hey, you don't care who it is? Well, you *better* care. That's the guy who made the fucking case, you jackass."

I spun around to see Guy Fisher, Wally's older brother and one of the defendants who was on trial with Nicky.

He gave me a respectful nod, one gladiator saluting another. A moment later, another marshal inside the courtroom peeked out, recognized me, and ordered the rookie to let me pass.

Once I even ran into Nicky Barnes himself in the hallway. We tried to avoid each other, but there was so much foot traffic it couldn't be helped. Because of the crush of bodies, we were pushed toward each other.

Even though I was facing a stone-cold killer, what I felt at that moment was a far cry from the terror that threatened to overwhelm me when I first saw him in person back at the parking garage months ago. It was almost pity. Almost.

"Hey, Nicky," I finally said to him. "Nothing personal. You did what you had to do, I did what I had to do."

"Knowing this," said Nicky, "I understand it."

And that was that.

THE TRIAL LASTED two months. All told, forty witnesses took the stand.

Throughout the testimony, Nicky Barnes remained unruffled. Always trim and dapper—a typical ensemble might include a muted gold tie from Armani, russet brown shirt tucked into tailored, olive trousers, lizard-skin belt, tan leather ankle boots, wool sports coat with gray and lavender weave, suede coat with sable collar, and, always but always, those purple-tinted Playboy sunglasses—he joked, doodled on notepads, waved to friends in the gallery.

His expression never changed. In his mind, there was no doubt about the outcome.

In his summation, David Breitbart argued that, notwithstanding all the undercover tape recordings, none of the heroin buys could be linked directly to Nicky.

He insisted that Geronimo had never heard Nicky talking about drugs. What's more, he argued, a man of Nicky's high position would never have done business with "trash" such as G, who he characterized as a sleazebag with an arrest record and a guy who had taken money to do the government's bidding.

Waxing eloquent, Breitbart sought to portray Nicky as a local Joan of Arc.

"Several years ago it became apparent to police officers that there was an uppity black man in Harlem . . . and he had the nerve not to be afraid to answer back when someone spoke to him. So some cop said anybody with that much money must be a drug dealer. 'Let's get him.' The prosecutors have engaged in an obscene conspiracy to persecute Barnes."

Breitbart was articulate, compelling, and utterly convincing.

In November 1977, the judge gave the case against Nicky Barnes and the fourteen other defendants to the jury.

While the jurors were deliberating, Nicky remained free on bail. But the government's effort to keep tabs on him turned into a comedy act worthy of the Keystone Kops.

To begin with, the U.S. attorney's office assigned me and Bobby Nieves to tail him.

Me.

The same guy who had infiltrated Nicky's organization to take him down. The same guy who, by all rights, should have been given twenty-four-hour protection, just like Geronimo and all the other prosecution witnesses.

Instead, I was being asked to shag Nicky for the next twenty-four to seventy-two hours—marry him, in effect, until the jury came back with its verdict.

But Bobby and I had a job to do, so we did it. After getting a quick bite to eat, we headed up to Harlem with other DEA teams, stopping at all of Nicky's known hangouts. At Jegazze's, an uptown nightclub, we spotted Nicky coming out with Shamecca, his beautiful, leggy lady, who was decked out in a $5,000 leopard skin coat. They got into Nicky's new white Mercedes and began heading downtown. Along with the other agents, Bobby and I trailed behind.

For a while, Bobby and I switched off with the other surveillance teams, piggybacking Nicky for several miles. Then it occurred to me that we were being silly. What the hell was the difference if he *knew* we were on him? Unless he was planning to shoot it out with us and go down like an Old West gunfighter, he had no way out.

So Bobby and I pulled up close behind him, nearly riding his bumper. Nicky knew we were on him, too. When we all got stuck at a light at Fifty-ninth and Broadway, our vehicle nuzzling his car's rear, he jumped out and started marching toward us, cursing, talking tough, rolling his shoulders.

Bobby and I reached for our guns.

As he neared our car, Nicky recognized us. And smacked his forehead, as if to say, *What the fuck! You guys? Again?*

Instead, he just leaned into my window and said, "Louie? What's up, man?"

"Nicky," I said, "you got my people worried. They just want to make sure where you are."

Nicky laughed. "Jesus Christ, ain't that a fuckin' bitch! Look at all this shit, all this shit, and they got you guys doin' *this*? I'll be damned! Can't they even give *you* a break?"

Nicky Barnes was showing me more respect than my own people.

"Well, man," Nicky continued, "I tell you what. No need to go crazy here. I'm just goin' down here to the Sheraton Hotel, where me and my lady are goin' to take care of business, y'understand?"

I smiled. "We got you, Nicky. So how about me and Bobby come along and put you to bed?"

"Fine by me," Nicky said.

And off we all went to get Nicky and his lady into their pajamas.

After Nicky parked his Mercedes on the street outside the hotel and checked in, some of our agents set up in the lobby. Others took up positions outside the hotel, including me and Bobby, who promised Nicky we'd sit on his car and safeguard it till morning.

Parking in front of his Mercedes, we killed the lights on our own car, pulled our seats back, and adjusted our rearview mirrors so we could see Nicky's ride. And there we sat through the night, just off the old West Side Highway, facing the Hudson River and the rotting piers, pondering the meaning of life and the majesty of the stars in the cold autumn sky.

* * *

WHILE SAT, WE chatted. Bobby figured we'd get promoted, receive major awards. Me, I wasn't so sure.

I was now thirty-one years old, but I was still at war with myself, a young Turk with a short fuse and a nitroglycerin charge. Thirteen years of parochial school education with the Marianist Brothers, Franciscan priests, and Sisters of Charity, who were anything but charitable. A father who made my worst drill sergeant look like an altar boy. A hair-trigger temper, a paper-thin skin, and a penchant for attracting and inflicting violence. How far could I ever really advance in my career?

The clock ticked slowly and, except for the city rats who scurried back and forth from one manhole to another under cover of the steam belching up from the pavement, the night was still and silent.

Eventually both of us fell asleep.

I AWOKE WITH a start, a new day's sun shining in my eyes, and instinctively I smacked Bobby in the chest. He nearly jumped out of his skin. We looked at each other and immediately knew that something was wrong. We both spun around at the same instant to see it.

Nicky's Mercedes was *gone*.

Bobby and I started screaming at each other. "How the fuck could you fall asleep!"

"Me? What about *you*?"

"Jesus Christ!"

"How could this have happened!"

"Fuck! Fuck! Fuck! Fuck!"

I jumped on the radio and reached out for the other agents who were parked outside the Sheraton. But no one responded to my radio calls.

"Oh, shit," I started to say. "This is worse than I thought!"

Finally I got a faint, groggy "10-4" from one of the other agents. But he hadn't seen Nicky's car either.

Bobby and I leaped out of our car and went tear-assing toward the hotel entrance. As we came flying into the lobby, we slid right past the other agents staked out inside, unable to get any traction or hit the brakes on the slippery marble floors.

Trusty old Rooney, a big, salty Irishman, looked up from his Styrofoam cup of coffee and his morning *Daily News.*

"What's up, boys? Out for a morning run, are yas?"

"Tommy," I blurted out breathlessly, "where the fuck is Nicky?"

"Where we put him. Up in his room."

"Are you sure?"

"Well," said Rooney, "unless he jumped out the window of the tenth floor, he's still up there, 'cause he sure as hell didn't come this way."

"Hold on," I said, and ran over to the front desk. "Hey, pal," I said to the clerk, "ring up to room two-fourteen, willya?"

He handed me the receiver.

"Yo," said the voice on the other end.

"Nicky?" I said.

"No, it's Jimmy Carter. Who the fuck you think it is, man?"

Thank you. Sweet Jesus, thank you.

"Sorry, Nicky. It's okay. It's Louie. Just wanted to make sure you were all right."

"What, you think I mighta split for the Bahamas or something? Jeee-zuss!"

"Shit, man, I'm sorry. Go back to bed."

Bobby and I smiled lamely at Rooney, who looked back at us with a half-assed, head-shaking grin as we dashed out the door again.

Jumping into our car, we peeled out, burning rubber, flashing our red light, blasting our siren.

"Shit!" I hollered. "Those fucking sons of bitches! *They towed his car right out from under our noses!*"

Tearing down West End Avenue at close to a hundred miles per hour, we arrived at the NYPD's Thirty-fourth Street tow pound. Speeding through the front gate, red light still flashing, we pulled directly into the warehouse.

And there was Nicky Barnes's Mercedes, dangling from the tow truck's hook, the truck driver walking back in its direction.

Cops from the NYPD were pulling in behind us. But, with a full tank of adrenaline now fueling my system, I ignored them, leaping out of our car and charging the tow truck operator like an enraged bull. When I got close enough, I hurled my body at him.

Turning around to see me, the driver dropped his clipboard. In the next instant, I had him pinned against the Mercedes.

"You motherfucker!" I seethed. "How could you have towed that car knowing we were the man?"

The driver sputtered, "I . . . I . . . I assumed . . . I didn't know . . . I was just doing my job."

I tried to cool down. But when the tow compound desk sergeant informed us that they wouldn't release the Mercedes without a court order—in addition to all his other crimes, Nicky had accumulated more than $3,000 in unpaid fines and was a scofflaw—I was ready to go to war all over again.

Bobby pulled me away before I could do any serious damage and, embarrassed and exhausted, we dragged our sorry asses back to the Sheraton. Adding insult to injury, when we returned, the guys staking out the lobby were pissed at us for leaving without telling them why. Then, when we gave out with the full story, they began laughing at us.

But leave it to Rooney to have the last word: "That was good thinking, boys, real good thinking, having Nicky's car towed. No way he'd get away then."

Bobby and I shot each other sheepish looks. Was he giving us an ingenious out? We couldn't really be certain.

At about 9:30 a.m., Nicky walked into the lobby, doing his usual cock-of-the-walk strut. Bobby and I approached him tentatively.

"Good morning, Nicky," I said. He read my face like a road map.

"Yo, what's up, man? C'mon, Louie, I know something's happened. So what's up?"

"Well, Nicky, I got bad news. And I got good news."

Nicky waited for the rest of it, his eyes looking like missiles ready to launch.

"The bad news is they towed your car and there's nothing we can do about it."

"And the good news?"

"Bobby and I will be giving you a lift to the courthouse."

AT 3:00 P.M. on December 2, 1977, the jury filed back into Judge Werker's courtroom to deliver its verdict.

Nicky Barnes was convicted under the drug statutes of being the head of a continuing criminal enterprise. Along with twelve of his cohorts, he also was convicted of other felonies and narcotics violations. "Bat" Saunders and Wayne Sasso were acquitted. The jury hung on Guy Fisher.

On January 19, 1978, Nicky and his convicted codefendants reappeared for sentencing. True to his customary sartorial splendor, he showed up wearing a Hermès tie, a chalk-stripe Saint Laurent suit, and his omnipresent designer shades.

Stevey Baker, Bo Hatcher, "Fat Stevey" Monsanto, and two other Barnes associates all got thirty years. Another lieutenant got twenty years. Joseph "Jazz" Hayden and Petey Rollock got fifteen years. Wally Fisher got eight years. One other member of the gang got six years.

But the judge saved the harshest penalty for Nicky Barnes: a triple-life term with no parole. It was the single stiffest sentence in the history of Manhattan federal court.

He was "Mister Untouchable" no more.

NICKY CONTINUED TO direct drug deals from jail. But five years into his sentence, he learned that his old partners were cheating him. Against his orders, they also were doing drugs themselves—using them in front of his two young daughters—and messing with his wife and girlfriend.

Enraged by these betrayals, Nicky agreed to cooperate with the government in gathering evidence against his friends, associates, and rivals. Over the next seven years, he helped send more than fifty people to jail.

Thanks to Nicky's testimony, Guy Fisher, who had eluded the RICO rap the first time around, was convicted and given a life sentence.

Nicky's cheating girlfriend, who had been doing Guy while Nicky was cooling his heels behind bars, also was busted. Released on bail, she was shot three times in the back of the head in December 1982 while sitting in a Washington Heights tavern.

Because of Nicky's cooperation with the government,

Rudolph Giuliani, at one point the U.S. attorney for Manhattan, sought a reduction in his life sentence. Eventually he was resentenced to thirty-five years and placed in the prison's witness protection unit. His daughters also were relocated and given new identities.

While still in prison, Nicky graduated from college and won a national poetry contest.

In 1998, after twenty years behind bars, Nicky Barnes was released, given a new identity, and relocated under the Federal Witness Protection Program.

Meaning he was still out there somewhere.

CHAPTER FOURTEEN

AFTER THE VERDICT CAME back on Nicky Barnes, the good guys threw a big party at an Irish pub near the courthouse. About seventy-five people—DEA bosses, Justice Department officials, prosecutors, NYPD commanders, detectives, cops, agents, clerks, secretaries—crowded together to hoist their glasses and bottles in celebration of Nicky's conviction.

I put in an appearance but left quickly. I was uncomfortable with all the hoopla, ill at ease around some of the DEA bosses. All the drinking and back-slapping and speech-making rubbed me the wrong way. Victory seemed to have an awful lot of fathers that night.

I wasn't relaxed around the prosecutors, either. Although I liked some, certain others were of a different breed, not the kind of straight-up, hardworking, middle-class Joes I liked to mix it up with—they were prep school/Ivy League, but might as well have come from another planet.

It didn't sit right with me that we were feting Nicky's downfall. Sure, I felt proud at having been the guy tapped to take him down, that I had been at the top of my game, that I had managed to come through in one piece. But I was superstitious by nature, feeling that whatever I put out there, good or bad, would eventually come back to me. So celebrating some other person's defeat, even though it might be deserved, was just asking for bad luck to come back at me somewhere down the line.

I also felt it was bad form. In the boxing ring, you didn't prance and dance around a knocked-out opponent's body; it was unsportsmanlike. Nicky Barnes was not some lowly street urchin—he'd been a formidable adversary, one of the best, and he deserved respect for at least that much.

AFTER THE BARNES case concluded, *Reader's Digest* published an article about my undercover role. Mama told me that Papa had actually shown it to everyone in the neighborhood. She also claimed that he had mailed copies of the Spanish-language version to my aunts in Spain.

I tried to make myself believe it. I so desperately wanted to believe it. But, in the end, I wasn't buying it.

A few years later, I journeyed to Spain with Iris and the kids to visit my aunts. One of them brought out a copy of the *Reader's Digest* article to show me.

"Your papa sent this to us!" she said, beaming.

I excused myself, and stepped outside, onto the patio.

And cried my eyes out.

THERE WAS ANOTHER side effect of closing the Nicky Barnes case that I hadn't counted on. After all the applause died down and the press moved on, I fell into a funk. I had enjoyed my fifteen minutes of fame, my moment in the spotlight. Now . . . I was invisible again.

The DEA group handling the Barnes case was dismantled and, along with five other agents, I was transferred into a different group. But I couldn't seem to get any traction. A few cases came my way, but none very exciting or challenging. Meanwhile, my burning need for attention and approval—a chronic affliction after all those years of being Papa's son—came roaring back with a vengeance.

I began to see myself as washed-up fighter who turns to wrestling for a paycheck, just like Anthony Quinn in *Requiem for a Heavyweight*.

IRONICALLY, IT WAS boxing that rescued me from my depression.

While sitting in my office one afternoon in April 1978, I got a call from Jim Hunt, the DEA's black-belt ass-kicker and articulator.

"Guess what, kid," he said. "The Police Olympics is going to include boxing this summer. So, in view of this most auspicious and momentous development, I want you to get your ass down to the doc's office for an immediate physical. I've already taken the liberty of making an appointment for you."

Other than hitting the heavy bag now and then and mitt-sparring with my pals DEA agent Mike Levine and NYPD detective Carl "the Duke" Schroeder, I had not put on the gloves since my discharge from the army in 1966. And here it was, twelve years later. Nevertheless, I felt jazzed. Maybe Louie D. could give it one more jolt.

After the doctor gave me the green light, I began training more seriously with Mike and Carl. Using my undercover name of Louis DelRey to conceal my true identity, I also joined Gleason's, the famed boxing gym around the corner from Madison Square Garden, and worked with some of its legendary trainers. By the summer I was in the best shape of my life.

At the New York State Police Olympics, I fought in the middleweight division. After a couple of byes, I knocked out my first opponent in the first round and won a unanimous decision over my second opponent that same night, capturing the middleweight championship. From there I went on to the International Police Olympics boxing championships in San Diego, where I scored an upset win over a highly ranked middleweight named Marty Jimenez.

When I returned to New York with my gold medal, everyone in the DEA office welcomed me back as a conquering hero. Jim Hunt was beaming with pride. “My boy, you’ve succeeded in bringing the quintessence of glory to this fucking agency,” he said.

I felt flattered. But frustrated as well.

I had busted Nicky Barnes, was among the more prolific casemakers in the New York office, and had won two boxing championships for the pride and glory of the DEA. Yet, after all that, I could not snag a bump in rank.

Some agents who, like me, held the civil service rank of GS-12 bypassed the usual channels for promotion by requesting that the federal government’s Office of Professional Management audit their positions for a possible upgrade to GS-13, a team leader. Not only did they fail in their efforts, but also the DEA, furious that they had gone outside the agency to advance their careers, actually *demoted* them.

Given the climate of hostility toward agents with that kind of ambition, the chances of a go-getter like me ever getting bumped up were bleak. I fell into a fresh funk.

Transferring into a new group, I slowly started to recoup, and I teamed up with a new partner, Agent George Papantoniou.

George, whose parents had been born in Greece and who spoke Greek himself, always dreamed of one day being assigned to the Athens office of the DEA. He and I knew each other from our days as recruits at the DEA Academy. Once we were teamed up, we caught fire. From December 1979 through the following year, we nearly outdid the entire DEA-NYPD Task Force combined on our stats, arresting close to thirty class one narcotics dealers, seizing more than twenty kilos of dope, and confiscating luxury vehicles, firearms, and more than $300,000 in cash.

And then a real doozy of an investigation tumbled into our laps, one that would require me to deal with a whole different breed of gangster in a totally unexpected setting.

IT BEGAN ONE morning during a stakeout in midtown Manhattan. We had set up in a luncheonette across the street from P. J. Clarke's, a well-known Third Avenue speakeasy turned celebrity saloon and burger joint. A kilo of cocaine was due to be delivered to a guy named Charlie, who supplied drugs and call girls to high rollers on the Upper East Side.

George and I already had busted Charlie and flipped him. Now we were just waiting for his supplier to show up. Given that this was a brand-new connect for Charlie, none of us had any idea of what the supplier looked like. There were hundreds of pedestrians, any of whom could be the supplier, streaming past us.

But along comes one in particular who set off alarms—long blond hair, mustache, street clothes, windbreaker . . . he just rang my bell.

His whole appearance fit the classic profile of a scumbag drug dealer, which gave us sufficient probable cause to roust him. Georgie and I stepped from the luncheonette and into his path.

"Hey, bud, howya doin'?" I asked. He was startled.

"Huh?" he said.

"Federal narcotic agents," I said, flipping open my credentials. "Got some ID on you?"

As he fumbled for his wallet, I could see a fine layer of sweat beading on his upper lip.

"You mind if I pat you down?"

"N . . . n . . . no," he said, his jittery behavior further bolstering the profile.

Inside his jacket, I found a package tied with a belt to his torso. "Whoa! What's this? Hot pastrami sandwich?"

He frowned. "C'mon, man, you know what it is."

"So where you goin' with it?"

He shook his head and gave out with a long, slow sigh of defeat. "Aw, shit," he said.

We put him in our car and worked our magic on him. He agreed to take the dope up to Charlie's apartment, as originally planned. Only we would be right behind him to bust them both once Charlie took possession of the delivery. This way we could go through the motions of taking Charlie down without letting on that he previously had given up his connection.

Back at headquarters, we put the drug dealer, Scott, in one room and, as a ruse, put Charlie in another. Knowing that Scott had a lot more to give us, we stepped on him hard. He was desperate for a deal.

"Hey," Scott finally said to us, "I just gave Charlie up. That should be worth something, right?"

"Sorry to tell you this, Scott," Georgie said, playing the game, "but Charlie tells us you danced many times before on this. We'd love to go with you instead of Charlie, but you'll have to do better than that."

As Georgie kept putting the screws to Scott, I went through the stuff we'd found in his pockets. For some reason, he'd been carrying his passport. The pages bore so many entry and exit marks that the document looked like a foreign stamp collection.

"Quite the world traveler, ain't you, Scott?"

"Hey, man," he said. "I'm just a mule. I get paid for delivering the shit."

Now he had my interest. "By the Colombians?" I asked.

"Aw, no, man, no, I'm not goin' there. I'm not lookin' for no fuckin' Colombian necktie." Colombians were notorious for a particularly nasty form of execution by ripping an informant's tongue out, then feeding it back down his throat and yanking it out front again through a fresh hole gouged in the informant's neck.

"Well, we need more from you, something else," I said. "Otherwise you know where you'll be ending up."

Scott wiped his mouth. "Look, I've done business overseas. Muled cocaine to Europe. There were these guys in England, part of a syndicate. Tough motherfuckers. Cut your balls off, you so much as look at 'em cross-eyed. I kept putting 'em off, but they've been dying for me to mule heroin back into the States."

"This heroin, where's it coming from?"

"Iran. The Sicilians bring into England. Then these English fuckers find a buyer. And, lemme tell you, they'd cream in their jeans for a steady customer over here."

"So how do you propose to get us into these people?" George asked.

Realizing he had no choice, Scott threw in the towel. "I have their phone numbers," he said.

George and I immediately rigged a tape recorder up to the phone. "Call 'em," George instructed.

When Scott got through to England, he talked in code.

"Hey, man," he said, "remember that situation we discussed regarding Uncle Henry? Well, guess what? I met a living cousin of Uncle Henry's in the States, right here in New York."

We heard the party on the other end say, "Well, that's tremendous, mate, 'cause Uncle Henry has been dying to meet his relatives in New York and establish an ongoing relationship."

The Englishman offered to send a sample—that he would be "mailing a book with a letter in it from Uncle Henry."

After the call ended, we sent word to the DEA's London office with the local phone number Scott had dialed. London reported back that the number belonged to Bobby Edwards, a big-time crook who had been linked to narcotics, extortion, counterfeiting, and murder. The organization he worked for was believed to be headed by another British gangster living in Spain.

Now things were really getting interesting. Armed with the info on Bobby's criminal past, we had enough to officially open a new case, dubbed Operation Henry.

A week later, the package from England arrived at Scott's local post office box. We brought it to DEA headquarters. Sure enough, a thick book was inside—*Country Bizarre,* filled with essays and illustrations touting the old-fashioned pleasures of the English countryside, its harvests, its arts, and its crafts.

Stuffed between its pages was a blue envelope on which somebody had written,

Happy Birthday
Lots of Love
Henry, et al.

But when we searched inside the envelope for "the letter," we came up empty.

Scott put down another call to London. "Hey, we just heard from Uncle Henry," he said to his English counterpart. "We got the book. But we can't find the letter."

"Hey, where's your spine, mate!" the voice on the other end spat back.

As soon as he hung up, I tore open the binding. A clear plastic package filled with white powder tumbled out. I opened the package and did my field test, which came back positive for heroin. Our lab later confirmed that it was 80 percent pure.

Tallyho. We were in business.

GEORGE, SCOTT, AND I were met at London's Heathrow International Airport by the country agent from the DEA's London office and officers from Her Majesty's Customs and Excise Department, which traditionally investigated smugglers. The customs officers whisked us back to their London headquarters. Eventually Scott phoned Bobby to arrange a meeting.

BOBBY EDWARDS WAS one nasty-looking motherfucker.

Thin, medium build, pasty white complexion, deep-set eyes, long hair, nasty scars crisscrossing his high cheekbones, and a gold earring dangling from one lobe. He looked like a pirate.

When we met up with him at a London pub, he had two others with him. I was pretty certain all three of them were packing.

I was dressed casually in a Ralph Lauren polo shirt, pressed slacks, Italian leather shoes, and a tweed sports jacket. I had shaved off my facial hair after the Barnes trial, just in case some friend of Nicky's might have been looking to whack a bearded Louie D., but I had recently grown back the mustache. Georgie looked his Brooks Brothers best.

"Nice to meet you boys," Bobby said in a thick Cockney accent.

I introduced myself as "Louie Canelda" and George as "my partner, the Greek." Then, lapsing into my best Red Hook mob accent, I gave Bobby my pedigree, explaining that I was related to a "particular family" in New York. "I'm sure you heard of our thing. New York, Chicago, you know what I'm talking about, right?"

Bobby smiled, revealing a mouthful of broken yellow teeth. "Right on, mate, I kinda figured that about you."

"Well, these are the guys you're gonna be dealing with. You got a problem with that?"

"No problem at all," said Bobby.

"Good," I said. "We are in the market for a dependable source of supply. High quality. Reasonable price. Steady flow."

"I think we can do business," said Bobby.

"Okay, but there is one caveat."

"Hell, man," said Bobby, flashing me a big smile and pointing to his ruined teeth. "I've already got too many of those!"

"No, not cavity," I said. "I mean *one condition.*"

"Oh," said Bobby. "Spit it out, mate."

"Once we get rolling, we expect this to be an ongoing thing. We're not gonna get into this piecemeal. Now, of course, I know, like in any business, there will be some hitches. But outside of what's normal, I want this to be a smooth-running operation."

"Understood," said Bobby.

I went on. "Now, to facilitate our first purchase, I have certain contacts. Matter of fact, I have a relative at a U.S. Air Force base here in England who's in charge of loading and dispatching all the C-130 transport planes back to the States. We go through him, we can fly your product straight into New Jersey, no U.S. customs inspections, no hassles, no delays, clear sailing all the way."

Bobby's eyes lit up. He said, "Well, that opens all kinds of doors. Maybe you guys can use your military connection to help us get our product to other parts of the world. We could bring you in on that, too."

I held up my hands, playing the ever-cautious businessman. Never wise to be in too big a hurry during the romancing phase. "All is possible with the proper cooperation," I said. "As long as we have a gentleman's agreement, as long as we are honest with one another, there's no end to what we an do together."

Bobby was beside himself. He had the supply routes and the product, but he hadn't been able to come up with the outlets. The chance to bring his dog and pony show into the States was practically giving him a woody. "So whattya wanna start with?" he asked.

"Well," I replied, "we would like to ultimately do a forty-kilo deal. But let's start out with a dry run for four kilos up front and, say, $50,000 for each kilo."

When Bobby agreed to the terms without trying to push the price higher, I immediately knew we were dealing with the kingpins of the operation. The closer you got to the source, the cheaper the dope. It meant there were fewer middlemen taking their cuts—the more palms you needed to grease, the higher the cost . . . as much as $150,000 a kilo.

We were negotiating directly with the big guns.

* * *

AFTER THE MEET, George and I hopped on the London Underground. We were scheduled to rendezvous with our counterparts at British Customs and report back on our meeting with Bobby Edwards.

And that's when my survival instincts suddenly kicked in.

As we rode the Tube, I stole a glance into the next car. Yep, just as I thought. Then I looked at George.

"George, let's go to another car."

"Why?" he said. "I'm fine in this one."

"I think we're being followed."

"Followed? Followed by who?"

"Followed by those two shitbirds in the next car who keep giving us the hairy eyeball."

George whipped his head around.

"Jesus, George, please don't turn your head around. Whattya doin'?"

"You're crazy, Lou. You're seein' things. C'mon, what's with this dramatic shit?"

"Georgie," I said, grabbing him under the elbow, "you never fucking pick up on what I'm tellin' you! You gotta get smart about this shit!" Fortunately, George and I could say just about anything to each other without ruffling any feathers. Just before hustling him into the next car, I deliberately dropped my keys on the floor. This gave me an excuse to kneel down, pick them up, and put a good eye on the tails. The two of them were definitely moving on us.

As we slammed the car door shut behind us, I told George, "Next stop, we get off. Then we count to three and jump right back on again, just before the doors close. Like in *The French Connection*. Got it?"

"Got it," said George.

When the stop came up, we did our subway shuffle, leaping back on the train an instant before the doors closed again.

"I see 'em, I see 'em!" said George.

Looking royally pissed off, the two tails stood on the platform, muttering and cursing as our train pulled out again and left them in its wake. "That's the way the blokes do it over here," one of the Customs officers later told us. "No matter how well things might be going, they always put a tail on their associates."

After that, we spotted even more of them. I came to believe that one of the clerks at our hotel's front desk was actually a Bobby man, by the way he looked at us every time we came into or walked out of the lobby.

AT OUR SECOND meeting with Bobby Edwards, he had someone else with him.

Unlike Bobby, this new player didn't look like a street pirate—he was tall, white-haired, perfectly coiffed, clean-cut, and smartly dressed. And he sounded like he was schooled at Oxford. Bobby introduced him as Ron Leslie.

Leslie had brought a heroin sample with him, which he gave me for a taste. When I went into the men's room to do my field test, it came back righteous.

Back at the table, we finalized the price for the four-kilo purchase. But Leslie insisted on one more step before consummating the deal. "You know, gents," he said, "it's like when we were little kids, playing doctor and nursie. I've shown you mine. Now you need to show me yours."

We needed to prove that we were good for the money.

"I'll have my bank wire a letter of credit to the Bank of England," I said. "Once it arrives, I will bring you into the bank and show you the money personally."

"Splendid," said Leslie. And he got up to leave with Bobby.

"Oh, one last thing," I said. Leslie turned back to me. "I've told you who I am, my history, my connections, et cetera, et cetera, et cetera. And, with all due respect, when I do business with someone, I like to know who I'm dealing with."

Leslie smiled. "Perfectly understandable, old chum," he said. "So I suggest you gents take a look at the chronicles from the sixties. Especially the part about a train."

Chronicles? Train? What the fuck was Leslie talking about?

FORTUNATELY, THE BRITS were able to clear up the mystery.

A search of old newspapers turned up a 1968 interview that Leslie had given to *News of the World*. He claimed to have sprung a fellow named Ronald Biggs from London's Wandsworth Prison three years earlier.

And Ronald Biggs, as nearly any Englishman with a noggin could have told you, was perhaps the most celebrated participant in the biggest heist in English history: the Great Train Robbery.

Along with fifteen cohorts, one of whom could have been Leslie, Biggs had boarded the Glasgow-to-Watford mail train in 1963 and made off with mail sacks containing £2.6 million (which, adjusted for today's inflation, is equivalent to roughly $56 million in U.S. currency).

Captured by the police, Biggs had been sentenced to thirty years in prison. But fifteen months into his sentence, he escaped. And Leslie had taken credit for helping to orchestrate his getaway.

Recruited by a pal over a pint of beer at an East London

pub, Leslie had purchased a secondhand furniture van. The roof of the van was cut away and outfitted with a special platform. After driving the van up to the prison wall, Leslie had tossed a rope ladder over the thirty-foot wall, enabling Biggs and three other inmates to scale the wall and drop through the van's roof, onto several piled mattresses. The escapees then scrambled into a getaway car, with Leslie at the wheel.

After his escape, "Biggsy" had gone on the lam, using a fake passport to flee first to Paris, where he acquired new identity papers and, thanks to plastic surgery, a new face; then to Australia and finally to Brazil, where he married a nightclub dancer and sired a son. Over the years, he had repeatedly eluded Scotland Yard and become the stuff of legend back home in England.

Many things about Ron Leslie were not known. Had he actually participated in the Great Train Robbery itself? It was not clear. Nor was it clear why he had chosen to give his tell-all interview to *News of the World* in the first place. Not wanting to bring suspicion upon ourselves, George and I did not press Leslie for answers to these questions. However, the paper later reported that he had received $26,000 for helping Biggs escape and had served 3½ years in prison.

What was unmistakably clear was that Leslie was now consorting with big-time drug dealers such as Bobby. If we could make a solid case against Leslie, the Brits felt they could pressure him into luring the fugitive "Biggsy" back to England to serve the remainder of his sentence.

IT WAS TIME to bring Scotland Yard into the investigation. British Customs and Excise arranged a meeting.

Dressed in their buttoned-down blue tunics and starched

white shirts, the two Scotland Yard inspectors spoke with crisp, courtly accents, and their elegant, refined manner unnerved me. We talked about our status as American DEA agents operating on English soil. Technically, we were functioning as agents provocateurs, foreign undercover operatives trying to entice English nationals into committing crimes. While everybody felt it was a historic first, technically it was also illegal. So it was agreed that, for the record, neither George nor I were actually in the country.

We laid out the planned meet with Ron Leslie at the Bank of England. Scotland Yard agreed to pull the strings to make the necessary cash available for us to show him. They also introduced us to a team of police sharpshooters who would protect our backs.

GEORGE AND I met up the next day with Leslie outside the Royal Bank of England. As the three of us entered, I glanced over at one of the uniformed security guards in the lobby.

Jolly good day there, sharpshooter one.

We were escorted to the office of one of the bank officers. When we entered, he was busy going over some records with his assistant, who gave us a bored look.

Tickety-boo, sharpshooter two.

After the introductions and handshakes, the bank officer and his phony assistant escorted us to a private conference room. Walking with them down the hallway, we passed a handyman who was polishing some antique lamps.

Keep your pecker up, sharpshooter three.

Farther down the hallway, we had to step around a janitor in overalls and workman's cap who was mopping the floors.

Balls to the wall, sharpshooter four.

Once we were seated inside a private conference room, two tight-lipped men in dark, pinstriped suits entered, carrying aluminum safety deposit boxes, which they carefully placed on the table in front of us.

Hail Britannia, sharpshooters five and six.

As soon as all the others had left, I flipped open the lids on the boxes and flashed Leslie $2 million in U.S. currency and British pounds sterling. He thumbed through the American bills. Then he picked up one of the pound notes and ripped it in half, neatly decapitating Her Majesty, Queen Elizabeth.

Bringing the ragged edge of one torn half up close to his eyeball, he marveled, "See that silver thread going through there, gents? The British pound sterling is one of the greatest notes ever made," he said as he turned the torn note over and over in his hands. "It is just about impossible to counterfeit."

"You seem to know a lot about that sort of thing," said George.

"Well, gentlemen, this, after all, was my game," said Leslie. "At one point, I produced enough counterfeit peseta notes to undermine the entire economy of Spain. But my warehouse caught fire and burned to the ground. Every one of my beautiful pesetas . . . What can you say? Life can be so cruel."

Satisfied we had the money to pay for the forty kilos of heroin, Leslie was ready to do the test run.

THE EXCHANGE WOULD take place in a London hotel. George and I had booked two rooms—one for ourselves, one for Leslie. A third room was commandeered by British Customs agents and Scotland Yard sharpshooters.

Inside our room, George and I double-checked the

$200,000 we had brought to pay for the four kilos. Inside his room, Leslie readied the four kilos. And in the third room, a dozen British law enforcement agents donned bulletproof vests and loaded ammo into their rifles and machine guns.

The plan was for me to bring Leslie to our room so he could see the cash. Then I would accompany him back to his room so I could see the heroin. From there, I would telephone George to let him know that Leslie and I were on our way back in our room with the merchandise.

The *real* plan, however, was something quite different. If, for any reason, I returned with anyone but Leslie, or in addition to Leslie, George was to treat it as a rip-off. He was to stall for time, then immediately call the command post so the British cops and agents would rush our room.

If, upon coming back to our room and announcing myself by saying "George, open the door," that would signal George that the guy or guys accompanying me had their guns out. And George would know to wait for our backup. If I said anything other than that, it meant the people accompanying me did not have their guns in hand and he could, if he chose to, open the door to us and wield his own gun, which had been given to him by British Customs. Either way, he could count on me to back his play. And either way, Leslie and his boys were going down. But it was still a very dangerous situation, since the guys accompanying me would be armed.

The first part of the plan went off smoothly. Leslie came to our room and inspected the $200,000 in cash. Then I returned with him to his room and saw the four kilos of heroin, along with the two Sicilian goons Leslie had brought along to safeguard his stash, both of whom looked like professional assassins.

Inside Leslie's room, I did my standard Marquis field test

on a sample. It came back righteous. But when I tried to put the call down to Georgie, I couldn't get through. Fucking English telephones! No matter how many times I tried, the hotel operator simply could not make the connection.

Leslie grew edgy. Finally, to my dismay, he said, "We'll reschedule for another time." Then he nodded to the two Sicilians to pack up all the heroin. Out the door they marched.

Scrambling for the room phone again, I finally got through to George. "Georgie!" I said, gasping. "Cocksuckers are in the wind!"

George alerted the Brits. What happened next was straight out of a cartoon. Doors ripping open, then slamming shut. Bad guys dashing out of one room, cops and agents barging into another. Then vice versa. Then bad guys and cops huffing and puffing up one hallway, racing down the next, then charging up to the next floor to repeat this madcap relay race all over again. Then the entire lot of cops and bad guys exploding into the stairwell, everyone bonking headfirst into everyone else and toppling en masse into a pile of writhing, sweating, cursing flesh.

When it was all over, Leslie and his two Sicilian goons were under arrest. And so were Georgie and I.

The idea was to throw us into jail right alongside the others. That way we might be able to glean even more information, maybe even come up with the rest of the forty kilos.

Unfortunately, the whole prison ruse turned out to be a bust. Once we were all in our cells, the real gangsters clammed up. And I had to spend the entire night with one eye glued to my bunkmate, the bigger of the two Sicilians, whose ripe body odor was industrial-strength and whose face looked like it had run into the business end of a butcher knife.

Within a week, George and I were back on a plane, for all

intents and purposes being "deported" back to the States. There was no official record of us ever having been in Britain, much less having worked an undercover investigation with the British authorities. In effect, it had never happened.

But thanks to the inroads we had made working undercover, the Brits did arrest Bobby Edwards and his merry band of cutthroats, eventually seizing more than fifty kilograms of heroin.

BACK HOME AFTER England, I began angling again for that promotion.

Midway through 1981, DEA headquarters in Washington notified New York that it could promote six agents to GS-13. My phone started ringing off the hook with congratulatory calls from other agents across the country, all certain that one of those promotions was earmarked for me.

On the day the promotions were handed out, I sat behind the desk in my office, waiting for the call. From my desk, I watched the other five agents walk one by one down the hallway toward the office of the associate regional director, who was giving out the good news. All of them were good guys and fine agents, and all of them had seniority. But given my job performance, I felt I was at least as deserving as they were.

By 5:30 p.m. there was one slot left to fill. Just before six o'clock, a sixth agent walked past my door.

I waited several minutes, until the sixth new GS-13 had shaken the boss's hand and left to celebrate. Then I marched into the director's office. The minute he saw me, he knew why I was there. My expression told the whole story.

"Settle down, Louie," he said immediately. "You were right

up there. It was so close all around that it came down to throwing darts to make the picks."

"My life is not a fucking dart game," I snapped. "How the fuck could you do this?"

The director hemmed and hawed and made lame excuses, whereupon I shouted at him, "This is so fucking wrong, man! As far as I am concerned, you can kiss my ass in Macy's window!"

I spun around, walked out, and went straight to see my group supervisor, Jeff Hall, who had been pushing hard for my promotion. Realizing what had happened, he shook his head with disgust.

"I'm going home," I told him. "And I have no idea when I'll be back."

He nodded glumly. There was nothing he could really say.

I was gone for more than a week, technically AWOL, but Jeff covered for me so there wouldn't be any repercussions. During my time away, I did some heavy soul searching. And eventually I came to a conclusion about what I needed to do next.

No, I wouldn't quit. I had never done that before, and I wasn't about to quit now. I would rather die on my feet fighting.

I would come back stronger than ever. Fight even harder.

And when I finally did return, I did exactly that, working more good cases, both with and without Georgie. I also went up to see the New York office's personnel director, Joe LaRocca, who had always been a booster, especially after my boxing triumphs.

"Joe," I said, "what do I have to do get my damned GS-13?"

He got up and closed the door. Then he sat down on the edge of his desk, leaving only a few inches between us. He lowered his voice.

"Look, Lou," he said, "you never heard this from me, okay? But if you go through the chain of command and get the green light from your immediate superiors, you can actually request an *internal* field audit by DEA headquarters in Washington. It's rarely done, but it is a way to be reconsidered for promotion without going outside DEA channels and getting all the bosses' bowels in an uproar."

Jeff Hall, my supervisor, quickly got on board for this unorthodox move. But when I went in to see the new associate regional director, a hard-core paper pusher, he threw up his hands. "You do this, Lou, and you'll be risking your career," he said. "Remember what happened to those other agents who pushed for an audit? They all got knocked down to GS-11s. Is that what you want?"

My anger rose. "Fuck it," I said. I slammed my shield and gun on his desk. "They demote me, I resign."

The new director sighed and shook his head. He pushed my shield and gun back toward me, then said, "It's your funeral, Lou. Go ahead if that's what you want to do. I'll authorize your request. Just don't come crying back to me if you get kicked in the nuts, which you most assuredly will."

IN THE SUMMER of 1981, I officially submitted my request for an internal audit to Joe LaRocca, who forwarded it to Washington. It wasn't until October that an audit was conducted by an administrative officer in Washington. Shockingly, while many of my cases were reviewed, Nicky Barnes was not one of them.

Timelinewise, it did not fall within the requisite parameters for review.

But as God would have it, on December 13, 1981, I was promoted to GS-13—the first DEA agent ever to receive a promotion by way of an internal audit. I had once again risked it all in a very different fight for my life—the eternal struggle of office politics—and emerged victorious. My actions kicked down the door for other good agents to gain their own well-deserved GS-13 promotions by following a similar path.

CHAPTER FIFTEEN

IT ALL CAME DOWN to this: When I was on the job, at the wheel, in the spotlight, I felt fulfilled and happy. When I was a supporting player, not operating at full strength or actively involved in a case of my own, I fell into a funk.

The job became the centerpiece of my emotional life and my self-esteem, the spine on which all else depended. And if it wasn't going well, I would take a nosedive.

After Operation Henry ended, that's exactly what happened: George and I hit a full-on dry spell. Other agents in the office started making the big cases. Then George's longstanding dream came true and he snagged a transfer to Greece. Left on my own and relegated to a supporting role, I slipped into depression.

I needed a change, so I landed a transfer into the DEA-NYPD Joint Task Force. I had wanted to move into this unit because it offered a new environment and new challenges. I would be working not just with federal agents but with city cops and state troopers as well. The task force was more proactive than other units I had been assigned to, preferring quick strikes to prolonged investigations. In it, I could take a break from being the lone casemaker. Everyone in this unit was a casemaker. I bounced around the task force for close to two years, but my task force tour did nothing to help me shake the blues. I felt like a candle that has burned out at both ends. Something dramatic needed to happen.

I was fried in New York.

WHEN I HAD first joined the DEA, my dream had been to one day relocate to Southern California. Iris's parents and sister Gladys had moved to California shortly after we married. And about four years into my DEA stint, my own family—Mama, Papa, and Alfonsito—relocated to Ventura County, a coastal area northwest of Los Angeles. So there were plenty of reasons for us to go west.

I had tried on and off for ten years to transfer to California, without success. At one point I had put in for a group supervisor's position in San Diego. The job went to someone else.

Looking for a way to jump-start my career again, I pulled a few strings and got myself reassigned to the DEA squad at John F. Kennedy International Airport, a fifteen-minute drive from home. It turned out to be a dumb move. While the location was great and the work was easy, few of the cases were generated by DEA. Almost all were hand-me-downs from U.S. Customs after its agents had made airport arrests and drug seizures. The investigations seemed secondhand and trivial, the environment was sterile, and many of the other agents, though decent guys, seemed to be operating as though they were just serving out their sentences—hardly the kind of go-getters I liked to run with.

The airport gig plunged me into an even gloomier state of mind. The only way was I was able to keep my sanity was to pick up my gloves and start boxing again, which I was able to do when my old buddy, an ex-sparring partner in the DEA-

NYPD Joint Task Force, Carl Schroeder, asked me to help him train the NYPD's newly formed boxing team.

Then, out of the blue, an opening cropped up in the DEA office in Santa Ana, California. I jumped on it with both feet. If I wanted it, I learned, it was all mine. Iris and I were giddy with happiness.

But just as quickly, fear washed over me: What was I doing?

My son, Louis Jr., was doing well at high school in Queens, playing second base on the JV baseball team and having a stellar year at the plate and in the field. My daughter, Maria, was about to graduate from grammar school. Both had wonderful friends, most of whom they had known since they were little kids. Iris and I had devoted our lives to our children's happiness, yet now we were putting it all at risk. How many times had I heard horror stories about other agents who had hopscotched from one city to another or from one country to another, with tragic consequences? Taken away from their friends and families, their wives had become angry, sullen, and depressed, and their kids, feeling disconnected and rootless, had screwed up in school, fooled around with drugs, or gotten into trouble with the law.

What the fuck was I doing?

I began to suffer sleepless nights, break into cold sweats, pace aimlessly around the house. Flip-flopping endlessly in my feelings, I drove Iris nuts.

First it was . . . *It's a great opportunity for us. We'd be fools not to take it. Besides, I've reached the end of my rope in New York. I'm fried, unmotivated, depressed, constantly frustrated. I need to make this change for my own peace of mind.*

Then it was . . . *How the hell can we do this to the kids? Uproot them? Take them away from all their friends? From their schools, where they're doing so well? How can we be so cruel and so selfish? We must be insane.*

The deadline was fast approaching . . . and in May 1985, I made the decision.

I apologized to Iris for subjecting her to all my paranoia, worrying, and second-guessing, and told her we would move to California.

THE FIRST FEW weeks in Costa Mesa, California, were hell.

A satanic serial killer, Richard Ramirez, aka "the Night Stalker," was on the loose in Southern California. When news broke that he had killed a couple not far from Costa Mesa, we were all badly shaken. For nights on end, the kids slept with Iris and me in our bedroom. Lady lay on guard at the foot of the bed. It wasn't until the end of August, when Ramirez was finally captured, that we felt we could let down our defenses.

Meanwhile, I struggled with a totally new and unfamiliar law enforcement milieu. Although good guys, the California cops seemed like they were from some other planet. They had professionally styled haircuts, neatly trimmed mustaches, even polished fingernails. They wore form-fitting, custom-tailored shirts and pants, their buttons perfectly aligned with their belt buckles. Their brass and silver insignia sparkled in the endless sunlight. Their patent leather shoes and holsters gleamed. Their handcuffs, nightsticks, and other equipment were all positioned with textbook precision. To me, they looked like male Barbie dolls.

But they lacked the chutzpah I was accustomed to.

Then there was my new DEA office in Santa Ana, run by Frank Briggs. Frank and I had as much in common as salt and pepper—I was an ethnic street guy from Brooklyn, and Frank was a cowboy-style Marlboro man. But Frank turned out to be a solid boss and a stand-up guy, and he helped me make the transition into my new gig.

But it was a whole different story with the other agents in the Santa Ana office. They were decent guys, but cut from a very different cloth than I was. With them, my personality went over like a lead balloon. Instead of being accorded the respect I had earned as a senior agent in New York, I was treated like a washed-up, self-promoting whack job. Out here, nobody even knew who Nicky Barnes was. I had no standing, no history, no clout. What's more, I had no contacts, no informants, no markers to pull in. I didn't know any DAs or assistant U.S. attorneys. I didn't even know how to get to the DEA's office or the federal courthouse in Los Angeles, and I developed a real phobia about going up to either, since it required driving fifty miles north in bumper-to-bumper freeway traffic. To me, L.A. seemed like a plastic wannabe city, one big, sprawling, ugly shopping mall with no heart, no spirit, no substance, and no purpose.

Out in the field, I had a hellish time with surveillance details. With all its causeways, freeways, highways, and whatever-the-fuckways, California made me dizzy. I'd drive around with one hand on the wheel and the other on a big map, constantly flipping it over and inside out, trying to figure out where I was and where I was heading. I knew New York City like the back of my hand, yet out here in Orange County I was a bumbling idiot. It was particularly embarrassing when I tried to keep up with everyone else in a surveillance and suddenly found myself stranded and alone in unfamiliar territory. The other units would radio back to pinpoint my location, but I couldn't give it to them . . . because I myself had no fucking clue.

The cases themselves were different, too, especially those involving Mexican drug dealers. I just didn't have a good handle on them. Plus, they trafficked in brown, Turkish taffy heroin, which they sold in chunks secreted inside balloons. Given its consistency, I couldn't use my field kit to break it down the way I did with the powdery white and beige heroin back in New York. The only way to break it down would have been to put it in a blender, but out here no heroin dealer in his right mind would have stood for that shit. So I pretty much focused on the handful of Colombians who were dealing cocaine. As a result, I felt like a bench player, underutilized.

The funk permeated my personal life as well. The homes in Costa Mesa were immaculate, their lawns meticulously manicured. The neighbors were cordial, fit-looking, and laid-back. Pristine ocean beaches lay just a mile away. The weather was glorious.

Then I'd glance out the window of our new house and see . . . nothing. Absolutely nothing.

It was dull. Dreary. And lonely.

Our families were out here, but they weren't exactly around the corner. Iris's sister was sixty miles away, our parents forty miles farther. The drive north to see them, which we made every weekend, was grueling.

Meanwhile, my son, Louis Jr., suffered a crushing setback when he learned that he wouldn't be starting at second base on the high school team after all. The coach, intending to keep him in reserve all along, had sold me a crock of bullshit when I first came out to talk with him. Game after game, I had to watch my kid sitting on the bench, looking like the stuffing had been kicked out of him. Knowing he harbored fantasies of one day playing in the pros, I was stricken with guilt over what I felt I had done to him, and I would have to walk away from the field so nobody could see me cry.

At night, I'd toss and turn in bed, then drag my ass out the next morning completely exhausted, my sleep-deprived brain wracked by all kinds of ugly thoughts. The paranoia, worrying, and second-guessing that I thought I had put to rest in New York had come roaring back into my life with a vengeance.

What the fuck have I done to my son? Have I completely ruined his life? Have I ruined it for the rest of the family, too? Have I wrecked my own career? My future? My happiness? What a selfish fool I was to have dragged us all out here!

No matter how hard I tried, I couldn't turn it off. And then, because my feelings were getting to me in such a big way, I'd worry that I was allowing myself to become *mushad* (an Italian-American slang word for overcooked and soft, like pasta).

Finally, at work I got into dustups with other agents. Given my fragile and depressed state of mind during this period, I was hearing every other word as a dig, an insult.

When a boss jumped on me about my paperwork in front of everyone else, I wanted to tear his heart out and eat it. I let it be known that if he ever did it again, no matter when, no matter where, I'd rearrange his face.

Out in the field, when one of the agents broke my balls about getting lost— "Hey, fellahs," he radioed over the DEA's airwaves, "let's pull over for a siesta and wait for Lefty Louie"—I went berserk. After catching up, I yanked him out of his vehicle and jacked him up against the side of his car. "You think this is funny, motherfucker?" I spat at him. "You wouldn't make it for one day in New York, you fuckin' prick."

Nobody else said a word.

Obviously I was not in a good place.

Iris could see that I was struggling with my self-esteem and mired in misery. She worried that I was bringing everyone else in the family down with me. She insisted I get help.

The DEA had an employee assistance program that

offered counseling. I made an appointment with the therapist who ran it, Cecily Kahn. In the interests of confidentiality, she suggested we meet somewhere away from the DEA's office. We picked a local coffee shop.

On the day of the appointment, I was nervous. I had never opened up to an outsider about my deepest, darkest feelings. It seemed unmanly and mushy—totally out of character for a tough-as-nails guy like me.

When I arrived at the coffee shop, I brought a huge bouquet of fresh flowers and handed it to Cecily. She was surprised, maybe even a little irked. This was not something new patients ordinarily did. Was I trying to romance her? Win her over? It was a professional therapy session. Just what was I trying to pull here?

But after I explained how ill at ease I felt, how I needed to behave in the Old World ways I had been taught since childhood and how meeting a woman for lunch for the first time required certain gentlemanly gestures, Cecily seemed more accepting of my offering. It was something I needed to do to feel like a man. Cecily, to her credit, realized that.

Cecily immediately put me at ease. After our first session at the coffee shop, we arranged to meet again, in her office. Over a period of months, I began to learn things about myself. For instance:

That my depression stemmed from other triggers besides uprooting my family and myself from New York.

That it also resulted from my lifelong quest to gain approval from a disapproving parent.

That even if he was approving, Papa would never, ever show it.

That I was always trying to measure up to him, but in my own mind, I never could.

That, notwithstanding all of the above, I was consumed with the need to be a better father to my own kids than Papa had ever been to me.

That lots of other agents of my generation, particularly in DEA, had grown up with abusive fathers.

And that, just like me, many of those agents had turned to careers in law enforcement as a way of resolving their issues with authority and power.

I began to understand that I was not alone. It was an epiphany. Over the coming weeks, Cecily and I continued to meet and talk.

But there were setbacks.

One day, while riding in an elevator with another DEA agent, I spotted some guys who gave me a bad vibe—in fact, they looked downright menacing. So I instinctively opened my jacket and tapped my gun so they could see it. But some of the other passengers freaked at the sight of my gun and bolted off the elevator at the first opportunity. After it was over, the other DEA agent pulled me aside and said, "Lou, you gotta take it easy here. You're starting to scare me."

I hashed over the incident with Cecily. Realizing I could eventually end up hurting myself or someone else, she urged me to confide in my supervisor, Frank Briggs, the one guy I totally trusted and respected in my new DEA office.

With Cecily's encouragement, I made a painful decision.

I would voluntarily give up my guns.

Frank agreed to temporarily lock my weapons in his safe. When the time was right, he would give them back to me. No one else would know about this because no one else would be notified and no report would be written. Nothing would ever go on my record. The whole thing would be kept hush-hush, just an informal understanding between Frank and me.

Outside of my therapy, some positive things started to happen. Iris found a nursing job a couple of miles from our house in Costa Mesa and came to love working there. My daughter, Maria, made lots of great friends at her new school. After the kick in the teeth he had suffered at the beginning of the baseball season, Louis Jr. beat out his competition for the starting position at second base and excelled on his new team. My old friend in Queens, Ray D'Angelo, and my ex-partner at the Equal Employment Opportunity Commission office in Jersey, Pat Matarazzo moved to the West Coast and settled in San Diego. Two other couples from back home moved to nearby Las Vegas. Other, newer friends came into our lives.

Slowly but surely, my thinking began to change. New York no longer loomed as some lost paradise, the magical kingdom of my past glories. The more time that went by, the more I realized how tense and stressful it had all been for me back east. California was not such a terrible place after all.

Back on the job, I got my guns back. And my mojo, too. I started to roll with the punches, not take everything so personally, using my noodle instead of my knuckles.

When a local police lieutenant insisted on a prolonged, puffed-up, self-important round-table discussion with twenty other cops about an undercover buy I was about to make with a state narc, I resisted going off on him like I would have done in the old days. Instead, I resorted to a little psychology to show him the futility of his talking about "operational procedures" and "deep cover strategies."

"Lieutenant," I said, "with all due respect and with all your experience, you don't actually think the deal is gonna go off according to plan, do you? Because, if you do, you are leaving out two very important elements. First, the bad guys ain't looking to cooperate with your plans. And second, they've got plans of their own, which my partner and I, being on the inside, should have the right to agree with or not agree with. Bottom line, don't you think that, for the most part, it should be our game and our calls?"

It got so quiet in that room that you could hear a mouse pissing on cotton a block away.

But the other cops and agents welcomed my forwardness and my way of looking at things, and the lieutenant eventually came around to my way of thinking, too. It was a turning point for me. In the end, we arrested two subjects and seized two kilos of cocaine. And the lieutenant and I actually became friends.

As I got a bit more familiar with the streets, I started pulling some of my old daredevil driving stunts . . . wheelies, illegal U-turns, speeding in reverse or the wrong way down one-way streets, running lights.

When one of the local cops got "stuck" at a red light, I radioed him to just "pop" the light because we needed him to take point on our surveillance detail. The cop later tried to read me the rule book: "We don't do that out here. We obey all the laws and all the traffic regulations."

I smiled and gave him a friendly pat on the shoulder. "Look, pal," I said, "a lot of jobs give their employes perks. Bakers get to take home a loaf of bread. Pressmen get to take home a daily newspaper. And cops get to bust a fucking light when they have to."

Yeah, I was the old Louie D. again, back in form, kicking ass.

But I still needed one more thing to make me complete. A case that would get my old juices going. A case that would put me back in the driver's seat. A case that would challenge me by pushing me to my limits. A case that would put me in real danger.

Well, I got it. In the grand scheme of things, it would turn out to be bigger than I ever could imagine.

CHAPTER SIXTEEN

THE EXISTENCE OF THE Medellín cartel had not become fully known to the DEA until the early 1980s.

It was unearthed in Chicago as part of Operation Blast Furnace, a sting operation engineered by DEA agents Mel Schabilion and Harry Fullett. When a Colombian middleman came looking to buy thirteen hundred barrels of ether, an essential ingredient in the conversion of coca paste into cocaine, he was steered to a building near Chicago's O'Hare International Airport. Inside the building, Schabilion and Fullett, posing as brokers, offered to sell the Colombian the thirteen hundred drums, each containing fifty-five gallons of ether, for $400,000.

The first shipment was to contain seventy-six barrels. But before it was sent off, DEA technicians rigged two of the barrels with battery-powered transponders—automatic devices that receive, amplify, and retransmit signals. A spy satellite tracked the barrels south, through Central America and into South America, to an area deep inside the jungles of Colombia. The location was so remote that the drug traffickers had dubbed it Tranquillandia or "land of tranquillity."

Alerted by the DEA, the Colombian National Police raided Tranquillandia in March 1984. What they found defied imagination: a huge complex of airstrips and laboratories built to facilitate the refining and shipping of cocaine on a massive scale. Nearly fourteen metric tons of cocaine, worth more than

$1 billion. Ledgers, receipts, and other records—including a death list containing the names of high-ranking Colombian officials.

The next day, the Colombian police burned Tranquillandia to the ground. Enraged, the notorious kingpin of the Medellín cartel, Pablo Escobar, put contracts on the heads of the chief of the drug police and the minister of justice. Both were eventually assassinated.

The bloody retribution was in keeping with Escobar's long history of violence, an ongoing slaughter that claimed the lives of informants, competitors, cops, drug agents, police chiefs, journalists, judges, prosecutors, governors, and even two candidates for Colombia's presidency.

Specific targets were not the only ones marked for death. Anyone in proximity to those targets—wives, children, mothers, fathers, cousins, nieces, nephews, grandchildren—also were fair game. When it was finally over, the corpses of an entire family would be left lying in pools of blood.

In the mid-1980s, the mayhem expanded beyond targeted assassinations. Bombs were detonated at police headquarters, newspaper offices, shopping malls, high-rises, and bull rings. In November 1985, an assault by a 35-member guerrilla team on Bogotá's Palace of Justice resulted in the taking of 300 hostages and the slaughter of the building's administrator, its security guards, half the members of the Colombian Supreme Court, and close to 100 others. Army units later freed 200 of the hostages. It was widely assumed that Escobar had masterminded the attack as a way to dispose of courthouse documents relating to several criminal investigations targeting the cartel. Many of these documents were destroyed in the siege. Finally, in November 1989, bombs planted aboard an Avianca Airlines passenger jet carrying five police informants exploded in midair, causing the plane to crash and taking the lives of all 107 passengers on board. Drug traffickers called a radio station to take credit for the bombing.

Meanwhile, Escobar and the other cartel kingpins continued to pump a ton or more of cocaine worth of billions of dollars into the United States each week.

While the original sting operation had curtailed the flow of ether from the United States to Colombia, the DEA realized it would have to become even more creative if it wanted to truly cripple the cartel. Simply locking up its street dealers was about as effective as picking grains of sand off a beach. As soon as one was knocked out of commission, another would pop up to take his place.

There had to be some other way, some means of striking directly at the cartel's higher-ups. And preferably from the inside.

From experience, the DEA knew that, although relatively indifferent to the arrests of its dealers, the cartel still had one overriding worry: retrieving its money. While they were netting millions from their cocaine sales, the Colombians still had to get the proceeds out of the United States. They couldn't simply bring boxes and bags full of cash to an American bank. U.S. government regulations required that any bank deposits exceeding $10,000 be reported to the Internal Revenue Service. So the Colombians were always searching for new schemes that would allow them to operate below the government's radar.

Realizing this need, the DEA took heed of a tried-and-true adage in criminal investigations: *if you want to get to the real bosses, follow the money.*

* * *

EURIMEX, A MIAMI-BASED company, was an elite money-laundering enterprise. It had multiple bank accounts and a worldwide network of branches ranging from Hong Kong to the Cayman Islands. Its operatives were empowered to wire cash from one account to another until the money eventually made its way to banks in Latin America, where it could be safely withdrawn by the *narcotraficantes* of the Medellín cartel.

Unbeknownst to the cartel, Eurimex was a sham. It had been set up by DEA Special Agent J. D. Miller, a goateed Texan who was faking the Colombians out of their jockstraps.

Miller had created Eurimex to track the money flow and unearth the cartel's bank accounts. Each and every cash transaction was being methodically recorded by the Drug Enforcement Administration. Ultimately, once enough evidence had been accumulated and enough players implicated, the drugs could be seized, assets could be confiscated, and American prosecutors could go before American grand juries and seek RICO indictments—not just against the coke peddlers in the States, but also against the cartel kingpins themselves.

The entire operation had been given a deliciously ironic code name: Pisces.

In astrology, Pisceans are considered easygoing, affectionate, and submissive, never threatening or challenging to stronger and livelier figures.

They also are said to be highly gullible.

At first, the focus was Miami and New York. But, at a certain point, Special Agent Miller learned that one of the cartel's biggest earners, José Lopez—aka "el Tío," aka "the Uncle," aka "Uncle Lopez," aka "Uncle Pepe"—was eager to begin laundering drug money on the West Coast.

This presented the DEA with a golden opportunity. José Lopez was a heavyweight. He owned his own coca plant fields, operated his own laboratories, flew his own fleet of planes. He transported cocaine into the United States for Pablo Escobar. Lopez had a lavish house in Colombia surrounded by a high fence and machine-gun-toting bodyguards. His drug riches had enabled him to purchase vast tracts of land and businesses in Mexico. He even had his own emerald mine.

Someone like José Lopez would come to the hook, but first would have to be lured.

Special Agent Miller had brought Lopez part of the way there by making cash pickups for him in Orange County and San Francisco. But, based in Miami, Miller had to commute regularly between two coasts to manage these transactions, and the time, travel, and paperwork involved were taking their toll. His workload had become untenable.

Miller needed help. A fresh piece of bait, so to speak. Enter Louie D. Given my Mafia-flavored seasoning, my fluency in Spanish, my past undercover drug buys, and my history on the Nicky Barnes case, particularly in washing Nicky's heroin money, the DEA higher-ups figured I could be the fresh minnow to dangle in front of José Lopez's greedy jaws.

Clearly, the assignment would be high-risk. Along with Pablo Escobar, cartel operatives such as Lopez were known to be ruthless killers. And I would be regularly handling significant amounts of his precious cash. These would not be the piddling $10,000 and $50,000 bundles I had moved for Nicky Barnes back in New York. A single pickup for el Tío might contain $150,000 to more than $1 million. One little slip and I could wind up fitted for my very own Colombian necktie or, at the very least, a double tap to the head. Bang bang and bye-bye, Louie D.

Still, I was back, baby. Big time.

The danger I would be facing was a plus, a pick-me-up, a

tonic for what had ailed me. *This* is what I needed to push me back to the top of my game, to pull me out of my despair and depression.

In a strange way, facing almost certain death would make me feel alive again.

FRANK BRIGGS, THE boss of the Santa Ana office of the DEA, and Joe Day, originally out of the Los Angeles office, knew that I had been struggling. They also knew that giving me a role in the investigation would be like throwing me a lifesaver. So they tapped me for the job. After they brought me up to speed on Eurimex, Special Agent J. D. Miller put the wheels in motion for my undercover debut.

First, he instructed the DEA's informant in Bogotá to sell me to el Tío as the West Coast's most deft drug financier and money launderer.

Then, again communicating through his informant, Miller encouraged Lopez to have his coke dealers in Southern California begin delivering their cash proceeds to me for purposes of laundering it.

Using beepers and phones, the dealers started to reach out to me to arrange the pickups. When we spoke on the phone, we would never refer to the money outright. Instead we would talk about "contracts," "statements," "suits," or even "pairs of shoes."

For example, "twenty-five statements" meant $250,000. The dealer would tell me he had the twenty-five statements ready, and I would reply that I was happy to "sign" them. Or he'd say he had fifty suits to be picked up, and I would give him a time and a place to deliver them.

With a surveillance team of agents and local cops watching

my back, I began criss-crossing Orange County, making pick-ups in the parking lots of hotels and restaurants. Often I would pull up in a black Lincoln Continental. Then another car would slide in next to mine. Once I got out, the driver of the second car would emerge, pop the hood of his trunk, and pull out the box, suitcase, gym bag, whatever, that contained the drug money. I would take the box or bag, put it in my own trunk, and depart.

It was like driving up for takeout. Only instead of leaving with a Big Mac and a chocolate shake, I'd pull out with several hundred grand in cold cash.

Maneuvering along the highways in a roundabout, helter-skelter manner—with my backup team now following me—I would make my way back to the DEA's Santa Ana office. Meanwhile, the local cops, who'd also been in on the stakeout, would key on the dealer, tailing him back to his home or "stash house" to begin building a collateral criminal case against him.

At the DEA office, the cash I had collected would be locked in a safe. The following day it would be carried across the street to the Sun West Bank, counted by automatic cash machines in the presence of the bank's director. The count was always pretty much on the mark, never off by more than a few hundred dollars. The money was then wire-transferred to the Amerfirst Bank in Miami. At Amerifirst, the money would be deposited in an account belonging to Eurimex, the sham corporation run by Special Agent J. D. Miller.

Once the money was in the Eurimex account, 7 percent to 10 percent of the total would be deducted as Eurimex's "commission"—it was actually used to help finance the Pisces sting operation. The rest would be wired into the Panama branch of the United Bank of Switzerland. There, it would be deposited in the personal account of the DEA's Bogotá-based informant.

The informant would then cut a personal check to Medellín kingpin José Lopez or wire-transfer the funds into Lopez's personal account.

Sometimes the money would be withdrawn directly from the Eurimex account and, on orders from Lopez, used in the States to purchase gold, real estate, airplanes and helicopters, eighteen-wheel tractor-trailers or whatever other big-ticket items Lopez happened to fancy.

If it all sounds confusing, remember that was the name of the game. The point was to keep the money hopping, skipping, and jumping from one account to the next and the next and the next, until its route became so convoluted and muddied that it was virtually impossible to trace it back to the coke dealer who had handed it to me in that California parking lot in the first place . . . which was exactly what el Tío, José Lopez, required. In that way the cash could never be tracked directly to him.

Unless, of course, someone happened to be clandestinely watching its progress at each step along the way.

Like the DEA was right now.

THE DEALERS WERE usually Colombian males, sometimes accompanied by women. When I would meet up with them, I would begin a little innocent and naive chitchat. But I would always be trolling for tidbits of useful information.

"How ya doin'?" I'd casually ask as some guy was handing me a satchel from the back of his car. "You feelin' okay? Any problems gettin' here?" or "Everything workin' out for you?" or "Yeah, okay, you know, a lot of my customers live around here" or "You been here long? You miss Colombia?" Make them feel comfortable. Lull them into a false sense of security.

"Nice car you got there," I'd say. To which the scumbag dealer might reply that it was rented, or that he owned it. Either way, I'd make a mental note of the license plate number, which might later yield the dealer's real name, age, home address, and, if he had one, criminal record.

Or, just to tweak a sore spot and play on their machismo, I might remark, "Oh, I thought you guys were just a pickup team for Uncle Lopez."

This would invariably make the dealer bristle. "No, no, this is money for *my* product," he'd fire back. "I only owe *part* of it to el Tío."

And *bam,* I would have the guy dead to rights not once, but twice—first for admitting to peddling the drugs, then for admitting that he was peddling the drugs on behalf of José Lopez. All of which would be nicely recorded on my concealed wire.

After a while I became a sounding board for the dealers, a confidant they felt they could open up to. My cover name was "Lucho," but over time, as I gained their trust, I came to be known as "Don Lucho," as a way of showing respect. Growing increasingly at ease in Don Lucho's presence, the dealers began to talk more openly about their business dealings.

For example, several complained that their product was "fucked," and it was causing their customers to suffer nosebleeds. It turned out that el Tío had been using benzene instead of the now-scarce ether to dilute the cocaine paste, and this substitute cutting agent was highly disagreeable to the nasal passages.

This revelation was significant for two reasons. First, it corroborated that the earlier DEA sting, Operation Blast Furnace, had successfully disrupted the flow of ether from the United States into Colombia. And second, I was later able to work it into conversations with other dealers I was romancing, prompting them to voice similar complaints, and thereby linking themselves to José Lopez's drug-peddling conspiracy. With just a little prodding, I usually could nudge one dealer into acknowledging that he knew, worked with, or worked for one of the other dealers and that all of them took their marching orders from el Tío.

I asked a dealer named Freddie Benitez how he managed to get around Orange County so easily, given that he'd been in California for only eight months after leaving Colombia. Freddie volunteered that he was selling huge quantities of cocaine to a car dealership in Los Angeles. In return for the coke, the car dealership supplied Freddie with cash, cars, phony drivers' licenses, fake registrations, you name it.

More information filed in the back of my head.

Sometime later, I met up with another dealer, Rogelio Rivero, to launder a large amount of cash. When Rogelio let slip that he had a big customer in Marina del Rey—a car dealership—the alarms went off.

"Nice," I said. "Maybe you can get me a good price on a new car?"

"Absolutely," Rogelio said. "And we could also get you whatever kind of phony identification you need—license, registration, the whole nine yards."

"Wow!" I said. "You wouldn't happen to know a guy named Freddie Benitez, would you?"

"Sure, I know Freddie!" said Rogelio. "We have the same connection."

"Huh!" I said, trying to make myself sound completely clueless. But at this point I decided to take a big swing, aiming straight for the fences.

"That wouldn't be Tío Pepe, would it?" I asked.

"Tío Pepe, yeah! How did you know?"

I smiled. "What do you think I'm doing here? I work for him as well!"

Rogelio grinned. "Tío Pepe! El Tío! *Exactamente!*" An open admission that he was moving coke and money for el Tío, the main target of our operation. Grand-slam home run, baby.

Rogelio said he needed to call the car dealer. But after he tried a couple of times on his car phone, he started to get angry. "Shit!" he muttered.

"*¿Qué paso?*" I asked.

"My phone is fucked!" he said.

Thinking quickly, I volunteered my own car phone. "Here, why don't you use this?"

Gratefully, he accepted my offer and made his call.

Later, back at my DEA office, I retrieved the number Rogelio had punched in from my car phone's memory bank. After I traced it to a Chevrolet dealership in Marina del Rey, surveillance was set up on both the car dealership and Rogelio's residence. Over time, probable cause was established. Search warrants were executed. Along with arresting Rogelio, the car dealer, and a bunch of other associates, the DEA and the local cops recovered hundreds of kilos of cocaine and hundreds of thousands in cash.

IN MY BUSINESS transactions with the dealers, I always insisted on timeliness and accuracy.

Show up late for a meet, and I'd deep-six the deal. Give me fewer "statements" than originally promised, I'd back away just as quickly. I needed to maintain my reputation as a reputable professional, someone who could not be trifled with. Any kind of monkey business or corner-cutting simply would not be tolerated . . . despite the potential for violence by the Colombian dealers.

Then again, misunderstandings sometimes could be exploited in eliciting new information. And sometimes I'd provoke them on purpose.

Meeting with one of José Lopez's biggest coke distributors, I agreed to launder a new sum belonging to el Tío. But despite having been told earlier what it would be, I deliberately exaggerated the amount of money. The dealer insisted I had the figure wrong. I threatened to back off the deal until somebody accounted for the missing money—"and that somebody sure as hell ain't gonna be me."

Flustered, the dealer dragged me to a telephone booth and called José Lopez personally in Colombia, even putting me on the phone with him. Speaking in Spanish, el Tío reconfirmed that the amount to be laundered was less than what I had stated. I apologized profusely for the confusion and agreed to the deal as I now understood it.

Then I said my good-byes, quietly celebrating that I had just gotten my conversation with the local dealer and my conversation with el Tío, both of which were highly incriminating to each, on the concealed wire I was wearing.

WHILE I WAS doing my dog-and-pony show in California, J. D. Miller was delivering an Academy Award performance of his own in Miami. Posing as wealthy financier "James Menzer," the putative head of the money-laundering organization that employed me on the West Coast, he was dealing daily with his Colombian informant and, through him, with el Tío.

In fact, el Tío was so pleased with the way it was all going that he decided he wanted to meet Miller in person. So he invited Miller to visit him in Colombia.

José Lopez's home in Bogotá was palatial. Each room was on its own separate level, and the house contained a dance floor with a three-story waterfall. The house was surrounded by a stone-and-iron fence and patrolled by Uzi-carrying bodyguards. Inside this enclave, J. D. Miller talked new business with Lopez, the DEA's first-ever face-to-face encounter with the Medellín cartel.

Over single-malt scotch and the finest Havana cigars, Lopez acknowledged for the first time that he was not just a money-changer but also a major drug lord. He was using his fleet of planes to fly cocaine into Mexico, where it could be trucked across the border into California and Texas. He wanted the Americans to help him expand his empire, purchasing businesses for him, making him loans, buying more airplanes for his fleet. He asked for a helicopter to shuttle him between his coke labs and his landing strips. Miller agreed to buy him a helicopter.

The meet between Miller and Lopez came off so well that Lopez decided to kick up my West Coast business another notch. In January 1986 he notified Miller that he wanted me to connect with a Colombian husband-and-wife team, Eduardo Pantaleone and Clara Velez, on a new wash.

The amount this time? More than a million bucks.

Eduardo Pantaleone was a man of few words, eerily quiet. But below his difficult-to-read exterior I sensed a short fuse and a real propensity for inflicting pain and suffering. I had been around guys like this before, so there was no mistaking what he was: a stone-cold killer.

I met Pantaleone in the rear parking lot of a Mr. Steak restaurant in Anaheim. The million-plus in cash, contained in a large brown duffel bag, was in the trunk of his rented car.

But he spooked me so much that after we parted company and I drove away from the parking lot with the cash, I became convinced that he had enlisted a team of assassins to follow me, rip me off, and make sure I was never seen again. With all that money now sitting in my trunk, I began driving with near-lunatic abandon, speeding up, slowing down, making sudden turns off the freeway, then jumping right back on again to shake possible tails.

With one hand on the wheel, I used the other to radio my backup team. But I couldn't raise anyone on my portable. Waves of fear swept over me. Face-to-face I never feared any of these banditos, but what might be going on behind my back was a whole other matter. Finally I pulled off the road completely, parking behind a motel.

Walking a short distance away from my car to get better reception, I tried my portable again. All I got was squelch.

As I turned back to my car, my heart leaped into my throat.

The lid of the trunk was ajar.

A cold sweat beaded up along the back of my neck. Had I forgotten to close it? Had the cash tumbled out during my mad drive? Had I already been ripped off by Eduardo's assassins? Was I a walking dead man?

I rushed toward the trunk, yanked up the lid. The duffel bag was still there, the cash inside it.

Just then I sensed someone tiptoeing up behind me. Pulling my snub-nosed .38, I wheeled and pointed, ready to blow his head off.

"Freeze, motherfucker!"

A potbellied, middle-aged Mexican yelped and stumbled backward, falling hard on his ass. He was the motel's gardener.

I took out my badge and credentials and, helping him to his feet, apologized profusely in Spanish.

Then I drove around to the front office, where I was able to telephone our DEA base in Los Angeles. Ten minutes later, my backups were at the motel. I was still shaken when they arrived.

AT THIS STAGE, we had moved a total of $8 million into el Tío's accounts. So impressed was he with our performance that he asked for another meeting with Eurimex, only this time on American soil.

Flying into Miami with his chief lieutenant, Alfonso Reyes, Lopez met with J. D. Miller and his DEA supervisor, Richard Gorman, both of whom posed as Eurimex executives. New business was hashed out during a leisurely cocktail party on a fifty-seven-foot Hatteras motor yacht, which the DEA had wired with hidden sound and video equipment. The discussions continued late into the evening at an expensive steak restaurant on the Intercoastal Waterway in Fort Lauderdale.

After Miami, el Tío flew on to Las Vegas, where he proceeded to lose $50,000 at the gaming tables. Then it was on to Los Angeles.

It was time for el Tío to meet Don Lucho in person.

I WAS WAITING outside the lobby of the Marriott Hotel on Century Boulevard in Los Angeles when el Tío pulled up in a rented white Lincoln Town Car with Alfonso Reyes. One of our confidential informants was at the wheel, acting as his chauffeur. I got inside the car with them.

Lopez was bubbling over with excitement. "So this is *the man*!" he exclaimed in Spanish. "The wizard! The magician! The amazing Don Lucho!"

I took stock of el Tío. In his late thirties, thin, clean-shaven, and olive-skinned, Lopez clearly had meanness in his eyes. Indeed, there had been talk he could be unforgiving and ruthless with anyone who dared violate his rules.

While we exchanged pleasantries, the parking lot attendants, bellhops, desk clerks, and guests perusing their morning newspapers in the hotel lobby occasionally shot glances our way. All of them were undercover cops or DEA agents.

We drove to another Marriott, this one in Marina del Rey. In the parking lot we met up with Ricardo, a relative of Lopez and one of his biggest California dealers. Lopez ordered Ricardo to retrieve a gray cloth Samsonite suitcase from the back of his own car. Inside it was more than $300,000 in cash. As Lopez and Reyes stood by my sides watching, Ricardo placed the suitcase in the trunk of our vehicle.

After Lopez and his party headed off to Rodeo Drive to do some high-end shopping, the informant and I brought the Lincoln back to the Marriott on Century Boulevard. Agent Joe Day and the rest of my DEA team were waiting there to take possession of the suitcase full of cash.

It was critical evidence, and it marked a significant breakthrough. For the first time ever, el Tío had involved himself directly in a money wash.

The next day I met Lopez and Reyes for dinner at a seafood restaurant. Over three-pound lobsters and French champagne, el Tío began to muse about the future.

"You know, Lucho," he said, "I like it here. I like it so

much, I'm thinking of buying a home in this place. It's easier to conduct my kind of business in California."

"Yeah," I said thoughtfully, "I know exactly what you mean."

AFTER RETURNING TO Colombia, el Tío sent word that he wished me to launder more money for Eduardo Pantaleone and his wife, Clara Velez. This time I met both of them them outside a restaurant in Costa Mesa. Pantaleone gave me a suitcase containing $390,000.

Ten days later, at the Marriott Hotel in Inglewood, I picked up $135,000 from another dealer.

I was on fire. And so was the rest of the Operation Pisces team. Our undercovers were now moving $12 million to $15 million each month through Eurimex's accounts.

Lopez met again with J. D. Miller to talk business, only this time in Panama. On his trip to Panama, Miller was accompanied by a pregnant woman, whom he described to el Tío as his girlfriend. In reality, she was Tammy Connelly, another DEA agent whom he had brought along to bolster his cover story.

During their meetings, Lopez complained that he had "lost" three of his planes en route to drops in Mexico—they had been seized by the authorities. Left without sufficient air transport, he wanted to borrow one of Eurimex's planes to fly a four-hundred-kilo shipment up from Colombia. Miller said it could be arranged for a fee of $150,000. Lopez agreed that the money could be deducted from the proceeds on the sale of the four hundred kilos.

Piloted by two DEA informants, the plane landed in La Estrella, an area on the northwestern tip of Colombia just outside of Medellín. After picking up its cocaine cargo, it flew back to an airstrip in West Palm Beach, where the four hundred kilos were off-loaded and placed inside a rented U-Haul driven by two other DEA agents. Accompanying the truck, Miller followed it to a drop point in West Palm Beach, where he was to surrender the keys to a member of Lopez's gang. But the gang member showed up two hours late.

So later that night, when the Metro Dade police "intercepted" the truck in South Miami, arrested its occupants, and seized all the cocaine, Miller pinned the blame for the bust on the tardy gang member.

Thankfully, Lopez never became suspicious about who *really* had tipped off the cops.

TO FACILITATE THE pickups in Southern California, we decided to rent an apartment in Newport Beach.

I told the dealers that the apartment would offer us more privacy for our transactions, especially since the building had an underground garage that would better conceal the physical movement of their monies. Unbeknownst to the dealers, the apartment had been rigged with hidden surveillance equipment, allowing us to conduct our launders for the benefit of DEA tape recorders and video cameras. Laying all the cash on a large coffee table, I could thumb through the stacks of tens and twenties and spin the bundles while the drug dealers who sat across from me watching were being secretly recorded.

The agents in my surveillance team would set up in the apartment directly next door to ours and observe us on the hidden cameras. "If it looks like a 'rip,' don't even bother coming around to my door," I told the other agents. "Just break through the fucking wall."

In mid-June, Freddie Benitez brought $185,000 to the

apartment. He warned me to be extra careful—"The managers of these apartment complexes often work closely with the police, you know," he explained.

"Thanks for the heads-up," I deadpanned.

Ten days later, Eduardo Pantaleone showed up with $315,000. "I know you didn't get this selling shoes," I joked.

"Some of the money from the sale of a hundred kilos that el Tío sent me," he said. "He gives it to me for twenty thousand bucks a kilo. Anything I make above the twenty thousand, I keep."

"Nice," I replied, continuing to spin the bundles while the recorders picked up his verbal admissions of criminal activity.

Five days later, at a parking lot outside a Holiday Inn, I topped my previous record for pickups when another dealer handed me a zippered suitcase and a nylon carry bag containing $1.6 million.

The next day, back at the undercover apartment, two other dealers brought me $700,000. And a month after that, another dealer brought me $640,000, part of which was contained in a Kotex Thin Super Maxi box.

With amounts like these, I had stepped up to a whole different league. I was becoming the J. P. Morgan of money launderers. It reached a point where I was routinely handling so much cash that, just to amuse myself, I would dream up ways of absconding with it, giving myself a vulgar thrill. Sometimes my fantasies became so vivid that I would break out in a cold sweat, sickened by the realization that I actually felt temptation. But ultimately I never could come up with an entirely foolproof plan, particularly when it came to protecting my family. Had I actually dared to carry out any of my harebrained schemes, el Tío's cutthroats surely would have come looking for me and my loved ones.

After a while, however, the money began to disgust and nauseate me. Literally. Because of the powdery green dust spit out by the bank's automatic bill counters or coated to the insides of the boxes and bags of cash I was retrieving, I would hawk up and sneeze out green mucus that had accumulated in my throat and sinus passages.

AT THE URGING of el Tío, I discussed doing more washes with Eduardo Pantaleone and Clara Velez. But in July 1986, less than a month after doing my last deal with Eduardo, his temper finally got the better of him. At point-blank range he shot and killed another drug dealer who had been stealing from him. Then he fled to Miami.

The news of Eduardo's cold-blooded act threw a whole new scare into me. Could I be next? Just imagine what this guy was capable of doing if he ever found out who I *really* was. And now he was on the lam, God knows where. I kept my fears to myself, but for weeks I kept wondering where and when the hit might come.

Then, in mid-August, came word that Eduardo had returned to Los Angeles and been stopped on the San Diego Freeway for a minor traffic infraction. When the California Highway Patrol searched his car, they found a 9mm automatic pistol with a silencer. He was arrested and later charged with first-degree murder and conspiracy for the possession, sale, and distribution of a controlled substance.

Finally, I could breathe a little easier.

Right around Labor Day, as I was about to get back into the swing of things on Operation Pisces and do more and bigger money launders, my new supervisor in the Santa Ana office, Richard Canas, dropped a bomb.

"Lou," he said to me one day, "I got some heat on me from Washington to put you on something else."

"How the fuck can they do that!" I protested. "We're in the middle of Pisces."

He tried to mollify me. "Look, I'll pick up the slack while you're gone. But they need a Spanish-speaking agent on this and I don't have anyone else."

I knew he was right. The year before, I had dodged a request to work a border sting in Mexico against traffickers who were bringing coke across the U.S. border. They had tapped another agent for the job, but I couldn't stick him again with the gig. But I stalled as long as I could.

"Well, I ain't fucking going!" I snapped. "Where is this going to end? You think you got your life together and they pull this shit whenever they want to. They say you're indispensable, but the truth is I'm just another fucking body. I don't want to hear any of that shit. I'm tired."

"Down the line," said Canas, "they'll make it up to you."

"They never make it up to you," I replied. "They're just playing on my pride."

Canas had no answer for that. Finally I asked, "So where do they want to send me, anyway?"

Raising his palms toward the heavens, Canas made one of those what-the-fuck-you-gonna do? faces. "Bolivia," he said.

For one of the few times in my life, I was at a loss for words.

CHAPTER SEVENTEEN

LYING ATOP MY COT, peering down at her, I held my breath, every muscle of my body frozen in place.

Clinging to one of my cot struts, she looked back at up me, each spindly leg slowly drawing her bulbous body nearer to my own.

It was a Bolivian stare-down, both of us giving each other the hairy eyeball.

The only difference was that her eyeballs—all eight of 'em, to be exact—actually *were* covered by hair. Fine, dark, slender bristles.

Just below her eyes and directly forward of her mouth, I could make out the *chlicerae* containing the glands that would pump the venom out through her fangs.

Another tippy-toe step upward, executed with the grace and precision of a prima ballerina, and she came within striking distance of my forearm.

She pushed another hairy leg forward. Her eyes seemed fixated on the soft flesh inside my elbow.

Ever so slowly, I reached over and grabbed my M-16. Then, in one lightning move, I banged that fucker off the cot leg.

I couldn't remember how many that made. It was either the fifth or the sixth tarantula I had dispatched that morning.

It had become a ritual. Every morning, as the first rays of equatorial sun peeked through my tent flaps, I awoke to a greeting party of giant spiders. "*¡Buenos días, Señor Louie!*

¡Ahora, vamos a comer!" they seemed to be saying as they hungrily skittered toward me.

And every morning I smacked them away. I was also careful to turn my combat boots upside down and bang them a couple of times on the side of my cot, since the bastards loved to crawl inside.

The Bolivian jungle was an idyllic place. The temperature started off at 65 degrees in the morning, rising to 80 degrees in the afternoon. Each day, I gazed out on palm trees, rolling mountains, and deep blue skies and breathed a sigh of wonder. Tropical vegetation so lush it could swallow you up like breakfast. Flowers so vivid that their colors would hurt the eye. Lagoons, rivers, brooks clear as glass. Wildlife that took my breath away. Riotously colored macaws, toucans, parrots, and motmots. Pink, freshwater dolphins that swam in the rivers, along with alligators, *surubí, piranha,* and *pacú.* Blue *morpho* butterflies as big as kites. Countless varieties of monkeys. Three-toed sloths. Giant anteaters and tapirs and armadillos. Wild peccaries. Jaguars. And the largest and weirdest-looking rodent on the planet, the *carpincho,* which can grow to a weight of more than a hundred pounds.

But along with the magic, the jungle seethed with danger. While out on patrol, one of my men was charged by a spotted leopard, which he shot and later skinned. Another was wounded with an arrow fired by a hostile hiding in the bush. And, along with the tarantulas and lizards, our tents were regularly invaded by jumbo unidentified flying insects.

WHY THE HELL was I here, anyway? In August 1986, the United States had announced that it was sending U.S. Army troops to Bolivia to assist in the war in drugs. By the end of that month,

I had been drafted, landing at the airport in La Paz, the capital. Upon deplaning, I was greeted by eight Bolivian soldiers wearing khaki uniforms and baseball caps. They marched toward me with their machine guns at the ready.

"Agent Diaz," one of the soldiers said in Spanish, "we've been waiting for you." They put me in a car and whisked me away from the airport.

Forty-five minutes later, I had found myself in the DEA's office in downtown La Paz. There, the DEA's country attaché briefed me on my mission: Working with officers and personnel from the U.S. Army's 210th Combat Aviation Battalion, a Blackhawk helicopter assault unit out of Panama, I was to lead commandos from UMOPAR, Bolivia's specially trained drug police, into the Beni and Chupari jungles, locate clandestine cocaine-processing labs, and destroy them. More than a hundred labs were said to be operating in these areas. Our mission was to put them out of commission.

It also was our mission to arrest the *narcotraficantes*—which meant there could be a lot of shooting.

For the next few days I was given more specific briefings about the terrain and the support I would receive. Meanwhile, I tried to cope with my altitude sickness—La Paz is twelve thousand feet above sea level—by brewing mata tea from coca leaves I purchased at one of the open-air markets.

Three days into La Paz, I was driven back to the airport, placed on a fixed-wing Cessna, and flown to Trinidad. When I deplaned, I looked around and saw what looked like a staging area for mercenaries. Heavy trucks and U.S. Army vehicles were stuck in the mud. All sorts of equipment was still on the pallets. Men in fatigues were barking orders to other men marching about in formation. Barbed wire, armed sentries, and machine-gun emplacements surrounded the facility.

Blackhawk helicopters from the 210th Combat Aviation Battalion, DEA Cessna aircraft, and a vintage DC-3 sat on its airfield. This would be the rear base camp for our jungle raids.

I immediately spotted a familiar face, that of Jim Bradley, my old instructor from my DEA academy days. Jim still looked and sounded like a cowboy—weather-beaten face, bushy mustache, barrel chest, and a Texas drawl so smooth it could melt butter. Fluent in Spanish, Jim would be the DEA liaison between the La Paz office and the jungle operations.

Then we drove about a mile to the Hotel Ganadero, where the DEA agents and intelligence officials would be housed. Inside the hotel, I spotted fifteen armed guards stationed in the lobby and the hallways. All were uniformed members of the Leopardo Brigade, UMOPAR's mobile jungle patrol unit.

"Hey, Jimmy," I said as we walked up the stairs, "not for nuthin', but what the fuck's with all the armed guards?"

He quickly put a finger to his lips to silence me. "Not here," he whispered. "Can't talk."

He hustled me toward my room. I used my key to open the door.

Once we were safely inside, he handed me a .357 Magnum. "Watch your ass," he said.

"From those guys?" I asked.

"From *everyone*. This place is crawling with spies, double agents, and snitches working for the cartels."

Speaking in hushed tones, Jimmy warned that everyone was suspect. And the consequences could be dire. The week before, four botanists who had stumbled upon a coke lab in the Bolivian jungle had been brutally assassinated by the narcotraficantes. First, they had been tortured, then dismembered. Suspected informants succumbed to similar fates—beaten, burned, shot, macheted, and disembowled, their dripping innards left hanging from tree limbs as a warning to others.

"Nice of you to tell me these things," I said. "What a fucking mess."

"That's the least of it," said Jimmy.

"What do you mean?"

Jimmy warned that our own people could be just as dangerous as the drug traffickers. The Leopardos, he explained, were simple, backwoods peasants, most of whom spoke their own dialects and not much Spanish. They were great at following orders, but they were not very good at thinking for themselves. Tell them to pull the trigger, and they would immediately begin shooting, no questions asked. They were cold-blooded killing machines, just like the wiseguys back in Bensonhurst who were looking to make their bones.

"So what do we do?" I asked.

"Watch our asses."

I eventually got to meet the Leopardo's commanding officers, who were better educated than the foot soldiers and spoke perfect Spanish. But Jimmy cautioned that they were not to be trusted either. Colonel Velez, a small, courtly man in his fifties, was a consummate professional and a mesmerizing commander. But he was rumored to be on the payroll of the narcotraficantes, bribed to protect the very coke labs we were trying to locate and destroy. Years earlier, it was said that he had participated in a plot to kidnap Bolivia's president, then fled into exile in Spain, returning home only after a new president took office.

Velez's second-in–command, Captain Basilio, was a different breed. Arrogant, posturing, standing with his hands on his waist, goose-stepping around in his polished leather boots with his lower jaw jutting out like a preening Mussolini, he had

Spanish blood, came from a rich family, and had gone to the best military school in Spain. But he behaved like a prima donna, a little Lord Fauntleroy in combat fatigues strutting through the Bolivian jungle.

He also was a complete sadist.

Many times I would watch in horror as he and his sergeants beat their Leopardo foot soldiers. Most of these poor fellows had ragtag uniforms. Some didn't even own shoes. Basilio and his lackeys would smack them so hard in the head that they would fall to the ground. Or they would beat them with sticks until they bled. On seeing these acts of brutality, my knee-jerk anger and disgust for abuse of power quickly kicked in. I wanted to tear their fucking heads off. But I forced myself to keep calm, knowing that to do otherwise would be a very bad move.

When I asked why the officers were treating the men so brutally, one of the sergeants said: "They are so stupid, these campesinos. You have to beat them to death before they learn how to be soldiers."

Unlike their commanding officers, I tried to treat the Leopardos with respect. And because I showed them respect, they began addressing me as "Colonel" Diaz, which was a considerable relief to me.

Once our raids began, these were the guys who would be at my back with loaded carbines. So I sure as hell didn't want them to think I was just one more ugly gringo from el Norte who didn't give a damn about them or their customs, or that I couldn't connect with them on a basic human level. I wanted them to know I was their compadre.

It could end up saving my life.

* * *

IN TRINIDAD, I began debriefing a Bolivian informant who had agreed to work with us.

One day, on the roof of the Hotel Ganadero, Colonel Velez invited me to join him and a group of friends over drinks. While we sat, another man came to our table. Large, tanned, extremely well-dressed, decked out in lots of gold bling, he proved to be a lively and compelling raconteur. He and Velez obviously knew each other well. In fact, when the man first approached us, Velez jumped up and hugged him like a brother.

While we sat schmoozing, I happened to spot my informant across the deck, on the other side of the pool. He appeared to be giving me a signal.

So, excusing myself, I got up and walked into the men's room. A few moments later, my informant followed me inside.

After making certain no one else was in the bathroom with us, my informant said, "That man who just joined you at the table? That friend of your Colonel Velez? He is involved with the narcotraficantes."

Oh, just fucking fantastic.

IT WAS TIME to get the next phase of the operation rolling.

Boarding Blackhawk helicopters in Trinidad, we flew to the eastern lowlands of Bolivia, landing in a hilly area around San Javier, where a Jesuit mission had been built in the late 1600s.

We pitched our tents in an open field used as grazing land for cattle owned by Bolivia's president. Since I didn't fancy surviving on military-style, ready-to-eat meals, I had brought along four cases of cranberry juice, beef jerky, canned tuna, sardines, canned deviled ham, dried ramen noodles for soup, and crackers.

One morning at 5:00 a.m., about a week after I had first arrived in La Paz, I held a briefing with the U.S. Army officers who were piloting the helicopters. A communiqué had arrived from Trinidad with intel about our first target, a jungle coke lab. Nobody was privy to the communiqué's contents except me and the American pilots.

And with good reason.

We knew the Leopardos had been leaking information to the drug lords. Velez was a likely suspect. And Basilio had been much too curious. Sidling up to me like we were old school chums, he kept peppering me with questions. "Where are the targets? Where are you going? When do you expect to arrive there?"

"En boca cerrada, no entran moscas," I had replied, using an old Spanish proverb. *In a closed mouth, no flies will enter.*

So here in Bolivia, everything would be handled on a need-to-know basis. Neither the Leopardos nor their commanders would be told our destination until we actually got there.

Shortly after the predawn briefing, I gathered up my.357 Magnum, M-16 machine gun, twelve-inch Rambo-style hunting knife, grenade, smoke flare, garrison belt with 120 rounds of M-16 ammo, notebook, and pen. The Leopardos carried M-1 carbines. Together, about twenty of us boarded two Blackhawk helicopters. The four American pilots were veterans of combat in Vietnam.

Our flight took us several hundred miles into the jungle. Flying "nap of the Earth style" at two hundred miles per hour, a mere twenty five feet above the tree line, we followed the land contours. Whenever we approached a hill, the helicopter would suddenly zoom up over the top, then drop down quickly again, leaving me with a queasy gut. Wild buffalo, cattle, and parrots scattered at the loud whirring of our rotor blades. But the local campesinos loved it, frequently looking up, smiling, and waving at us.

Other army air teams or DEA pilots had pinpointed the locations of the jungle labs and noted their latitudinal and longitudinal coordinates. But we still had to corroborate the existence of the sites by observing concrete "land signatures," many of which could not be confirmed until we got closer to the ground.

Suddenly we saw the signs. A small, makeshift airstrip. A heavy canopy by the side of a river. Near and under the canopy were sure to be pits, vats, and metal drums. The pits, lined with plastic, were used to dry the coca leaves, which were then mixed with solvents (kerosene, benzene, sulfuric acid) and base chemicals (magnesium permanganate, ammonia, cement carbonate). The vats held the benzene after it had been filtered off from the gooey coca paste created in the pits. The drums, big enough to hold fifty-five gallons each, contained the ether needed to further process the cocaine, one drum for every ten kilos.

I told the pilots to drop us close to the lab. The booming, terrifying sound of the helicopters' rotor blades would be sure to flush out any narcotraficantes who might be inside or around the lab, making it easier for us to spot them from the sky. It also could encourage them to surrender without a fight.

The pilots balked, complaining that there was too much danger from possible enemy gunfire.

"Bullshit," I replied. The time it would take us to walk from the drop point back to the lab would give anyone inside the lab too much of an opportunity to escape. So I goaded the pilots, "What the fuck's wrong? You ain't got hair on your ass? You flew in Vietnam and you won't drop us here? What kind of pussies are you?"

When I put it that way, they agreed to fly within two hundred yards of the lab. As the choppers lowered themselves toward the ground, my men and I jumped out, some of us rappelling down ropes to the jungle floor. As soon as we hit the soil, the choppers flew off. Or maybe they'd take their time, considering how I and my big mouth had just ripped into the pilots.

Slowly and quietly, we began creeping toward the coke lab. I worried that the narcotraficantes, having heard our helicopters, might by lying in wait for us. With my M-16 machine gun at the ready, I kept the Leopardos moving gingerly through the jungle to avoid any booby traps, like horsehair-triggered dynamite or sharpened pungie sticks.

Suddenly one of the men whispered excitedly, "*¡Allá!* There!"

Up ahead, hanging just above the tree line, I could see tarps, the makeshift roofs of the the lab. I also could hear a generator running.

Unlike the other labs we had hit, this lab had not been abandoned. Somewhere up there were people. People with guns. But I could not see any of them.

Using hand signals, I motioned everyone to hit the ground. For a few minutes, we waited. But we saw no one.

I signaled the Leopardos to split into two teams, one approaching from either side. Slowly, each team began to crawl forward on hands and knees toward the tarps.

I gave another series of hand signals.

Everyone raised his weapon. Took aim. And waited.

Then, on my command, we all began firing warning shots over the top of the lab.

Suddenly, and unexpectedly, came a response. A volley of rounds directed back at us from somewhere near the lab.

Ping! Ping! Ping!

Bullets ripped into the tall trees and thick brush around me. Small-arms and automatic weapon fire. The Leopardos began returning fire.

I threw myself into a body roll and scrambled for cover. Kneeling behind a rotting tree trunk, I came up again with my weapon and jacked off all the rounds.

The bullets ripped through the canvas sides of the lab, blowing a mosaic of holes in the flaps. Some tore through the thatched roof, shredding its leaves and branches.

I emptied the clip, then jammed a fresh one in to replace it. From all around me came the sound of more gunfire as the Leopardos trained their carbines on the lab. It was like the Gunfight at the O.K. Corral.

After ten minutes of fighting, everything turned quiet. I shouted to the Leopardos,

"*¡Adelante!* Charge!"

En masse, we all ran forward at the same time . . . only to find the lab deserted.

They couldn't have escaped through the jungle—our forces had completely surrounded the lab from the jungle approach. So they must have made their getaway in the opposite direction, running down to the riverbank. Dammit.

Could we intercept them in time?

Machine gun at the ready, I raced toward the shoreline. Out on the river, I thought I could make out the churning tail of a fresh wake. But then, just as quickly, it dissolved into the river's flow and disappeared.

"Fuck!" I said out loud. We had just missed getting them all.

Using small boats that must have been hidden ahead of time in the underbrush, the narcotraficantes were well on their way downriver. Looking down past my boots, I could see fresh footprints in the mud, as well as the imprints of the keels of boats that had recently been dragged into the water.

I also spotted droplets of fresh blood on the ground. We must have hit someone.

I jogged up the shoreline, hoping to spot one of the boats before it turned the bend. But, at this point, whoever had been at the lab was long gone.

Doing an about-face, I headed back to regroup with my men. After checking to make certain that none had been wounded, I began to do a closer inspection of the lab. It consisted of one big tent, or rather a canvas tarp stretched out over a log frame. Around it were smaller structures, also consisting of tarps stretched over propped-up logs. Under the tarps we found wood benches, on top of which sat heating lamps, rolls of cheesecloth, and shallow plastic containers, each two feet wide and three feet long. Steel drums full of ether sat atop a wooden platform or piled in stacks. Other processing elements—bottles of hydrochloric acid, sacks of potassium, bags of cement mix—were nearby.

We also found huge generators. Radios. And quantities of processed cocaine. Ledger books left behind by the narcotraficantes indicated that this particular lab had been producing three hundred kilos of cocaine each week.

Last but not least, we found a trailer. Bearing Texas license plates.

After removing these items to our base camp, I radioed the Blackhawks. "Zulu One to Zulu Two, we're looking to evacuate. We're setting the blaze. Ten-four. Roger and out."

I laid out a trail of cheesecloth, a hundred feet long, bringing one end up to the drums of ether. Then I used my M-16 to put big leaking holes in the drums. Finally, after pouring ether over the cheesecloth, I ignited the far end of the cloth with my pocket lighter.

And I ran like hell.

In ten seconds flat, the entire lab whooshed up in a giant fireball. No explosion, just a fast-moving spasm of red and orange flames, intense heat, and thick, black smoke.

Over a period of three months, from September through November of 1986, we would burn a dozen labs like this one to the ground. Each time we did, we would deal a blow to the narcotraficantes, since it would take at least six months to build a new lab.

In the meantime, we would accumulate a trove of valuable information. Notebooks and ledgers contained names. Supplies bore serial numbers. Blankets had tags. Ether drums displayed lot numbers, traceable back to their source.

Sent back to the DEA's intelligence unit in Washington, this information would generate names, nicknames, associates, locations, streets, and phone numbers. As in the case of the trailer that bore those Texas license plates, which turned out to belong to a major Texas drug dealer, who eventually was arrested by the DEA.

Except for the one lab where we took fire, the others were all deserted. Even when we first flew over them, the Blackhawks kicking up a ruckus, we never saw people running out and trying to escape. Despite my precautions, never revealing to the Leopardos the targets until we actually got there, somebody was tipping off the cartels.

The fuckers were ratting us out.

The entire operation was beginning to look like a farce.

* * *

AT ONE POINT, we received fresh intel on a promising new location.

The target this time?

An entire *town*, populated with five thousand inhabitants. Once a Jesuit mission, Santa Ana was in the northeastern flatlands of Bolivia, near the Beni River. An idyllic little enclave, it was surrounded by fields of fresh-growing papayas, lemons, bananas, and coconuts.

But its natural beauty belied the menace it harbored. Santa Ana was the headquarters of Renato Roca Suarez and his brother Jorge Roca Suarez, two kingpins of the Bolivian drug trade, along with eighteen other narcotraficantes. As such, it offered plenty of bodies, plenty of suspects, plenty of chances to lock them up and shut them down once and for all.

Given the size and importance of this new target, an operation on a whole different scale would be mounted. Instead of the usual twenty Leopardos, more than a hundred were assigned to the strike team. Instead of two Blackhawks, seven would be deployed. In addition, a Faulkner twin-engine transport plane would be flown in to carry back any prisoners we might capture.

In preparation for this massive assault and sweep operation, Bolivia's attorney general issued twenty search-and-arrest warrants, each signed by the nation's president.

Despite my misgivings about Colonel Velez, he and his men, rather than the American DEA agents, would be given the job of executing the arrest warrants. Better to have Bolivians arrest Bolivians than enrage the local populace by having gringos lock them up.

Back at our rear base camp in Trinidad, Jim Bradley told me it would be better if I did not actively participate in the roundup of the narcotraficantes. But Colonel Velez insisted that I be given my own unit of Leopardos to command, and Jim eventually relented. While I might have mistrusted Velez, he knew I could be counted on to have his back.

Also participating in this raid would be five other DEA agents who had arrived in Trinidad from Cochabamba, Bolivia's third-largest city, including Mark Trouville, the resident agent in charge of the Cochabamba office, with whom I had worked back in Los Angeles. He was a go-getter and a hard driver. Even though Mark technically outranked me, I would carry plenty of weight on the raid, owing to my extensive undercover experience, my proficiency in Spanish, and my rapport with the Leopardo foot soldiers.

Early on the morning of October 12, 1986, while it was still dark outside, we boarded our Blackhawks. Then, along with the Faulkner transport plane, we lifted off from our base in Trinidad and headed south and west, toward Bolivia. The eighty-mile flight to Santa Ana would take about forty-five minutes.

The raid itself would begin before the sun rose.

SINCE THERE WAS no real airstrip in Santa Ana, we landed in an open field. With dawn slowly approaching, the booming bleats of red howler monkeys were already echoing from the jungle.

The Leopardos quickly deplaned and split into ten teams, ten men per team. Each team was to target a house known to be inhabited by a drug peddler. The houses had been painstakingly mapped and pinpointed before our departure from Trinidad.

The town was still asleep as we moved through it, and we wanted to keep it that way, not causing any undue ruckus that might scare off our targets. It was a stereotypical little village, one you might find in Spain or Mexico. A big church sat at the center, a large, open cobblestone plaza in front of it. The narrow streets branching off from the plaza were lined with low, attached houses constructed of light brown cement and red tile roofs. The farther you walked from the center of town, the bigger, more elaborate, and more freestanding the houses became.

Thanks to our intelligence, we knew that the drug dealers lived in more substantial houses, on the outskirts. Using a map, my team trekked silently toward the home of Jorge Roca Suarez.

Roca Suarez's casa turned out to be a single-level, white alabaster structure with a pink-tiled roof. It sat on a neatly manicured green lawn surrounded by tall coconut palms and flowering shrubs. It looked like the kind of appealing, Spanish-style home found in Palm Beach or even back home in Costa Mesa.

After the Leopardos surrounded the house, I knocked on the front door, with my UMOPAR lieutenant by my side. It was opened by a woman, small, dark, and pretty. Behind her I could see a couple of young children.

I identified myself. Then, flashing the signed search warrant in front of her nose, I told her we needed to enter her house.

She objected vehemently.

Speaking in Spanish, I said, "Señora, we have the right to search your house. It will go a lot better for you if you let us in than if you don't."

She relented and backed away from the door.

As we entered, I politely asked her to take a seat on the sofa. One of the Leopardos stood guard over her.

Then my men and I fanned out and began to search the other rooms. The house was bright, spacious, and modern. It was filled with beautiful, handcrafted wood furniture and wood carvings, big fluffy throw cushions, and colorful Indian rugs. The walls were adorned with large oil paintings. All in all, it looked like it could be the abode of a prosperous lawyer or a physician.

The other rooms were empty. If someone else had been inside the house, he was long gone. So I returned to the living room, where the woman sat on the sofa, now holding her two children close to her.

"Where is your husband?" I asked her.

She hesitated. Then she said, "In town."

I was skeptical. Just then, my lieutenant reappeared. In his hand, he held a silver-plated Smith & Wesson .357 magnum. He had discovered it in the drawer of a night table.

He displayed the gun to me, saying nothing. But I saw the want in his eyes.

In return, I gave him a nod, signaling him that if he wanted it, it was his to keep. I knew that guns like this were virtually impossible to come by in Bolivia and that, even if they were, the lieutenant could never afford to buy one on his salary. It might cost as much as a thousand bucks. Letting him have the gun would ensure both his gratitude and his loyalty.

Regrouping outside the house, I led my team back toward the center of town. Hopefully, the other teams would be having better luck than we had had.

In the town plaza, near the huge church, I met up with Mark Trouville and his team of Leopardos. From here, Trouville and I would monitor the rest of the operation.

Mark and I took a position by the entrance of the church. And waited. Radio reports started coming in, one by one, from each of the houses the Leopardos had hit.

Nobody. No drugs. No narcotraficantes. No nothing.

Shit! We'd been sold out again.

* * *

HOPING FOR SOME kind of miracle, I momentarily left Mark outside and stepped into the church.

Built by the Jesuits, it had the feel of an Old World cathedral, a huge, high-ceilinged interior, big columns, massive altar, lots of marble, religious statues, and burning incense candles. Dark and imposing, it was, in the characteristic manner of most Spanish churches, designed to comfort, guilt, and terrify you all at once. A couple of elderly parishoners sat in the front pews, saying the rosary.

I knelt in front of the altar. Crossed myself. And said the prayer my Abuelita Adela had long ago promised would always protect me:

O Michael, prince of the Heavenly Host, right hand of God, Our Father, be my shield and sword if need be. Cast into hell Satan and all the other evil spirits who wander through the world seeking the ruin of souls.

Suddenly, overhead, the huge iron church bell began clanging, again and again and again, reverberating loudly throughout the chapel.

As I got up to leave, I dabbed some holy water on my forehead. I crossed myself again. Then I stepped outside and straight into hell.

TWO OF THE Leopardo units were standing in the plaza. But, summoned from their thatched-roof houses by the clanging church bell and tipped by neighbors that Yankees from el Norte had invaded their town, a thousand villagers now stood around them, shouting in anger, "*¡Viva Bolivia! ¡Muerte a los Americanos! ¡Asesinos!*"

Meanwhile, more people were flowing into the plaza from

the outskirts. They were carrying machetes, sticks, and God knows what else.

An old woman began shouting into a megaphone in Spanish, "Injustice! Good people, don't allow this! Fucking gringos! Who are they to come here?"

In this neck of the woods, the people relied on the narcotraficantes for their livelihoods. The drug dealers kept the locals employed as mules, wholesalers, truck drivers, guards, maids, and gardeners. So they were not happy to see gringos from el Norte coming in to take away their benefactors and cut off their lifelines.

The old woman wheeled on me. "We don't want you people here! You must leave now! We will die defending this town from you Americans!"

I glanced past the crowd to see the two units of Leopardos standing lamely off to the side. But the other units and Colonel Velez were nowhere in sight.

The mayor joined the fray, rousing the townspeople to further fury. Taking the megaphone from the woman, he picked up on her irate refrain: "Why are you so concerned with this town where there are so many other things wrong in Bolivia? The government should clean up its own house!"

I wanted to spit in his face. According to our intel, this guy was a two-faced dirtbag who took bribes from the narcotraficantes to let them stay in business.

But the mayor, who had puffed himself up like a rooster, was just getting started. "We have been invaded by the Drug Enforcement Administration and the Americans, who come with Bolivian soldiers and police! This is the only village in Bolivia that can stand up to these people! And stand up we will, for that is the kind of pride and dignity we are known for!"

The crowd, which had now swelled to about two thousand, roared its approval.

Looking around the plaza, I suddenly spotted reporters from the BBC, the States, and Bolivia, with their cameramen pushing toward us. But wait a minute. What the hell were *they* doing here? How did they get here so quickly? We certainly hadn't invited them. Someone must have tipped them beforehand about our raid. Someone had betrayed us. Could it have been Velez? Basilio? Could it have been someone inside the U.S. embassy, which was aware of our raid plan from the very beginning? Whoever it was, extensive footage of us would later appear all over Bolivian television.

Some of reporters began shouting questions to Mark and me, but we refused to answer them. Meanwhile, the church bell kept ringing. The voices grew louder and angrier, the crowd larger and unrulier.

It was balls-to-the-wall time. I knew we had to get out of there. And fast. People were screaming, shouting, waving Bolivian flags, making death threats.

Our Blackhawks were back at the airfield, about a mile outside of town, and we would have to walk down a dirt road past all these screaming villagers to get to them.

More Leopardo units joined our ranks. Mark and I told the men to move out slowly. They were to walk deliberately, not run as if they were scared. *"Tranquilo,"* I said. *"Manténganse. No responden."* Easy. Stay together. Don't respond.

Two Leopardo units were still missing. They would have to find their way back to the airfield on their own. And still there was no sign of Colonel Velez.

As we trudged warily toward the airport, more and more people lined up to taunt us with death threats. Some began pushing. Others threw rocks. Fortunately, the Leopardos held steady. Keeping their guns pointed to the ground, they forged on.

A little girl in the crowd, no more than eight or nine years old, caught my eye. By way of signaling my fate, she drew her index finger in a slicing motion across her throat. A guy on a passing motorcycle actually flashed a handgun at us. I quickly raised the barrel of my M-16 machine gun to let him know what awaited him if he tried anything. He wisely tucked his gun away and zoomed off.

By the time we reached the airfield, the crowd had swelled to almost three thousand, more than half the population of the village. And they were carrying serious armaments—shotguns, carbines, pistols, knives, machetes, pitchforks, you name it. These people were out for blood. *American* blood. *My* blood.

Suddenly I saw something that made my balls leap into my gut. One of the missing Leopardo platoons, standing outside a tiny community center with a V-shaped roof, was detaining twenty of the locals, trying to prevent them from joining the fray. But in so doing, they risked infuriating the rest of the populace, which already was clamoring for our scalps.

Jesus Christ! I thought. *Just what this mob needs to see. How fucking stupid could they be?!*

I rushed up to the leader of the Leopardos. "Lieutenant, do you know who I am?" I demanded.

"Yes, you are Colonel Diaz," he replied.

"Release these people, Lieutenant. *Immediately*. We have three thousand people coming here ready to kill us. They'll kill us a lot faster if they see their townspeople being held. Let these prisoners go and get your men out of here. Pronto!"

The lieutenant saluted, then ordered the prisoners cut loose.

But the damage had already been done. Already seeing

their compadres taken into custody, the furious townspeople surged toward us. “Kill the Yanquis!” they screamed.

As they moved to cut off our egress, the Leopardos finally lost it and began firing their carbines into the air. Someone fired back at them. *Here we go.* Mark and I ducked for cover. Other people fell to the ground or turned and bolted, running pell-mell into each other.

I shouted at the Leopardos, “*¡Para de tirar!*” Stop the shooting! Stop the shooting!

Slowly, they lowered their weapons. The mob began to regroup. “Kill them! Kill them! Kill them!” they chanted.

We were within sight of our aircraft now. I shouted to the Leopardo lieutenant, “Get your men on those fucking helicopters!”

He quickly led his soldiers toward the waiting Blackhawks that sat about fifty yards to my left. The Faulkner transport plane was a hundred yards to my right.

“Get those choppers going!” I shouted to the pilots.

The mob might try to follow us across the field and toward our helicopters, but with the seventy-mile-per-hour winds created by the Blackhawks’ rotor blades and the heavy .60-caliber machine guns affixed on tripods inside their cabins, I knew they wouldn’t get far.

I turned back to face the mob. The mayor of Santa Ana was now front and center again, back on his high horse. Even though I knew he was a viper, I tried to buy time by reasoning with him. Behind him, the villagers were still screaming for my blood.

“Hey, man,” I said to him in Spanish, “I understand what this is all about, but the fact of the matter is you guys are harboring drug dealers. There’s gonna come a time when you’re addicted, your children are addicted. Then where are you gonna go for help?”

The mayor turned his back to me to face the crowd. Shouting right over me, he piously declared, "They are exaggerating the situation! We don't have a drug problem here!"

I wanted to get my ass out of there, but I couldn't. Not yet, anyway. Colonel Velez still had not returned. Much as I suspected that he was responsible for what was now happening, I couldn't just leave him behind.

All of a sudden, the mayor stopped his grandstanding. Then he melted back into the crowd. An instant later, something rolled toward my feet.

A hand grenade.

I leaped out of the way. Then, along with everyone else, I hit the dirt and stuck my fingers in my ears, waiting for the explosion. It never came. Instead, thick, choking smoke poured out.

Coughing and waving my hand to fan away the effects of the smoke grenade, I looked around again for Velez. Off in the distance, I could see him finally approaching with the last of the Leopardos.

The Blackhawks and the Faulkner had begun to rev up their engines. But a bunch of guys on motor scooters drove onto the tarmac and surrounded the Faulkner, determined to block its takeoff until they could search the plane and be certain we were not trying to fly off with any of their compadres. They swarmed like angry bees into its cabin.

As the mob kept surging forward, I stuck my index finger in the air and wiggled it furiously, signaling the Blackhawks to kick up the speed on their rotors. A blast of high winds and ear-splitting roars quickly followed.

Colonel Velez boarded a Blackhawk with the last of his men. Mark Trouville pulled me away from the crowd and together we ran toward one of the other choppers, fighting the fierce winds kicked up by the Blackhawks.

Then, as the crowd waved their machetes and fired their guns into the air we took off. Satisfied that it was not carrying any prisoners, the villagers let the Faulkner take off, as well.

"*¡Se van! Se van!*" the villagers shouted triumphantly. They're leaving! They're leaving!

Our mission in Santa Ana had been a failure.

Sabotaged from the very beginning.

BACK AT OUR forward base camp at San Javier, I crawled into my tent, exhausted and disgusted, and fell into a deep sleep. And I began to dream.

Not of the Bolivian jungles, but of the old haunted house in the churchyard in front of our apartment on Clinton Street in Brooklyn. Of the fireworks that lit up the skies of Red Hook every Fourth of July. Of a Roy Campanella home run ball I snagged in the bleachers at Ebbets Field. Of my pal Mikey Colavito. Of a garlicky slice of freshly baked pizza from Sam's, where Marilyn Monroe and Joe DiMaggio once walked in while Mikey and I were waiting for a pie to go. Of the hot crumb buns and those tart, savory homemade Italian ices my Abuelita Adela and I would pick up from a Court Street bakery. Of my mama's wonderful paella, her *caldo Gallego,* her black beans with pork chops, and her arroz con pollo.

I awoke with a start. And realized I had to use the bathroom.

So I pulled on my fatigues and my combat boots and slogged wearily to the makeshift outhouse we had built about two hundred yards away from our tents. Inside, I walked up to the wooden commode and started to unzip.

Suddenly, off to one side, I noticed something moving.

Triangular head, about two and a half meters long, dark

green on its upper body, a faint yellow color on its belly. A forked tongue flicked in and out between its fangs as it slithered toward me.

It was a *jararacucu,* one of the world's deadliest snakes. One bite could inject enough venom to kill thirty-two people. One of these bastards snags you, and necrosis, shock, spontaneous systemic bleeding, and renal failure follow. Death, which is inevitable, comes as a blessing.

Hoisting my trousers up hurriedly, like a ship's mainsail, I leaped up on the commode and reached for the two-by-four over the door, ready to bash the fucker's head in. About a foot from the commode, he swerved to one side, made a U-turn, and darted back out under the door.

I waited a few more minutes before coming down from my perch. Then I opened the door and looked around to make sure he hadn't doubled back for an ambush. Walking slowly to my tent, I warily eyed the ground ahead and to the side of me. Entering my tent, I gave the aluminum legs on my cot an extra spritz of silicon spray.

From that day forward, I would do my business inside my tent. In a pail.

Yeah, Bolivia was a beautiful country, all right. And a lot of the Bolivians were beautiful people.

But at this point, I had had enough. Special request or not, I was out of there. Gimme the old U.S. of A. any fuckin' day.

CHAPTER EIGHTEEN

I HAD BEEN BACK IN Southern California for only a few months when I got the word. The bosses wanted me back on Operation Pisces.

While I was gone, another agent, Marty Martinez, had substituted for me whenever there was a call from the drug dealers requesting fresh money launders. Before leaving for Bolivia, I had brought him along on several of my pickups and vouched for him as Don Lucho's trusted assistant.

However, the U.S. attorney now felt that there was not enough conclusive evidence to link Eduardo Pantaleone to the murder of the other drug dealer who had ripped him off. More was needed before the case could be brought to trial. And in the minds of the prosecutors and my DEA superiors, I was the guy who could get it.

The key would be Clara Velez, Eduardo's wife and the mother of his two children. Reprising my undercover persona of money-laundering magnate Don Lucho, I would have to find a way to lure her into a conversation that would incriminate her homicidal, coke-dealing husband.

It was not an assignment I relished.

I had never been comfortable going after some guy's wife. Plus, I would probably be taking both parents away from those two kids forever. As a family man myself, it was not something that sat easily with my conscience or my code. It would force me to cross my own lines.

On the other hand, Eduardo had been responsible for taking the life of another person who also had kids, and, for me, a human life was sacrosanct.

I had a job to do. So, in the end, I had no choice.

After doing surveillance on Clara's known haunts, we discovered that she was staying at her mother's house in Canoga Park, an area about twenty-five miles northwest of downtown Los Angeles. So one day in February 1987, along with other DEA agents and members of the Orange County Sheriff's Department, we set up on Mama's place.

Shortly after noon, Clara came out and got into a white Ford sedan. Following her, we watched her pull up to a Giant Supermarket, where she went inside to buy groceries. When she came out again and got back into her car, I jumped from my car and made my move.

Just as she was starting to pull out of her parking space, I came up on her as if by accident. Peeking through the open window on the driver's side, I widened my eyes in recognition and chirped, "Clarita? *¿Eres tú?*"

She braked. Studying my face, she gave me a wary look.

"It's Lucho, Clarita. Don Lucho."

Finally she recognized me. *"Oh, sí, que bien,* Lucho," she said. "I was just going to get some coffee for my sister-in-law. She lives a few blocks from here."

"God, Clarita," I said, "long time no see. How have you been?"

She supplied me with the usual generalities. I danced around with small talk for a few more minutes. Then I made a grab for the brass ring. "How's Eduardo? How's everything going?"

And suddenly the floodgates opened. Clara began to pour her heart out. Eduardo, she confided, had been arrested for murder. He had emptied his gun into the face of another drug dealer, Oscar Gonzalez, after learning that Oscar had stolen $100,000 and three kilos of cocaine belonging to Eduardo and Clara. Oscar had been entrusted to guard a stash that contained $1 million of el Tío's cash and five hundred kilos of his cocaine. Because of his treachery, he had been marked for death.

At first, Clara and Eduardo had planned to hire someone else to do the murder. El Tío had even given them his blessing for the hit, agreeing that Oscar needed to be taken out. But when Eduardo ran into Oscar at Don Felipe's Restaurant in Los Angeles, the temptation proved too great. So he pulled out his 9mm pistol and did the job himself.

In anticipation of the fallout, Clara and Eduardo had already begun to wind down their cocaine business and clear out their "stash pads." Had Eduardo stayed in Miami, where he could have counted more reliably on the help of el Tío in avoiding the authorities, Clara said, he would have gotten away with it. But when he foolishly returned to California, he got himself arrested. What's more, the Feds had seized $113,000 and a large amount of expensive jewelry from Clara's safe deposit box.

"I've done all I can do to help my husband," Clara said. "Including silencing potential witnesses."

"Oh?" I said, milking it one more time.

Coolly, she explained, "I told them if they said anything, I would have them killed."

I nodded in understanding. Then I told Clara I had expanded my money-laundering business—now had my own corporation, in fact—and offered to help her with any future money washes she might require. She thanked me. We exchanged telephone numbers. And she went on her way.

Clara had indisputably linked Eduardo, herself and el Tío to the assassination of Oscar Gonzallez. And I had picked up her admissions clearly and fully on my concealed wire.

AFTER THREE YEARS, Operation Pisces had run its course. The DEA had identified all the key players in el Tío's operation and pinpointed all his assets. It was time to take Pisces down.

But before rounding up all the bad guys, there was one last piece of the puzzle that needed to be added to ensure total success.

The big boss himself, el Tío.

To arrest all his underlings but leave José Lopez at large would be an incomplete and unsatisfying final act. José Lopez was a powerful and vicious criminal and, if allowed to remain free, could easily exact revenge while building up a whole new drug franchise. Somehow he had to be taken down.

But how? The Colombians would never touch him. He was too influential and too powerful.

The only way he could ever be arrested would be to lure him into the United States. The odds of ever doing that seemed infinitesimal at best.

But then, J. D. Miller came up with an ingenious ruse. Knowing that Lopez had a fondness for lavish parties, Miller sent word that he was going to be married and he wanted Lopez to be a guest at his wedding. His bride would be Tammy Connelly, the same pregnant DEA agent who had accompanied Miller and posed as his girlfriend on his trip to meet with José Lopez in Panama.

"I'm finally gonna make an honest woman of her," Miller communicated to Lopez. And Lopez, charmed by this chivalrous gesture of love and devotion, said he would be delighted to fly from Colombia to Florida for the ceremony and reception.

A private plane was sent to Bogotá to pick him up. The plane carried some of the other "wedding guests." All were DEA agents.

Lopez boarded the plane with $5 million in emeralds, one of which he intended to give to J. D. Miller as a wedding gift.

When el Tío landed in Miami, the first thing he saw was his spanking new $300,000 helicopter sitting on the tarmac. It was the same helicopter that J. D. Miller had dutifully purchased for him after receiving instructions to do so during their meeting in Bogotá. Lopez beamed with pride.

Standing nearby was a smiling Rich Gorman, whom Lopez recognized as one of the other principals of the Eurimex Company. While Lopez was disappointed that Miller had not been able to come to the airport, he was heartened by the sight of Gorman, a familiar face and another valued business associate.

Gorman gave him a warm greeting. "Welcome to the United States, José," he said as several other men slowly moved around to Lopez's sides. "I hope you had a pleasant flight."

"Very much so," said Lopez. "Thank you for asking."

"Yes, well, I'm afraid I have a bit of bad news."

"Oh?" said Lopez.

Slowly raising his DEA shield, Gorman announced in Spanish, "*Mala suerte, mi amigo. Somos la DEA.* Bad luck, my friend. We are the Drug Enforcement Administration." Then he added, "José Lopez, you are under arrest."

El Tío's smile quickly faded to a look of full-on shock. Handcuffed from behind, he was escorted over to his new helicopter, placed inside it, and flown to the DEA office for booking and fingerprinting. It was the one and only time he would ever get to fly in it.

Once Lopez was in U.S. custody, the rest of the takedown could proceed. More than a hundred DEA agents and scores of local police took part in seizures of cocaine and arrests of el Tío's operatives all across the nation.

By the time it was over, the DEA had seized more than nine tons of el Tio's cocaine, freezed ten of his bank accounts, and seized $75 million of his cash and $15 million of his other assets (including his airplanes and his beloved new helicopter). And it had taken more than five hundred suspected members of his drug ring into custody.

U.S. attorney general Edwin Meese would later describe Operation Pisces as "nothing less than the largest and most successful undercover investigation in the history of United States law enforcement."

What made the sting especially sweet was that a sizable chunk of el Tío's drug proceeds—the "commissions" deducted by Eurimex for its money-laundering services—had actually been used to finance the federal government's undercover operation. In effect, as Meese would put it, "the drug traffickers paid for their own downfall." All told, $320 in million cocaine and other assets were seized.

Working undercover for more than two years on the Santa Ana facet of Operation Pices, I personally had arranged and participated in twenty-five money washes and handled more than $15 million in drug proceeds. With the help of other DEA agents from the Santa Ana office and local California police, we had seized nearly $24 million in cash and a thousand kilograms of cocaine and arrested twenty-five major narcotics violators, virtually all of whom chose to plead guilty before their cases ever went to trial. According to J. D. Miller and Rich Gorman, 40 percent of the overall seizures in Operation Pisces could be attributed to our Santa Ana office.

As for el Tío, his story had a sad and poignant ending. Following his own guilty plea in U.S. federal court, José Lopez's wife and his girlfriend took everything he had left in Colombia . . . and ran with it. Sentenced to spend the rest of his life in an American prison, el Tío would have plenty of time on his hands to contemplate their treachery.

NOT LONG AFTER Operation Pisces started to wind down, Richard Canas, the supervisor of the Santa Ana office, was transferred. Just my luck, his replacement turned out to be an agent I had never gotten along with in New York. Despite everything I'd worked for, I was toast. In no time at all, the new supervisor had me banished to "never-never land"—the Los Angeles divisional office, a fifty-mile drive one way from my home in Costa Mesa.

Being in L.A., however, brought me closer on a daily basis to our families, and, at this point in time, their needs were growing. Iris's dad, John, was dying of cancer. Mama and Papa often needed Iris and me to drive them or Alfonsito to their doctor appointments. We also did their shopping, cleaned their home, and took care of their bills and their income taxes. Alfonsito still was living with my parents, and I was always searching for some kind of day care or job training that might finally give him his independence. But, in keeping with his suspicious and controlling nature, Papa thwarted me at every opportunity.

Up in L.A., I was assigned to the intelligence unit, which was run by Charlie Lugo. Blessed with a deep, booming, radio broadcaster's voice, Charlie had worked undercover on a lot of dangerous cases in Mexico. Fortunately for me, we melded like bread and butter. In an act of real kindness, he even arranged for me to work out of an office in Long Beach, which was much closer to my home in Costa Mesa.

By this point, President Ronald Reagan had announced a "war on drugs" and named his vice president, George H. W. Bush, to spearhead the effort. I was assigned to Bush's national drug task force, liaising between the DEA and the U.S. Coast Guard but also working with the army, the navy, and local police and sheriffs in amassing and analyzing drug-related intelligence.

My stint in the task force lasted two years, and I enjoyed every minute of it. I liked working with the coast guard and I loved the view I had of the Pacific Ocean from my office. As the DEA's representative on the task force, I would pass along requests from the DEA to the military for any drug-related intelligence they might have had on suspects or ships, boats, or private planes believed to be transporting illegal drugs. I also would pass along DEA requests for military involvement, such as flyovers that, with the aid of infrared devices, might detect clandestine amphetamine labs.

When it ended, I returned to the intelligence unit in Los Angeles, transferring into technical operations. The year was 1990, and drug dealing and its attendant crimes dominated the news almost daily. Panamanian dictator Manuel Antonio Noriega was arrested on charges of drug smuggling, racketeering, and money laundering. Marion Barry, mayor of Washington, D.C., was found guilty of cocaine possession.

Tech operations, which was known as the "black bag" group, provided infrared surveillance cameras, arranged for video surveillance and satellite spying, set up court-ordered wiretaps, installed clandestine listening devices in the residences or bases of suspected drug dealers, and planted tracking devices in cars or packages of drugs that would lead agents to their final destination. In addition to Los Angeles, we serviced DEA offices in Las Vegas, Hawaii, and Guam.

One day, as I went out to snag some lunch, I happened to notice a big commotion at the Bonaventure Hotel, which was a short walk across a small bridge that connected the hotel to the Los Angeles World Trade Center building housing our DEA offices.

Big trailers, big lights, big reflectors, big cameras, people with baseball caps and headsets scurrying back and forth, running heavy electrical cable lines, barking at one another.

I'd always been a sucker for the bright lights, so I decided to investigate. I moseyed toward the connecting bridge to get a closer look.

On the other side of the bridge I spied girls in scanty costumes parading back and forth. But a guy standing on the bridge particularly caught my eye. He had long hair and was well groomed and nicely attired.

He also was wearing women's high heels.

Well, this was not exactly the kind of crowd you'd expect to encounter on your lunch hour. So I decided I had better investigate further. I walked all the way across the bridge, toward the hotel's lobby.

Little did I realize as I crossed that bridge that I was about to step into the next major chapter of my life.

AS I ENTERED the lobby, I threw my jacket over one shoulder, tucked the *L.A. Times* under my other arm, and did what I always did in situations where I had not been invited, which was to walk straight into the middle of things like I owned the joint.

Inside the lobby, I saw a lot of people milling around, killing time. They were on a break from shooting a TV pilot called *The Oldest Rookie,* about a former deputy chief who returns to police work at age fifty. The star of the show, Paul Sorvino, was sitting on the set and sipping coffee. Sitting with him was a guy I recognized. His name was Lenny DiGiovanni—or Lenny D'John, as he was usually called—and he'd run with Crazy Joe Gallo's crew back in Brooklyn.

Even though I didn't know Paul, I'd always been a big fan. I decided I had to meet him. So I sauntered right up and, extending my right hand like we were bosom buddies, I gave him a load of 100 percent pure bullshit.

"Mister Paul Sorvino!" I said with snappy delivery and a big, toothy grin. "It's been a long time. How the hell are you?!"

It was a ruse, of course, something I had used many a time while working undercover. Greeted like long-lost friends and ashamed to say they've forgotten your name, people usually scramble to find some tactful way to respond without having to admit they don't have a clue.

"Ahhhhh," said Paulie, eyeballing me blankly, "howya been, kid?"

But Paulie's friend Lenny wasn't buying any of it. Plus, he was rightfully offended that I had barged into the middle of their private conversation. "Who the fuck are you?" he demanded.

So I did my usual soft-shoe shuffle and said, "Well, I'm like *you.*"

"What the hell does that mean?" he asked.

"Well, I'm from where you are."

"Oh, yeah?" he said, giving me the fisheye. "Where's that?"

"Brooklyn."

"No shit," he said. "Where in Brooklyn?"

"Red Hook." And I dropped the names of some local streets—Union, Sackett, Henry, Baltic, etc.

"Get the fuck outta here!" said Lenny. "That's my neighborhood!" To season the sauce, I threw in the names of some wiseguys I had known way back when. Lenny beamed. "Hey, I *know* them guys! I ran with some of them!" he said.

Pretty soon the two of us were talking like a couple of old pals at a high school reunion. So much so that at one point Paulie, feeling left out of the conversation, joked, "Hey, what about *me*?"

I never went back to work that day. The three of us hung out till 2 a.m., drinking and having a grand old time. Lenny brought us over to Vivaldi's in Van Nuys, where a bunch of actors, gangsters, and wannabe gangsters regularly got together once a week for some good, old-fashioned male bonding.

And I was invited to join their club.

I began going to Vivaldi's every Tuesday night and, thanks to Paulie and Lenny, I became friendly with guys such as Robert Forster, Frankie Pesce, Fred "the Hammer" Williamson, Gianni Russo, Bobby Miranda, the great character actor Eddie Lauter, and Carmine Caridi.

Along with the many actors and performers I met, I also got to know some other people who were not in the business—as a matter of fact, you didn't want to be associated with their line of work. They were mob guys, pure and simple, and some of them were pretty rough customers. After I was spotted talking to one of them, a gangster named Joe Dente, the FBI actually put a tail on me.

When I hung out with the wiseguys in these watering holes, I was very careful about what I said and what I heard. I did not want to be put in any situation that compromised me or anyone else I worked with. I was still on the job, a federal agent, and I made it clear that I didn't want the wiseguys to make their business my business. And vice versa.

Nevertheless, I took perverse pleasure in hanging out with them. It took me back to my youth, toughing it out on the streets of Red Hook, mimicking the guys on the corner, befriending Perky, and meeting Joey Gallo. And, with my heavy-duty South Brooklyn accent, I still loved being mistaken for a wiseguy—especially out here in bland, sun-baked, white-bread California, it was more of a kick than being taken for who I *really* was.

AFTER THEY GOT to know me, some of the actors asked me if I would do technical advising on their film and TV projects. Paul Sorvino came down to the range where I took target practice so I could teach him to shoot. Tony Danza and I swapped tales about boxing and the wiseguys back in Brooklyn. Harvey Keitel asked me to do a couple of weeks of consulting on a film he was shooting over in England in which he had to play a federal agent.

But, truth be told, I felt dissatisfied. I wanted *more.* During my many years of working undercover, I had honed my acting skills, giving convincing performances as "Louie DelRey," "Louie Canelda," "Lefty," and any number of other mobbed-up dirtbags.

Some of the actors I got friendly with at Vivaldi's, Matty's, and Frankie's encouraged me to give the acting thing a try for real. John Finnegan, a New York actor who had appeared in both *The Natural* and *On the Waterfront,* even told me I was born to be an actor. "It's in the eyes, Louie, it's in the eyes," he said. "And you got it, kid."

And so, I began to wonder. . . .

CHAPTER NINETEEN

WE WERE ABOUT TO raid the church where the serial killer was holed up. My team comprised more than a dozen cops, all wearing protective vests, some toting pump shotguns.

I would be leading the charge.

When we pulled up to the church, everyone came flying out of their cars, guns drawn, locked, and loaded. All of a sudden I realized my gun wasn't loaded. But before I could do anything about it, the uniformed cops stormed the church.

"Whoa!" I shouted, raising my hand to hold all the others back. "Easy! Easy! Set up a perimeter, hold your fire, wait for the shot—*that's* the way you do this, not go in like the Seventh Cavalry."

The cops pulled up short. Blinking and hesitating, walking around in circles, they all looked lost.

"Cut! Cut! *Cut!*" someone yelled. "Cut! Louie, whattaya doin'?"

Whoops. "My mistake," I said. "Sorry."

There's a tried-and-true principle in acting that says you have to be "in the moment, in the *now.*" You can't just play the role—you have to *live* it. Feel what your character is experiencing—the joy, the sadness, the pain, the guilt, the anger, the conflict. I knew a thing or two about that already from my undercover work.

But this time I had been a little *too* in the moment—I actually thought I was back at work, doing my job as a federal agent, leading a bunch of *real* lawmen on a *real* raid, looking to take down a *real* bad guy.

Sheepishly, I turned to the director, Bill Lustig, and asked, "Can we do it one more time?"

I was playing the detective partner of actor Robert Davi, and we were hot on the trail of a zombie cop, who had returned from the dead to wreak bloody vengeance on his assassins. *Maniac Cop III* was not exactly *On the Waterfront,* but it was legit movie work.

I had picked up the gig thanks to veteran actor Robert Forster, whom I had befriended during my Tuesday night soirees at Matty's Restaurant. Apparently, at one of these dinners, I had endeared myself to Bill Lustig when I let it drop that I had fought amateur, won a few championships, and worshipped Jake LaMotta, the legendary former middleweight champ and old "raging bull" himself, whom I had gotten to know back in New York. It turned out that Jake LaMotta was Bill's uncle—small world.

Before I knew what was happening, Robert Forster called me up and told me that Bill Lustig wanted me in his next movie, playing a detective. I was stunned beyond belief.

Now I figured Lustig must have wanted me for some small part or maybe as an extra, but it turned out to be a featured role.

When I showed up for my first line reading with Lustig, I impressed him by not only knowing all my lines, but also all the lines of every other actor I had to play opposite. And, more often than not, I nailed my scenes on the first take.

"I thought you said you never did this before," Lustig said.

"Oh, I never acted in a film, no. But I certainly acted when I was a cop." I neglected to mention that it also was standard operating procedure for me to know all my lines before I testified in court.

After *Maniac Cop III,* I was hooked. I joined the Screen Actors Guild. I had headshots made. I took acting classes at the Stella Adler Studio of Acting, the Lee Strasberg Theater and Film Institute, and the South Coast Repertory in Costa Mesa. Thanks to my good friend and fellow actor Bobby Miranda, I got myself an acting agent. To keep from being ethnically pigeonholed by casting agents, I came up with a stage name for myself: Lou Casal.

As time rolled on, my agent, Don Gerler, started to send me out on auditions. Sometimes I got the butterflies. When I was up for a major part in a TV series called *Land's End,* starring Fred Dryer, I learned that I would be competing with a lot of well-known actors. And I started to doubt myself.

But my friend and fellow New York actor John Finnegan reassured me. "Hey, Louie, they're all good actors, but ain't no one out there like you. So get out there, my boy, and nail the part."

Which was exactly what I did. Then I took some accumulated paid leave from my DEA job to fly down to Cabo San Lucas on Mexico's Baja Peninsula for the week-long shoot. Given what I had been doing for the DEA just a few years prior, there was a delicious irony in the role I played: the head of a Latin drug cartel.

The truth was that playing tough guys in a film or TV show was not really a big stretch for me. Hell, I had been playing characters like these for more than two decades, as an undercover agent for ATF and DEA. When it came to playing mobsters, in particular, I had no difficulty at all getting into character—I already *was* that guy.

I had to be careful, however, that "that guy" didn't overwhelm the fictional character I might be playing. And sometimes the lines got blurred. For example, during a break in shooting on a TV show called *Robbery-Homicide Division,* one of the stars started goofing around, twirling his prop gun and pointing it at me. And I went off on him.

"Listen, you motherfucker," I snapped at him, "put that fuckin' gun back in your holster before I ram it up your ass! Don't you ever point a gun at me! *Never.* You fucking hear me?"

When this actor learned who I had been in real life, he apologized to me.

Later, when I was rehearsing an episode of *NYPD Blue,* one of the producers disrupted my monologue by complaining out loud that my take on the character I was playing—a mob hit man—was all wrong. So I jumped in his face and said:

"You know, not for nuthin', my friend, but obviously you know that I can hear you, since you intended for me to hear you. First off, buddy, it's downright inconsiderate and unprofessional. And, second off, with all due respect to what you have to say, you've got to be there to know where I'm at with this thing. You've got to respect my moment, you know what I'm sayin'?"

The producer kept bad-mouthing me until Dennis Franz, one of the stars of the show, pulled him up by the short hairs and shouted,

"Why don't you lay off this fuckin' guy and let him do his fuckin' job! This guy's the real fuckin' thing! Now back the fuck off!"

And I went back to doing my lines the way I knew they should have been done in the first place.

My kids got a real kick of seeing me on TV or in the movies, and an even bigger kick when some of my new actor friends began coming to our house for parties or dinners. Mama became my most devoted fan. Papa, however, thought I was wasting my time and consorting with ne'er-do-wells—he regarded all actors as immoral, sleazy characters. There just was no pleasing some people.

While my DEA supervisor in Los Angeles gave me the okay to pursue my acting, I played it close to the vest with the rest of the agency. I never officially asked headquarters for permission, knowing they would likely refuse it. I continued to work for the DEA in Los Angeles while pursuing my acting career and, in 1991, I even snagged a promotion to chief of the L.A. office's technical operations unit. The promotion came at a good time for us. My parents, who were getting on in years, needed more and more attention, so the extra money I was making on the job, plus the money that was coming in from commercials and other acting gigs, would ease the burden from their rising medical and home-care bills.

Meanwhile, with both Maria and Louis Jr. grown and out of the house, Iris talked of scaling down, buying a smaller home, maybe even doing some traveling. So California was destined to be our home for the long term.

But then I ran into a new problem with the DEA. Under the agency's policy, after five years in a supervisory job like mine with tech operations, a boss at my pay level was required to move to a position inside headquarters in Washington, D.C.—no ifs, ands, or buts.

This, however, would pose a real hardship. Mama was experiencing high blood pressure, asthma, and heart problems. Papa, who already suffered from diabetes, had developed lymphoma. Then he suffered a major heart attack. And Alfonsito's epilepsy was worse than ever. Although my brother Rigel would later step in to help, at this point Iris and I were the only ones who could care for them on a regular basis. So now more than ever, we needed to be close by.

Nonetheless, in my fifth year as the boss of the tech operations unit, I got the dreaded call. Headquarters had set a date to transfer me to Washington, D.C., and there was no way out of it.

There was only one thing left for me to do at this point. So in February 1996, when I hit fifty, I put in my papers, surrendered my gun and my other DEA property, and retired.

If only it got any easier after that.

AFTER I SAID good-bye to the world of law enforcement and began to ease more fully into the Hollywood scene, things seemed to be looking up.

With the exception of Papa, everyone was excited about my new acting career. With the threat of a compulsory transfer to the East Coast no longer looming, Iris and I felt we could attend to Mama and Papa's health needs. Louis Jr. landed a great job as the public relations director for the Center Club in San Diego, a haute-cuisine dining club for business and social occasions. Meanwhile, Maria was planning for her wedding to her college sweetheart, Steven Lindholm.

As the date of wedding neared, in the spring of 1997, Iris went up to see Mama to help her pick out a wedding dress. When she came back home again, she complained of a headache, which was not at all surprising since Mama, funny as she could be, was a regular chatterbox, relentlessly asking what she could get for you. *You wanna piece of pie? No? Then how about an orange? No? Well, what about a nice cookie? No? Then how about . . . ?* And on and on and on it would go. My God, Mama could give a woodpecker a headache.

The next morning, however, when she stepped out of the shower, Iris said she felt a "pop" in her ear and heard a faint buzzing sound. We both dismissed it as one of those things, and Iris went off to begin her nursing shift at the Bristol Park Medical Group.

But during the next several days, she began to experience terrible headaches and nausea. On Easter Sunday, as we stood in church attending Mass, she nearly fainted, and I rushed her to the emergency room. A doctor ordered a CAT scan, which proved negative. We were all tremendously relieved.

Still, the headaches did not abate. And Iris began to slur her words and act confused.

Early in April, Iris went to visit her mother at the nursing residence where she was then living. I stayed home to work in our garden. A few hours went by. The phone rang.

It was a police officer.

Approaching a traffic light, Iris had passed out at the wheel and struck another car from behind. Nobody was hurt, thank God, but our Jeep was badly damaged and, when the police arrived, they found Iris crying hysterically. They thought she might be drunk or on drugs.

After I told the officer about her condition, he agreed to bring her home.

We decided to make a new appointment with her regular internist.

When Iris's sister Merci and her husband, Jimmy, came to visit, we all sat at the kitchen table, discussing Iris's condition. All of a sudden, Iris started to cry. Then her head went back and she blacked out. I immediately called 911.

At the hospital, the doctors performed a cerebral angiogram. A catheter was inserted into an artery and guided through the bloodstream to the arteries that led to the brain. The test indicated that Iris had suffered a cerebral aneurism, or ballooning of one of the blood vessels in her brain. There had been internal bleeding and they would have to operate right way. I penned my signature to the consent form.

Then we went back outside to the waiting room and sat for what seemed like hours. I was sick with fear. When a nurse called me on my cell phone to report that the surgery had been successful and Iris was out of danger, I dropped to my knees and thanked God. The many friends and relatives who had assembled in the waiting room went crazy with cheers and sobbing. When the surgeon came out to make it official, I leaned over and kissed his hands. Then I went home to catch up on some sorely needed sleep.

At about 4:00 a.m., the phone on my nightstand startled me awake. It was a nurse calling from the hospital. Iris had taken a turn for the worse.

When I arrived, I found Iris in the intensive care unit, hooked up to tubes but breathing normally. She looked peaceful and serene. I murmured in her ear, cheering her on, reminding her that Maria was going to be married in just a few short months so she needed to rally for this big occasion. Then the doctor came in. I went mute.

He leaned over Iris and flashed a penlight into both of her pupils.

"Let's step outside," he said.

In the hallway, I could see he was struggling with his words.

"I'm sorry to have to tell you this," the doctor said. "She's brain dead."

And I lost it. Reverting to "Louie D.," I grabbed him by the lapels and threw him against the wall. "No! No! No! You got the wrong person here!" I snarled at him. "This ain't happening! Not to my Iris! You ain't telling me this! No! *No!*"

The doctor, to his great credit, remained calm. When I

looked into his eyes, I could see that he was hurting, too. I relaxed my grip and collapsed against the wall behind me. I demanded more tests.

The doctor agreed to perform one new one, a nuclear brain scan.

I walked back into the intensive care unit and watched silently as the nurses hooked the brain-scanning device up to Iris. But then I was told to leave the room.

Outside, in the waiting room, I found Maria and Louis Jr. waiting for me. My anguish about what I had just learned from the doctor was excruciating. But I forced myself to soft-pedal the news I began to give my kids, saying only that there had been some complications and they were doing further tests. I simply couldn't bring myself to tell them anything more than that.

For an hour, the three of us sat huddled together, waiting, hugging, kissing, weeping, praying, dreading.

Then I looked up and saw the doctor walking toward us. He was straining to control his facial muscles, but I could read it in his eyes. I went cold, waiting for the avalanche that was about to bury me alive. I pulled Maria and Louis tightly to my sides.

As the doctor came closer, he began to shake his head. His lips parted. In what seemed like slow motion, he began to mouth the words.

"I'm so sorry . . . her body is alive, but her brain is gone."

The explosion in my ears was almost deafening. Maria slipped from my grasp, fluttering to the floor like an empty sheet that's just been yanked off a ghost.

When I pulled her up again, she began to speak as though in a trance. She said that she had just seen an angel, and it looked exactly like the guardian angel in the picture that had hung in her room back home since she was a child.

Through my tears, I looked up at the doctor. There was nothing I could say now, not a damned thing. Without any words, just a faint nod of my head, I acknowledged his grim verdict.

The doctor walked away, his head bowed in defeat. A nurse escorted us into a small private waiting room. Relatives and friends slowly arrived to join us there.

As word spread around the hospital, more and more people came to the intensive care unit—doctors, nurses, support staff, people I had never even met before. It seemed like every person who had ever known Iris at the Bristol Park Medical Center wanted to be with her in her hour of need. One little Filipino guy knelt by the side of Iris's bed, crossed himself, and prayed the rosary. Touched, I extended my hand and helped him to his feet. I later learned that he was one of the maintenance men.

I HAD AVOIDED telling my parents what had happened. Mama was especially close to Iris, and both she and Papa had weak hearts. But we couldn't keep things a secret much longer, so my brother Rigel agreed to drive with Louis Jr. up north to to break the news to them.

When Mama came to her door and saw Rigel standing outside, she knew right away that something was terribly wrong. She could see it in Rigel's eyes. As Rigel spelled it out, she fainted. She would have hit the floor had Rigel and Papa not been there to prop her up. Alfonsito also took it hard, and Papa, too. Although he was at a loss for words, Papa, like everyone else, had loved Iris deeply.

She was, after all, the devoted daughter he had never had.

* * *

THE NEXT NIGHT, I tossed and turned in my bed, breaking into a cold sweat. I felt lost, alone, and, for the first time in my life, very, very afraid. After a lifetime of confronting fear, daring it, even embracing it, I was now at its mercy. I agonized over what to do next.

Should I keep Iris on life support? Or should I tell the doctors to pull the tubes and let her go? And what about Maria's wedding? Should it be postponed? What would become of Louis Jr., who had always been so close to Iris? What would become of *me*? Iris had brought peace and sanity and goodness to my life. From the very first day I had met her, as a young student on those nursing residence steps back in Brooklyn, she had shown me nothing but love and patience and understanding. Without her, I would be lost.

I had no answers, only questions and more questions. And because I had no answers, I felt defeated.

At daybreak the next morning, I got up, sleepless and exhausted, and headed straight over to the hospital. Nobody else was there yet. I went into Iris's room. I held her hand. And I began to talk to her.

And then something strange and wonderful happened.

I heard God ask Iris if she wanted to come back to life, even if she could not be whole again. And I heard Iris reply that she had made a covenant with Him, and now it was time to honor that covenant. It was time for her to return to the Lord.

A prominent neurologist entered the room with my daughter, Maria.

"Given her condition, it would be best for Iris and for the rest of you if you let her go," he told us.

I asked one of the nurses to call for a priest. When he arrived, a few of our closest friends, along with Louis Jr., Maria, and my brother Rigel, gathered around Iris's bed and linked hands. The priest anointed Iris's forehead with sanctified oils and pronounced the last rites.

When the last rites had concluded, Iris's personal physician, Dr. Ahern came into the room. I asked everyone, including the doctor, to give me a moment alone with Iris. Then I pulled the curtain closed around us so it was just us two.

I looked down at Iris, taking in her features, closing my eyes periodically to imprint every aspect of her essence into my brain. I ran my hand over her body and kissed the scars on her right knee and her left ankle. I kissed her gently on the lips and whispered in her ear how much I loved her and how someday soon we would be together again.

Then I drew back the curtain and nodded to Dr. Ahern.

The doctor stepped forward. She threw her arms around me and kissed me. Turning to face Iris, she softly uttered her own farewell. Then she began to disconnect all the tubes and machines.

All through the process, I kept my hand on Iris's heart, feeling and living its every remaining beat.

And then it beat no more.

At the cemetery, a bagpiper played "Amazing Grace." Standing around the gravesite, all the mourners held a single blue and yellow flower in their hands.

It was, of course, an iris.

AFTER THE LAST friend had left, the real hell began.

Maria and Louis Jr. were still staying with me. Sometimes we would all sleep in one room and cry. At other times we slept in separate rooms and cried. In the beginning, when I heard my kids weeping, I would get up to comfort them.

Later, the mere thought of having to do so was so daunting, so painful, so devastating that I couldn't bring myself to get out of bed.

I had to sleep with the bathroom light on, like some little kid who's afraid of the dark. This Brooklyn tough guy was nothing but a ball of fear. I had no fight left in me. Night after night, I would toss and turn, then kiss the side of the bed where Iris's head had once lain. In the morning I would awaken before dawn, shivering in a cold sweat. Unable to sleep, I would drag myself out of bed, don a sweatsuit and sneakers, and go jogging for what seemed like a hundred miles.

The physical exertion and the sweating would get my heart going and my blood pumping. But once I returned to the house, the sick, empty feeling would pollute my soul all over again. By now, Louis Jr. and Maria had left to go to work. So I was again alone in my house. Instinctively, I would look around for my dog Lady, only to remember that she had died a year earlier. Then I would recall how crushed Iris and I had been when we had been forced to put her to sleep. And I would feel sad all over again.

When I wasn't crying, I was raging. I was angry with myself for being too overbearing and headstrong at home, for not recognizing sooner how sick Iris had been, for not acting more decisively to deal with her illness. Then I would be angry with my poor, ill mother, blaming her, irrationally, for giving Iris that headache in the first place.

Mostly, however, I was angry with God.

Looking around our house, I would see all the religious articles, medals, rosary beads, novenas, and prayers, all the symbols of devotion that Iris had faithfully accumulated over the years. I would remember that Iris had attended Mass every single Sunday, without fail, and that she had made sure the rest of the family attended as well. And I would become furious at her Maker.

Outside our house, I spotted the large, classic statue of the Virgin Mary that I had placed in our backyard. In my hurt, I picked up a sledgehammer and nearly smashed the statue to pieces. In church, I would stare up at the statue of Jesus and fantasize about machine-gunning him off His cross.

For a while I attended grief-counseling sessions, but the sessions made me feel worse. So after a couple of sessions, I just stopped going.

And the devil of despair came roaring back to dance with a vengeance.

Like when I put my .38-caliber revolver to my head, cocked back the hammer, and started to squeeze the trigger.

I was that close.

At the last instant, I realized that if I went through with this desperate act, I would be leaving my son and my daughter to cope with this ongoing nightmare on their own. Moreover, as a suicide I would never be allowed into the Kingdom of God . . . and therefore never be able to see Iris again.

I slowly let down the hammer, then put my gun away.

With time, I was able to channel my anger into prayer and ask for God's forgiveness. Still, Iris's absence felt like a gaping black hole. There were times I thought it was all a cruel joke and any minute someone would fess up to pulling my leg. At the end of each day, at about 5:30 p.m., I would picture Iris walking through our front door, still dressed in her starched white nurse's uniform, looking as beautiful as ever. Then, in a flash, it would hit me that she would never walk through our door again.

For weeks I couldn't even bring myself to leave the house. When I finally did start to go out, I was afraid of driving. My vision had become blurry, no doubt due to all the stress. And on those rare occasions when I did drive, I often found that I didn't know where I was or even where I was heading.

Despite all this, I decided we should go ahead with Maria's wedding.

"Mama would have wanted it that way," I told my kids.

ONE DAY, I happened to turn on the TV and watched a documentary about a World War I battle at city in northeastern France called Verdun. I was mesmerized. More than a quarter million young men killed, another half million wounded. Then I caught a second TV documentary, about another World War I battle, this one also in the north of France, at a place called Somme, which resulted in 1.5 million casualties. It was one of the bloodiest battles ever recorded.

All those lives snuffed out. All those bodies mangled. All those young men who would never have the opportunity to find love, marry their sweethearts, and have families of their own, like I had.

It was one small epiphany, a turning point that helped to pull me back from the brink.

MARIA AND STEVEN were married on June 28, 1997.

It was a beautiful ceremony, but a difficult one for me. I kept looking around everywhere in the church for Iris. And then came the toughest part of all . . . giving Maria away to Steven.

When I picked up Maria's veil to kiss her, I flashed back to my own wedding, nearly thirty years earlier, when I had picked up Iris's veil, looked into her beautiful eyes, and kissed her gently on her sweet lips.

AFTER THE WEDDING, Maria left home to start a life of her own with Steven. Louis Jr. took a new job that required him to move to Malibu. And I was left on my own again, to mull what once had been and what one day might be.

The paperwork alone plunged me into despair. Iris had always been the one to deal with our finances, but now I had to puzzle over our bankbooks, checkbooks, bills, and other statements. So many Mass cards and sympathy notes had arrived that I couldn't even bring myself to answer them.

Bobby Costanzo, an actor friend who also was from Brooklyn, pushed me to try for a role in a movie called *With Friends Like These*. The film told the story of three actor pals who compete for the part of a gangster in a new Scorcese film and run afoul of some real gangsters. In the middle of my audition, however, images of Iris flashed before me and I lost it. I couldn't finish. The part went to someone else.

Out of the kindness of their hearts, the filmmakers threw me a smaller role and asked me to do some coaching on how real wiseguys walk and talk. We ended up having a lot of laughs on the set, and the whole experience gave me a much-needed lift.

Hollywood extended another helping hand in September 1997 when an ex-DEA agent pal, Billy McMullen, called and asked if I would help him set up a security detail on a Steven Seagal film called *The Patriot*, which was filming on Seagal's ranch in Montana.

The story of some Montana paramilitary militiamen who

threaten to unleash a powerful chemical toxin on unsuspecting civilians, the shoot took an ominous turn when Seagal's people learned that some *real-life* militiamen were planning to sabotage the shoot or even commit violence against the cast and crew.

Flown out to Montana, I disguised myself as one of the truck drivers for the crew. But actually I spent my time identifying and observing the cars driven by the local mountain gorillas, recording their plate numbers and passing them back to Billy McMullen, who was able to come up with the names of the owners and, in the event they had outstanding criminal warrants, pass them along to the FBI. I myself even ran a few of the bad guys out of town.

The film work in L.A. and Montana was a welcome tonic. It brought me back to life again, gave me a sense of purpose. But once it ended, I fell back into that black hole, dwelling on the emptiness that made my days long and my nights even longer. I had returned from Montana just in time for the winter holidays, never a good time of year for those who are mourning loved ones. Thanksgiving was brutal. Christmas, which had always been Iris's favorite holiday, was even worse. I didn't hang one decoration or send out a single card. And New Year's Eve, without Iris by my side to kiss as the ball dropped in Times Square, was absolutely excruciating.

At one point I went to my dentist for a teeth cleaning. As the hygienist worked on me, occasionally touching my face to position her instruments, I thought how wonderful it felt to be touched by a woman again. It wasn't a sexual thing; it was more life-affirming. To be touched was to be nourished, to be warmed, to be reassured, to be connected, to be alive, to be *human.*

Yet here I was in my life, for the first time ever completely and totally alone.

It was becoming unbearable.

ABOUT A YEAR and a half after Iris's death, my daughter, Maria, encouraged me to visit the land of my heritage, Spain, and in particular my father's ancestral homeland in the northwest, Asturias.

"Go," Maria said. "Go and meet your relatives."

In Madrid I stayed with Papa's cousin, Manolo Canellada Diez. Then I flew to Barcelona, where I met up with several high-ranking Catalan law enforcement officials whom I had befriended in 1992 when I had helped with security at the Barcelona Olympics. After that came a trip to Palma de Mallorca, where I visited my aunts and uncle. Returning to Madrid, I rejoined Manolo for a drive north to Asturias to meet more relatives. In Gijon, a quaint seaport city on the Bay of Biscay, I met one cousin who not only looked like me but was a cop, to boot. And in Infiesto, I met even more cousins. Seeing how much alike we all looked, I felt safe and secure, knowing that I would never be totally alone in this world. And being with them in Asturias, a land embedded in Papa's soul, filled me with deep pride.

I fell in love with my family. I fell in love with Spain.

At one point we visited the tiny hillside village of Covadonga, which holds a mythical place in Spanish history. It was here, in the eighth century, that an Asturian warrior named Pelayo led a band of outnumbered Christian soldiers against a much larger Moorish army. According to legend, the Virgin Mary appeared to Pelayo and urged him on to a stunning victory.

To show their appreciation for the Virgin's help, Pelayo and his men built a shrine in a local cave. The cave, which is situated in the side of a mountain, contains a statue of Our Lady and sits above a pristine waterfall. Pilgrims come to drink its waters, which are said to ensure long life, happiness, and good fortune.

Trekking up the mountainside to the shrine, I, too, drank deeply.

When I came back down again to rejoin Manolo, I told him I had sampled the waters. Manolo put his arm around me.

"Cousin," he said, "do you know what the significance of that is?"

I looked at him blankly. He smiled at me.

"Whoever drinks from these waters is destined to find love within a year."

I WAS NOW into the second year since Iris's death. I decided I needed to meet somebody new.

I began attending dinners and dances sponsored by various Spanish fraternal organizations in Southern California, hoping to meet a native Spaniard. But I often found myself the third wheel at the table. Most of the Spaniards who came to these functions were married or already coupled off. All the women were spoken for. Occasionally I would dance with a wife or a girlfriend or somebody's mother-in-law, but I always knew it could never go anywhere. Disillusioned, I pretty much made up my mind that these gatherings were a waste of my time.

In October I received an invitation from the Casa de España for a dinner-dance at a naval officers' club in nearby San Diego. My first instinct was to throw it in the trash. But at the last second, I convinced myself that a trip to San Diego would give me a chance to visit with my old New York buddy Ray D'Angelo, who had relocated to Southern California, so, what the hell, I'd drive down the coast and give this meet-and-greet thing one last try.

At the dinner-dance I once again was seated with people who were paired up. There was one divorced woman at the table, a nice-enough person, but I felt no chemistry. However, trying to be a good sport, I invited her to dance.

As I guided her around the dance floor, I happened to look past her shoulder and I saw a group of people walking toward the outside patio. Among them was a young woman. She was dressed in a tasteful, lightly colored blue dress that accented her figure. Her soft, auburn hair seemed to flow as she walked. Suddenly she turned to look in my direction, and I caught a glimpse at her beautiful dark eyes and her striking cheekbones. The smile on her lips was radiant.

It was like someone had just thrown a hard right to my jaw. For a moment I forgot where I was. My dance partner noticed.

"What's wrong with you?" she asked.

I fumbled for an answer. "Er . . . nothing," I said. "I was just remembering an important telephone call I need to make."

I escorted her quickly back to the table, dying to get off the dance floor. Then I walked back and introduced myself to the stunner with the auburn hair. She told me her name was Maria José. That she was from Barcelona. And that she would be returning to Barcelona very soon. And for good, since her visa was about to expire. I felt like a man who had just been kicked in the belly by a mule. Nonetheless, I told her about myself and gave her my business card.

"If there is anything I can ever do for you, don't hesitate to call," I said.

Sometime later, I found a message from her on my answering machine. We made plans to have lunch in San Diego. We drove to a restaurant in La Jolla. Lunch was wonderful, as was the walk on the beach afterward. We talked easily about ourselves, our families, our friends, and I learned that she had never been married before. More lunches followed, one in Coronado Beach, another in San Diego's Mexican old town.

I was mad for her.

In the weeks that followed, the intimacy between us grew. There were times when I felt hesitant, fearing that I might be betraying Iris. Maria José was totally understanding. Had I not hesitated, she said, she would have thought less of me as a man.

During the time we were together, I came to realize that Maria José was a very different kind of woman than Iris. While Iris had been dutiful and deferential, very much in the traditional Old World style, Maria José was independent, opinionated, and liberated, a modern woman. At times she could be as ornery as a stallion, unafraid to stand up to me or speak her mind, and I realized I would have to learn to adapt to her free spirit and her outspokenness.

I brought Maria José to meet Mama and Papa. Mama and Maria José fell in love with each other immediately. Mama was thrilled that I had found someone, even more thrilled that this someone was a native Spaniard. Papa was cordial but cool and noncommittal. Mama later told me that he had difficulty seeing me with a new woman.

When I took Maria José to the airport for her return flight to Spain, I was not certain I would ever see her again. Before she left, I gave her my gold chain, from which hung a medal of St. Michael.

"He will protect you that same way he protected me all those years I was undercover," I told her.

Then she boarded her flight. My heart was roiling.

Christmas came and went. Then New Year's Day 1999. A few days after, Maria José phoned from Spain.

"Louis," she said, "I love you. I miss you. I want to come back to you."

On the morning of her return to Southern California, I bought six dozen red and yellow roses, which I carefully arranged throughout my house. I rented a huge white limousine and hired a chauffeur. When the limo arrived at my house, I got into the backseat carrying another dozen roses, a chilled bottle of Moët & Chandon, and two champagne glasses, along with a couple of CDs of Gloria Estefan love ballads.

When Maria José landed, we fell into each other's arms. And I thought, *Thank God. Thank God for this strong, beautiful, courageous woman who has rescued me from the prison of my despair. Thank God for this stunning creature who has finally, blessedly, brought me back to life again.*

OUR WEDDING TOOK place on December 3, 2000, at the Center Club in Costa Mesa. About fifty relatives and close friends stood inside a large, sunny salon decorated with beautiful paintings and tapestries and watched us take our vows.

Afterward, at the reception, Maria José; her mother, Loli; and her girlfriends had the crowd on its feet and cheering wildly when they broke into *sevillanas,* the fiery, flamenco-style folk dances that originated in the south of Spain.

My life was full and happy again.

I had been reborn.

CHAPTER TWENTY

THESE DAYS I SLEEP late, but not too late.

The Southern California morning usually dawns beautiful and sunny, not a cloud in the sky, not even in winter. The air is perfumed with a pleasing mix of smells, the briny tang of the Pacific Ocean blending with the scent from the rose bushes around my house and the freshly cut grass on my neighbor's lawn. Off in the distance I see royal palms swaying in the gentle breezes. At my feet, sparrows, drawn by the bread crumbs I have put out the night before, frolic in the new puddles left by my lawn sprinklers.

Even though I am now a Californian (of sorts), there are times when my mind flashes back to an old churchyard in Red Hook, Brooklyn, where we used to play ball. When I was a kid, I had gone to the lot one night and laid on my back, looking up at the stars, contemplating the vast universe and wondering how my life in it would eventually turn out. As I lay there that night, nearly fifty years ago, I had talked with God. I had asked Him to let me do good in the world, lead an honorable life, use my time on this planet to make a difference.

Over the years I had tried to take the right path. It hadn't been easy. On occasions, too many occasions, I had been compelled to dance with the devil. He had appeared to me in different forms. Spoken with different voices. Confronted me in all manner of locales. Red Hook. The U.S. Army. The gun and drug dens of New York City. He had taunted me in England, squared off against me in the parking lots and rented rooms of Orange County, played hide-and-seek with me in the jungles of Bolivia. And he had just about beaten me for good in a hospital intensive care unit in Costa Mesa. He came back at me again when Mama died and, three years later, Papa followed.

Papa's death was especially tough. Incredibly, he lived till age eighty-seven, surviving two major heart attacks, triple and quadruple bypass surgery, the removal of his spleen and gallbladder, diabetes, and even lymphoma. When his heart finally began to fail him, he went out like the lion he had always been, battling with me and my brothers, the doctors, the nurses, the orderlies, the hospital administrators . . . anyone and everyone who dared to tell him they knew better than he did or failed to live up to his high standards in meeting their responsibilities. At the end, however, beaten down by his aging body, the terrible suffering he had endured over the course of his own life, and his desire to be reunited with Mama, he finally gave in to the inevitable.

On his last day, I asked my brothers Rigel and Alfonsito to leave me alone with Papa in his room. For a while I just stood and contemplated his majestic, noble, still-handsome face. Then I laid down next to him, my face touching his face, and cried as I told him how much I loved him, how much I would miss him, and how a part of me would die when he did. And he surprised me.

"Luis," he murmured, uttering my name in Spanish. Then, right after that, he murmured, "Mama."

My crying turned into waves of uncontrollable sobbing. After a few minutes, I composed myself. A terrible weight lifted from my shoulders. Papa and I were finally at peace with each other. And I knew for certain that my papa had really and truly loved me after all.

That night, Papa died. My hero, my el Cid, was finally at rest. And so was I.

After Papa's passing, the devil threw another punch my way when I was diagnosed with cancer—non-Hodgkins lymphoma, to be exact—which I managed to tough out and beat, just like Papa once had.

Yet here I am, still on my feet. I may have danced with the devil, but I like to think I have walked with God. Looking back over the years, I am certain He must have listened to me back in that lot in Red Hook. And thanks to His benevolence and protection over the years, I am still going strong.

True, my life is different now. I feel like a retired gunfighter, watching from the sidelines, no longer dusting off my spurs to step into the middle of Main Street and draw down on my opponent. Instead, when I'm not due at an audition or on a film set, I visit the local schools to speak about acting, the perils of drug use, and my career with the DEA. Or I go to the gym, where I work out with weights, do some calisthenics, tug at the pulleys, hit the treadmill or the elliptical trainer. I also help train local amateur boxers who aspire to professional careers.

Whenever I can, I spend time with my grandkids. But often I find myself longing for the good old days. Working closely with smart, seasoned law-enforcement agents. Going undercover. Feeling the danger, the fear, that rush of adrenaline. Trumping the villains. Then going out afterward to celebrate with my ATF or DEA buddies by busting balls and laughing our asses off while we got stewed and stupid.

I don't do that now. And, like a lot of my fellow ex-agents, with whom I still keep in touch, I miss it terribly. I miss living on the edge, that special camaraderie. I miss the opportunity to do something important and meaningful for people other than my own family. I know who I am at this stage of the game, what I've become, but I'm not really at peace with it. I feel conflicted. I'm always asking myself what I can be doing better. And I still crave the spotlight and long for the applause. I actually fantasize about getting a phone call from the DEA at some point and a supervisor saying breathlessly, "Lou, we need you on something big. Get your ass get down here ASAP."

Occasionally I have dreams about making new cases.

But could I do it? I wonder . . .

I still have that penchant for a good fight. And I'm always on the lookout for possible danger. I never go to bed without looking out my bedroom window for suspicious cars or other activity. When I'm on foot, I still watch for shadows coming up behind me or peek into store windows to see who's at my back or off in the distance. And I'm always sizing up approaching pedestrians, their walk, their talk, their appearance, their attitude.

Just the other day, in fact, when I was out for a stroll in my neighborhood, I was about half a mile from my house when I spotted these three shitbirds shuffling toward me. They were street punks, with ugly tattoos and metal piercings, sweatshirt hoods pulled furtively up over their heads, trouser waists down below their asses. Cursing and trash-talking, they kept making crude comments about other passersby, and I knew that they were up to no good. Flashing back to my Red Hook days, I started to roll my shoulders as I walked, mentally bracing for what I might need to do next. Take the first one out quickly with a thunderous right to the chin, then polish off the other two with left hooks to the body and head—that was my game plan.

In the end, we just passed each other by wordlessly. And went our separate ways.

Even though I'm now on the sidelines watching, there's a

still a small flame flickering inside me. And sometimes it whooshes to life. Like when I'm watching a good action film. Never before did I get caught up vicariously in somebody else's act. But now, when I watch these movies, I begin to picture myself in the hero's role. I know it's bullshit, but my adrenaline kicks in, my heart picks up, my blood pressure rises. At home I yell at the TV and bang my fist into the furniture. In movie theaters I holler back at the screen. Other theatergoers know to keep their distance.

As for the future, who knows? Maybe I'll do more acting work. Become a script consultant on TV crime shows. Build houses. Maybe I'll even . . .

But then I start to wonder again . . .

Could I still match wits with the villains? Mix it up with the bad guys? Put my street smarts and my years of law enforcement experience to fresh use? And, if need be, bust some heads and kick some ass, the way I did in the good old days?

Then, just as quickly, I pull myself up short and think . . . do I really and truly want to do it anymore? Well, *do* I?

I'm retired now, but when I read the recent headlines, I worry. Just to cite a few recent ones: "Ten Alleged Mexican Drug Cartel Leaders Among 43 Defendants Indicted in Brooklyn and Chicago as Part of Coordinated Strike Against Mexican Drug Trafficking Organizations" . . . "Five Indicted for Plot to Murder U.S. Agent in Colombia" . . . "Manhattan U.S. Attorney Announces Extradition of Leader of International Money Laundering Organization" . . . and, in a real sign of the times, "Three Al Qaeda Associates Arrested on Drug and Terrorism Charges."

Things haven't really changed that much. That devil is still out there, looking to wreak havoc. He still needs to be shown who's boss.

Officially, I've danced my last dance. Yet I still have my health. I still have my instincts. I still know all the moves. Could I get back out on the floor with him one last time? Could I still do the dance?

Every day, I kick it around in my head.

And I wonder.

BIBLIOGRAPHY

The authors wish to acknowledge the following additional sources:

Books

Barnes, Leroy "Nicky," and Tom Folsom. *Mr. Untouchable.* New York: RuggedLand, 2007.

Biggs, Ronald. *Odd Man Out: My Life on the Loose and the Truth About the Great Train Robbery*. London: Bloomsbury, 1994.

Gosling, John, and Dennis Craig. *The Great Train Robbery: The Inside Story of the Century's Most Startling Crime.* London: W. H. Allen, 1964.

Reynolds, Bruce. *The Autobiography of a Thief.* London: Virgin, 2000.

Newspaper Articles

Koltnow, Barry. "A Tough Guy for Hire." *The Orange County Register,* March 27, 2001.

Martinez, Al. "Louie the Actor Is Back." *Los Angeles Times,* April 23, 1996.

Murphy, Jack. "A Cop Who Busts Drug Dealers, Jaws." *San Diego Union,* August 27, 1978

Various articles. *News of the World,* Great Britain, 1968–1985.

Magazine Articles

Adams, Nathan M. "Target: Mr. Untouchable." *The Reader's Digest,* June 1978.

Ferretti, Fred. "Mister Untouchable." *New York Times Magazine,* June 5, 1977.

Fleetwood, Blake. "Get Nicky Barnes." *High Times Magazine,* November 1978.

Jacobson, Mark. "The Return of Superfly." *New York Magazine,* August 7, 2000.

Television Programs

Cole, Judy, writer and director; Maddy Woodmansee; and Towers Productions. "Undercover: The Double Life of Louie Diaz, Operation Pisces." *ID Investigation,* Discovery Channel, September 3, 2009.

Crain, William, writer, director, and producer; and Stephanie Tepper, producer. "Drug Wars: The Godfather of Cocaine." *Frontline,* PBS, March 25, 1997.

Ullman, Tracy, producer and director; and Towers Productions. "Gangland Series: American Gangster." History Channel, November 24, 2008.

Theatrical Films

Dash, Damon, producer; Mary Jane Robinson, producer; and Marc Levin, director. *Mr. Untouchable.* Magnolia Pictures, HDNET Films, Dash Films, Blow Back Productions, September 30, 2006.

Web Articles

Lee, Rensselaer. "The Economics of Cocaine Capitalism." *http://www.cosmos-club/web/journals/1996/lee.html.*

U.S. Drug Enforcement Agency. "DEA History," *http://www.deamuseum.org/dea_history_book.*

Youngers, Coletta. "A Fundamentally Flawed Strategy: The

U.S." Washington Office on Latin America, September 18, 1991, *http://www, drugpolicy.org/library/tlcblvia2.cfm.*

Court Documents

U.S. Court of Appeals for the Second Circuit, Docket Nos. 84-1010, 84-1023, 84-1024, 84-1025, 84-1026, 84-1027, 84-1028, 84-1041, *United States of America v. Kenneth Thomas,* aka "Fat Kenny," aka "China," Guy Thomas Fisher, aka "Radio," aka "Stick," Ishmael Muhammed, aka "Samuel Jones," aka "Brother Jones," aka "Brother," aka "BJ," Frank Alphonso James, aka "Black Frank," aka "Alphonso James," Wallace Rice, Thomas Forman, aka "Gaps," James Wheelings, aka "Tippy," aka "Jay Wagner," Elmer Thomas Morris Jr., aka "Coco," aka "William Barhem," appeal of judgments of conviction entered on January 12, 1984, in the U.S. District Court for the Southern District of New York.

U.S. Court of Appeals for the Second Circuit, Docket Nos. 78-1040 et al., *United States of America v. Leroy Barnes,* aka "Nicky," Steven Baker, aka "Jerry," Steven Monsanto, aka "Fat Stevie," John Hatcher, aka "Bo," Joseph Hayden, aka "James Hayden," aka "Freeman Hayden," aka "Jazz," Waymin Hines, aka "Wop," Leonard Rollock aka "Petey," James McCoy, and Walter Centeno, aka "Chico Bob," appeal of judgments of conviction entered on January 19 and 23, 1978, in the U.S. District Court for the Southern District of New York.

ACKNOWLEDGMENTS

IT WOULD BE VIRTUALLY impossible to thank all of the people in my life who've contributed to my story in some form or another, but I will do my best to recognize and thank as many as I can.

My sincerest thanks to Gianni Russo for his undying support of me in good and bad times, and for bringing me to the door of my literary agent, Frank Weimann—a man who strongly believed in my story and made this happen; a big hug to my co-author, friend, and partner, Neal Hirschfeld, who skillfully and painfully drew the story out of my soul; everyone at Simon & Schuster for taking us on, and our editor, Ed Schlesinger, for making us better; my family in Spain, all the Canelledas, the Genaros, the Rodriguezes, and the Delgados for accepting me with open arms into their families and for encouraging me to write this book; all my Brooklyn childhood friends with whom I shared so many joys and experiences, especially Paul Coriaty and Nicky Estavillo, retired NYPD Chief of Patrol, the entire Gonzalez family, Ray D'Angelo, and Pat Matarazzo for a lifetime of encouragement and support, especially in the writing of this book; my dear family friends of old and new who supported us so vigorously and with whom we shared so many memorable occasions, particularly: the Coriatys, the D'Amicos, the D'Angelos, the Donovans, the Estarillos, the Fultons, the LaSpisas, the Lunds, the Palermos, the Matarazzos, the McTeigues, the Medinas, the Middletons, the Mirandas, the Neals, the Pantageses, the Reardons, the Reynolds, the Russos, all the Vegas.

To all my brother ATF agents and bosses with whom I first served in New York from 1972 through 1975.

To all my brother DEA agents and bosses with whom I served in the New York office from 1975 through 1985.

To my DEA-Group #13 brother agents who had my back during the Nicky Barnes investigation and with whom I shared so many fond memories: Group Supervisor Charly Casey, Special Agents Mary Buckley, Don Ferrarone, Ray Kobyra, John Lawler, Fred Marano, Bobby Nieves, Mike Pavlick, Tom Rooney, Pat Shea, Andy Smith, and Tom Ward.

To my DEA-Group #6 brother agents who were with me for a long run: Group Supervisor Jeff Hall, Special Agents Richard Bell, Celerino Castillo, Chris Egan, Gerry Franciosa, Jaime Forteza, Terry Hanna, Kieran Kobell, John Maddox, George Papantoniou, Danny Pavichevich, Arthur Reed, Billy Snipes, John Tully, John Tuttle, Terry Valentine, and group secretary Mary Ann Fernandez.

To DEA Administrators Peter Bensinger, Jack Lawn, and Michele Leonhart for personally acknowledging my accomplishments and supporting my career.

To all the great United States Attorneys and Assistant Prosecutors I worked with, for their guidance, respect, and faith in me, particularly: Dominic Amorosa, Robert B. Fiske Jr., Rudy Giuliani, Diane Giacalone, Robert Mazur, Reena Raggi, Benito Romano, Tom Sear, Bob Tendy, Fred Varela, and so many others.

To all my Los Angeles DEA brothers, bosses, and support personnel with whom I served from 1985 through 1996.

To all my Santa Ana Resident Group brother agents and bosses for their untiring support in "Operation Pisces," particularly: Group Supervisor Frank Briggs and Special Agents Paul Clayton, Bobby Corso, Steve Crane, Joe Day, Mark

Nomady, Marty Martinez, Rex McMillan, Dennis Stevens, and group secretary, Joann Evans.

For all my brother special agents who died in the line of duty and those who passed on well before their time.

To my most solid of DEA brothers and friends who have been there for me, especially: Larry Acevedo, John Andrejko, Victor Aponte, Jennifer Ballone, Jenny Briones, Ron Brogan, Danny Cabrera, Ron Catanese, Bobby Canales, Phil Chelsing, Ron Chepesuick, John Cheslett, Paul Clayton, Vinny Colandrea, Richie Crawford, Paul Doyle, David DeVorre, Arnon Drozd, Chris Egan, John Fernandez, Richie Fiano, Eddy Follis, Desi Gonzalez, Rocio Graciano, Simeon Green, Adriana Guzman, David Hererra, Lakita Hill, Steve Jennings, George Kontess, Doug Kuell, Brenda LaMott, Ed Lauter, Edie Lund, Tim Li, Laura Limon, Ralph Lockridge, David Ma, John Marcello, John McCaffrey, Jackie MacPherson, Jimmy Marchello, Ray Margarella, Jose Martinez, Ray Martinez, Vinny Mazzelli, Larry McElyn, Tony Medina, J. D. Miller, Bobby Miranda, Bobby Nieves, Peter Nieves, Myrna Opere, Gino Pagano, Bobby Palumbo, Susan Pantages, Tyrone Patterson, Anthony Paulmino, Roger Rangel, Tony Recevuto, Abel Reynoso, Chris Rose, Elizabeth Samaniego, Carl "Duke" Schroder, Don and Ann Shirey, Irma Silva, Danny Staffieri, Dick Slattery, Kurt Sorgenfry, Steve Spielsinger, Rev. Joseph Strubbe, Kelly Snyder, Jack Toal, Evette Torres, Madeline Valdez, Jim Vega, and Lance Williams.

To all the great police officers and police departments of Orange County, California, with whom I served, especially: Anaheim P.D., Santa Ana P.D., Costa Mesa P.D., Huntington Beach P.D., Newport Beach P.D. and Long Beach P.D.

To all my Catalan Police friends, "Los Mossos de Esquadra," for their loyality, friendship, and support of me in the writing of this book, particularly: Joan Miquel Capell, capo de tutti capi, and the "Mossos," de Hospitalet, and so many other of my dear Catalan friends who supported and encouraged me to write this book as well, especially: Carlos Civit, Tony Cruells, Andreu Martin, Carlos Quilez, and Xavier Vinader.

To my beautiful Isaac, Judit, Pau, and Anna for always making me feel so loved.

To all my Hollywood friends who encouraged, endorsed, and supported my second career as an actor, especially: Nicky Blair, Frank and Terri Compatelli, Bill Clark, Matty and Tony Danza, Robert Davi, Tom Davis, Lenny D'John, Robert Forster, Charly Guardino, Bobby Costanzo, John Finnegan, Sonny Grosso, Barry Koltnow, Ed Lauter, Bill Lustig, David Mills, Bobby Miranda, Kathy Moriarty, Bobby Morones, Phil Palermo, Frankie Pesce, Ray Rappa, Frank Stallone, Peter Henry Schroder, John Tracy, Mark Thomas, Harry Wiland, Fred Williamson, Burt Young, and of course my agents, Don Gerler and Richie Reiner.

To my doctors David Klein and Jeffrey Barke for getting and keeping me healthy, and Cecily Kahn for getting my head straight.

To all my Argentine friends for your constant support and encouragement.

And last but not least, thanks to Michael King, and all his staff, and fighters of the "All American Heavyweights," boxing program for taking me in as one of their own.